Selected Letters of Stéphane Mallarmé

D0126851

Selected Letters of

STÉPHANE MALLARMÉ

Edited and Translated by

ROSEMARY LLOYD

THE UNIVERSITY OF CHICAGO PRESS
CHICAGO AND LONDON

Rosemary Lloyd is a University Lecturer in the French Department at the University of Cambridge. She is the author of *Baudelaire et Hoffmann, Baudelaire's Literary Criticism,* and *Mallarmé: Poésies* and the translator and editor of *The Conquest of Solitude: Selected Letters of Charles Baudelaire,* published by the University of Chicago Press.

The translations in this volume are based on the texts of *Mallarmé plus intime,* ed. Henri Mondor (Gallimard, 1944), and Mallarmé, *Correspondance,* ed. Henri Mondor, Jean-Pierre Richard, and Lloyd James Austin (Gallimard, 1959–85).

The portrait of Mallarmé on p. ii is by James McNeill Whistler and was taken from the frontispiece for Mallarmé's *Vers et prose* (1910).

The University of Chicago Press, Chicago 60637
The University of Chicago Press, Ltd., London
© 1988 by The University of Chicago
All rights reserved. Published 1988
Printed in the United States of America
97 96 95 94 93 92 91 90 89 88   54321

Library of Congress Cataloging-in-Publication Data
Mallarmé, Stéphane, 1842–1898.
    [Correspondence. English. Selections]
    Selected letters of Stéphane Mallarmé / edited and translated by Rosemary Lloyd.
        p. cm.
    Includes index.
    ISBN 0-226-48841-1
    1. Mallarmé, Stéphane, 1842–1898—Correspondence. 2. Poets, French—19th century—Correspondence. I. Lloyd, Rosemary. II. Title.
PQ2344.Z5A4 1988
841'.8—dc19
[B]   88-1351
                                                 CIP

Contents

Translator's Note

So eager was Mallarmé to avoid anything hackneyed and trite, so important did he consider the rejuvenation of language, that even his letters, particularly in his later years, were written in a prose style whose vocabulary and syntax are determinedly idiosyncratic. In translating them I have attempted to reproduce the flavor of the original rather than smooth out or gloss over their deliberate strangeness. Titles of works to which Mallarmé refers have been translated only when this helps to explain his comments on them, since he occasionally makes punning allusions to such titles.

This translation is profoundly indebted to the scholarship and friendship of Lloyd Austin, editor of the eleven volumes of Mallarmé's correspondence, of which the following letters provide a mere sample. To him, and to his wife, Jeannot, I would like to offer my warmest gratitude.

R. L.

Chronology

1842   18 March. Etienne (known as Stéphane) Mallarmé born in Paris.

1844   25 March. Birth of his sister Marie (known as Maria).

1847   2 August. Death of Mallarmé's mother.

1848   27 October. Mallarmé's father remarries.

1857   31 August. Death of Maria Mallarmé.

1862   Mallarmé meets Maria (known as Marie) Gerhard, his future wife, and embarks on a trial marriage with her in London.

1863   12 April. Death of Mallarmé's father.

       10 August. Marie and Stéphane married in London.

       November. Appointed teacher of English at Tournon.

1864   19 November. Geneviève Mallarmé born.

1866   May. Publication in *Le Parnasse contemporain* of ten of Mallarmé's poems.

       October. Appointed English teacher at Besançon.

1867   31 August. Death of Charles Baudelaire.

       October. Appointed English teacher at Avignon.

1871   16 July. Anatole Mallarmé born.

       October. Mallarmé appointed English teacher in Paris at the lycée Fontanes, now Condorcet.

1872   23 October. Death of Théophile Gautier.

1873 Meets Manet.
      August. Mallarmé writes "Toast funèbre" in honor of Gautier.
1874 Meets Emile Zola.
1875 May. Publication of Mallarmé's translation of Poe's "The Raven" with illustrations by Manet.
1876 Publication of a deluxe edition of "L'Après-midi d'un faune," illustrated by Manet.
1879 6 October. Anatole dies.
1883 30 April. Death of Manet.
1884 Liaison with Méry Laurent.
      Appointed English teacher at the collège Janson-de-Sailly.
1885 Appointed English teacher at the collège Rollin.
1887 Publication of an edition of Mallarmé's *Poésies*.
1888 Publication of Mallarmé's translations of Poe's poems.
1892 July. Debussy begins work on his "Prélude à l'Après-midi d'un faune."
1893 November. Mallarmé retires from teaching.
1894 1 and 2 March. Oxford and Cambridge lectures.
1898 9 September. Death of Mallarmé.
1899 Publication of *Poésies*.

Introduction

Literature was entering a critical period when Mallarmé first discovered the creative writing of the age. The 1850s had been an exceptionally productive decade for poetry: in 1852 Gautier had published *Emaux et Camées* and Leconte de Lisle *Les Poèmes antiques;* in 1855 appeared Leconte de Lisle's *Poèmes et Poésies;* Hugo, still in exile, produced *Les Contemplations* in 1856 and *La Légende des siècles* in 1859; Banville's virtuoso masterpiece, *Odes funambulesques,* appeared in 1857, the year which also saw the most important poetic publication of the decade, Baudelaire's *Les Fleurs du mal.* Despite this activity, writers of Mallarmé's generation, seeking a voice of their own, were increasingly convinced that poetry had reached a time of fundamental crisis: language seemed to have been worked threadbare, the rules of prosody appeared too restrictive, Romanticism's stress on the individual, like the Parnassian emphasis on plasticity, struck them as outworn. While some poets, notably Verlaine and René Ghil, experimented with metrics and prosody, and others, particularly Gustave Kahn and Francis Vielé-Griffin, explored the potential of *vers libre,* Mallarmé's aesthetic revolution, which was to have such a profound effect on twentieth-century poetry, concerned the rejection of any mimetic function and the restoration to poetic language of its power to suggest.

"My entire life," wrote Mallarmé in his mid-twenties, "has its *idea,* and all my minutes work towards creating it" (46)*. Central to that idea was the desire to purify everyday speech, to use the language of his contemporaries, avoiding the abstruse and the hackneyed, while yet imprinting upon it the seal of his own personality. Above all, as he asserts in that marvellously concise and suggestive precept, he wanted to *"Peindre non la chose mais l'effet qu'elle produit [paint, not the object, but the effect it produces]"* (24). Freed from its traditional representative function, poetry is above all the art of evocation and suggestion, the perfect vehicle for expressing the "mysterious meaning of the aspects of existence" and thereby for "conferring authenticity on our time on earth" (98). Indeed he considered this Orphic explanation of the world "the sole duty of the poet" (103), "the only spiritual task there is" (98). This does not mean, however, that Mallarmé was a purely cerebral

*Numbers in parentheses indicate the letter from which the quotation is taken.

poet. The delight poetry gave him was also intensely physical: poetry, he once exulted, "is in love with itself and the pleasure it takes in itself drops deliciously into my soul" (48). And although he felt the poet should yield the initiative to words, rather than follow the Romantic propensity for personal lyricism, words themselves "must fade before the sensation" they recreate (24) and, like a chest of sparkling jewels, must "*reflect upon each other to the point of appearing not to have their own color any more, but to be merely transitions in an entire gamut*" (44). Poetry, for him, was not effusion but concision, not inspiration but elimination, and the pleasure for the reader, he asserted, consisted in gradual guesswork, leading little by little to an ever deeper penetration of the essential enigma. It was not that he sought obscurity for its own sake, as many of his readers (then and now) have blamed or praised him for doing, but rather that he believed the reverberative power of poetry demanded a language of particular density: "of course I'm obscure," he snorts in a letter to Edmund Gosse, "if the reader makes the mistake of thinking he's opening a newspaper!" (168).

The means and ideals of poetry are at the core of Mallarmé's letters, as they are of his entire life. Long, exploratory, self-analytical letters record the years spent in the provinces, when Mallarmé was supporting his wife and young daughter through teaching, that "obligatory pastime" (215), and undergoing a profound, deeply disturbing crisis which was partly spiritual, partly physical, partly the result of isolation from what in those days he saw as the necessary stimulus of Paris. Later, established in Paris and beginning to attract the attention and admiration of other writers, he responded in pithy thank-you letters to the gradually increasing flood of books received, illuminating both the particular work and literature in general.

Despite frequent complaints that letter-writing was a minor form of torture, rendering paper and ink abhorrent, breaking into hours sacred to poetry, this is a marvellously rich, varied correspondence, revealing not only the maturing of a major poet but also the personality of a warm and complex man. There are flashes of sharp description—Verlaine teaching his pupils to pronounce English perfectly; Claudel, shrugging his shoulders furiously as he sits on the Mallarmés' sofa—and images of witty comedy or intense beauty. Who could forget the "fat-bellied lawyers dancing like bottles on water at the Sub-Prefects' Ball" (31), or the pond of dreams, "the pond in which we only ever hook our own image, mindless of the silver scales of fish" (49), or that evocation of heat, when "the mind is as indistinct as an aquarium traversed by vague fins, formerly silver" (54)? But above all there are cameos of Mallarmé himself: Mallarmé at Valvins, sailing, or wearing the mottled smock of a housepainter, or calling to his cat, who prefers the company of the local tom, or staying on, alone, to delight in the red and gold of autumn; Mallarmé spending all day writing a lecture and leaping aboard the carriage to go and deliver it, his shoelace dangling; Mallarmé replying, tongue-in-cheek, to journalists wanting his views on the bicycle or the top hat; Mallarmé as friend, father, lover, mentor.

Marked, in childhood, by the death of his mother and in adolescence by that of his twelve-year-old sister, Mallarmé, as his letters to his grandfather clearly reveal, had acquired considerable strength of character by the time he left school in 1860. Resisting family pressure to make a career in the Records Office, he turned to teaching as a profession which would leave him time for poetry. However much he came to loathe his work as an English teacher, however ineffectual he may have been for many of his pupils, he remained in the profession (apart from various periods of leave granted on the grounds of ill-health) until permitted to retire at the end of 1893.

As his letters bear ample witness, he was a man who valued friendship. As early as 1861 he had formed with the ebullient poet and teacher Emmanuel Des Essarts, a friendship which was to prove long-lasting despite sharp differences in character and aesthetics and regardless of Des Essarts' condescending treatment of the poet he regarded as far inferior to himself. While their enthusiasm for literature united them, their individual tastes reflected a chasm opening up in contemporary poetry: Des Essarts delighted in the vast outpourings of inspiration; for Mallarmé concision and depth were of the essence. All the difference between Hugo and Baudelaire found its echo in the two young friends.

Through Des Essarts Mallarmé made two other friends, a young artist, Henri Regnault, who was to be killed in the Franco-Prussian War, and Henri Cazalis, who was to achieve social success both as a doctor and as a poet writing under the pseudonym of Jean Lahor. Mallarmé's love for a German governess, Marie Gerhard, his decision to marry her, his periods of bleak depression, and his developing aesthetic convictions are all expressed in the letters to Cazalis. Cazalis, for his part, confided in Mallarmé his love for Ettie Yapp, kept him in touch with literary life in Paris, and above all encouraged his friend's philosophical and literary questioning.

Mallarmé made another close friendship in the early 1860s, that with the engaging and intelligent Eugène Lefébure. An admirer of Poe from as early as 1857 and a poet whose notebooks and published poems reveal a far from negligible talent, Lefébure eventually abandoned poetry to become a highly regarded Egyptologist. It was to him that Mallarmé wrote some of his most revealing and moving letters about the philosophical crisis he experienced at Tournon. Lefébure's letters to Mallarmé, in turn, reveal a remarkable depth of friendship and comprehension for the struggling young poet. Although that friendship ceased abruptly in 1871, for reasons which remain unclear, Mallarmé nevertheless wrote to Lefébure twenty years later, on the death of the latter's son, and signed himself "Your very old friend."

By the end of 1863, he had also found a further friend in the poet Armand Renaud, whose anthology *Les Caprices du boudoir* had just been published. In a letter to Renaud accompanying his review of the collection, Mallarmé emphasises that for him the principal purpose of such an exercise is to describe not the work itself so much as the reflections stimulated by it: this early statement of principle remains valid not only for all Mallarmé's subsequent reviews but also for his thank-you letters for works sent to him.

If the correspondence suggests that no other friendships, except, perhaps, that with Valéry in the last decade of Mallarmé's life, had quite the intellectual intensity of these early relationships, it does reveal a wide range of acquaintanceships in the world of letters. After spending some ten months in London, to improve his English, Mallarmé set off in 1863 for the provinces and his first teaching post, together with his young wife, Marie Gerhard, whom he had married in August. Through Des Essarts, now teaching in Avignon, Mallarmé met the main figures in the movement which aimed to reinstate Provençal as a literary language, the Félibrige. Principal among these were the poets Théodore Aubanel, with whom Mallarmé was to explore Mount Ventoux by moonlight, and Frédéric Mistral, an increasingly conservative poet whom Mallarmé tried in vain to interest in an international society of poets which would have included both the Félibrige and the Spanish poets.

His summer vacation in 1864 proved the starting point for two more important friendships, with the effervescent Catulle Mendès and the aristocratic but impoverished Villiers de L'Isle-Adam, whom Mallarmé may have met in the preceding year. Mendès, who had founded the *Revue fantastique* when he was only nineteen, was in close contact not only with established poets—Baudelaire, Gautier, Banville—but also the central figures of the younger generation. In Villiers, whose work *Isis* Mallarmé had already read and admired, he found not only a writer with a vision of art nearly as lofty as his own, but also a close if unpredictable friend. Their relationship was to become of central importance to the development of Symbolism after Mallarmé's return to Paris in 1871.

Not even the friendships formed over these years could make Mallarmé's time in the provinces anything but deeply unhappy. The frustrations and difficulties of a career to which he was unsuited, the financial hardships the young couple faced, particularly after the birth of their daughter Geneviève, and the sense of isolation from Paris, the center of artistic and literary life, all combined to plunge Mallarmé into troughs of extreme pessimism. The letters of 1867 in particular suggest the depths of his despair. Nevertheless, Mallarmé began devoting his winters to the poetic evocation of the icy princess Hérodiade, and his summers to the erotic and aesthetic adventures of his faun. In 1866 *Le Parnasse contemporain* published ten of his poems, as a result of which parents of his pupils, horrified that their sons should be in contact with a poet, made formal complaints. These complaints, together with poor reports from inspectors, led to his dismissal from Tournon. Appointed to a lycée in Besançon in October 1866, he moved to a post in Avignon the following year and in 1869 began work on *Igitur*, where the spiritual crisis he had experienced is transformed into an enigmatic, evocative art-form, half poetry, half theater. It was not until 1871, the year in which his son Anatole was born, that Mallarmé managed, with the help of friends, to secure a post in Paris. The years of exile were over.

It is in the letters written during his years in the provinces that Mallarmé most frequently discusses his own poetry. In January 1864 he offers Cazalis a gloss of "L'Azur" and points to the particular difficulty of locking together the dramatic element and the "serene, calm lines essential to Beauty" (15), while he explains to Lefébure that the initial source of inspiration for "Hérodiade" was the name itself, a word "as red as an open pomegranate" (30). By mid-1865 he was telling Cazalis of his "heroic interlude," "L'Après-midi d'un faune," insisting on the "very lofty and beautiful idea" it contained, but admitting, with a mixture of emotion and bravado, that the need to make it quintessentially theatrical resulted in the lines being "terribly difficult to create" (32). By the following month the bravado has worn a trifle thin, as he confides, again to Cazalis:

if you only knew what nights of desperation and what days of reverie have to be sacrificed to succeed in writing original poetry (something I've never achieved up till now), and poetry which is worthy, in its supreme mysteries, of delighting the soul of a poet! And what study of the sounds and color of words, the music and the painting through which your thought must pass, however beautiful it may be, if it is to become poetry! (33)

On the last day of the year, Mallarmé sends Villiers de L'Isle-Adam both a summary of "Don du poème" ("Gift of the poem") and the formulation of his poetics: "to create the strangest impressions, certainly, but without letting the reader forget for a single moment the enjoyment given him by the beauty of the poem" (37). Strangeness, enjoyment: the quintessentially Mallarméan ability to delight and baffle simultaneously is summed up here in one of his most forthright statements. One of the last detailed comments on individual poems comes in 1868, when he provides Cazalis with a gloss on one of his most beautiful and enigmatic sonnets, "La Nuit approbatrice," later entitled "Ses purs ongles," "solely so that you won't accuse me of having deliberately tried to be bizarre":

> it is inverted, by which I mean that its meaning, if there is one (but I'd draw consolation for its lack of meaning from the dose of poetry it contains, at least in my view) is evoked by an internal mirage created by the words themselves. If you murmur it to yourself a couple of times, you get a fairly cabbalistic sensation. (54)

One can speculate on why, in the later letters, while continuing to debate aesthetic questions in general, Mallarmé falls silent about individual poems: probably the main reason was the presence of friends with whom he could discuss specific problems or general challenges, together with the increasing sense that his work should not be revealed until it was "complete and perfect" as he puts it.

Mallarmé's first decade in Paris brought friendships with the artist Manet, who was to paint Mallarmé's portrait in 1876, the novelist Zola, on so many of whose novels Mallarmé comments in his letters, and the poet Verlaine, who had sent him a copy of *Poèmes saturniens* as early as 1866. The letters of this period reveal the role he played in having some of Swinburne's poems published in Mendès' review *La République des lettres,* and his association with the Americans, Helen Whitman and Sarah Sigourney Rice, both of whom were trying to rehabilitate the memory of Edgar Poe. Mallarmé himself not only translated Poe's poems but also wrote in homage to him a sonnet, which elliptically and provocatively proclaims Poe's innovative artistic qualities while condemning the blindness of his contemporaries.

Although forced by financial necessity to publish some works of a more utilitarian nature—for instance, a fashion review called *La Der-*

nière Mode, an imaginative study of English, and a study of myths, this last making it possible to hire a pony and trap for Geneviève— Mallarmé also published his *L'Après-midi d'un faune* in 1876, a long essay on Manet and the impressionists, and some of his translations of Poe. December 1877 saw the beginning of the famous "Tuesday evenings," when Mallarmé would gather round him poets and artists to talk about literature and aesthetics.

In 1878 tragedy struck, when Mallarmé's young son Anatole fell gravely ill. After a long and painful illness Anatole died in October 1879. This loss was all the more shattering to Mallarmé in that he found it impossible to transform his grief into poetry through the projected but never completed *Tombeau pour Anatole.*

Nevertheless, Mallarmé's literary reputation was gradually establishing itself. The year 1884 proved a watershed. Verlaine had just published a study of him, together with several of the poems, in *Les Poètes maudits,* and early in that year Huysmans' novel, *A rebours,* depicted Mallarmé as one of the hero's favorite modern poets, focusing on him the attention of a much wider reading public than before. It was in 1884, too, that Mallarmé provided the journalist Léo d'Orfer with the following definition: "Poetry is the expression, in human language restored to its essential rhythm, of the mysterious meaning of the aspects of existence: in this way, it confers authenticity on our time on earth and constitutes the only spiritual task there is" (98). The same year saw the beginning of Mallarmé's love affair with Méry Laurent. Born Marie-Rose Louviot in 1849, Méry had been an actress and model before meeting her protector, Thomas Evans, an American who had been Napoleon III's dentist. A friend of many poets and painters, she lived in the same street as Mallarmé and met him through Manet. Even after the moving letter of 11 September 1889, in which Mallarmé told her he now sought only her friendship, they remained very close until the poet's death. Their relationship inspired some of his loveliest poems, and it was for her that he wrote many of his best occasional poems, little verses sent as greetings or to accompany gifts.

January 1885 saw the publication of the poem that most sharply divided the literary public into implacable enemies or enthusiastic partisans of Mallarmé's poetry: "Prose: pour des Esseintes." Increasing numbers of young writers sent Mallarmé copies of their works or wrote asking his advice: the list of works received included at the end of each volume of the French edition of Mallarmé's correspondence is awe-inspiring. Pierre Louÿs and André Gide were early visitors to the Tuesday evenings: later, they were joined by Paul Claudel and Paul

Valéry. Valéry, whose first letter to Mallarmé, dated 20 October 1890, had convinced the older poet that here was a writer of exceptional promise, was to become a particularly close friend.

The passing years, however, brought deepening divisions within the symbolist group. In 1888 René Ghil was expounding his belief in the predominance of the intellect, when Mallarmé quietly asserted: "One cannot do without Eden." Ghil's attempt to systematize verse mathematically is far removed from Mallarmé's interest in exploring the subtle variations that can be created within the traditional forms.

Far more distressing was the condition of Mallarmé's old friend Villiers, who was painfully and slowly dying, in such poverty that Mallarmé sent a circular letter to fifty writers and artists to raise money for him. A further problem arose over the question of legitimizing Villiers' son Victor, the difficulty for his friends lying in the need to persuade him that he could no longer afford to delay. Eventually, however, Villiers did consent to the marriage ceremony taking place and Mallarmé's letter recounting the episode shows both his despair at having had to force his friend's hand and the sincerity of his belief that such an act was essential for the material well-being of Villiers' wife and son. Villiers died on 19 August 1889, saved from a pauper's grave only by the efforts of his friends. Mallarmé paid tribute to him in a lecture opening with the evocative sentence: "A man accustomed to dream comes here to speak of another, who is dead." Mallarmé's support continued after Villiers' death in other ways, too: with Huysmans he arranged for the publication of *Axël* and *Chez les passants,* and he helped Villiers' wife and son in later years.

Freed from school-teaching at last, Mallarmé found time in 1894 to travel to England, lecturing at Oxford and Cambridge on a question frequently raised in his drama reviews, the relationship between music and literature. It was in this lecture that he announced the changes taking place within the traditional prosody of French verse, particularly with regard to free verse, and asserted that music and literature were the "alternate faces" of what he termed the sole phenomenon, "the Idea."

These years also saw important publications, many of them revealing the value Mallarmé placed on the physical appearance of his works and his close friendships with impressionist painters. There were articles written for periodicals: his meditation in 1886 on Wagner's "unique challenge to the poets," in which he explores, in a prose of singularly demanding density, the power of music and its role in the theater; the series of drama reviews for the *Revue indépendante* in 1886 and 1887, in which he seizes on the opportunity to explore the aesthetic concepts of theater and ballet again in that characteristically elliptical and complex language which both demands and rewards the kind of close reading usually reserved for poetry. In 1887 appeared the collection *Poésies,* the first anthology of his poems, in a limited edition using a photolithographic technique to reproduce the manuscript itself. In 1891 he published a collection of prose poems, theater reviews, and other prose writings under the title *Pages,* with a frontispiece by Renoir. *Vers et Prose* came out in 1894, illustrated by a lithographed portrait of Mallarmé by Whistler, and at a price more accessible to the ordinary reader than had been the case for *Poésies.* In 1895 his *Variations sur un sujet* appeared in the *Revue blanche.* In May 1897 he gathered together many articles that had appeared in periodicals and published them under the title *Divagations,* introducing them with the following explanation: "These pieces will provide the reading public with a contemporary curiosity, in revealing the extent to which a very perspicacious and direct writer can acquire a notoriety in sharp contrast with his qualities, for having, simply, excluded clichés, discovered a suitable mold for each sentence, and practised a form of purism." Finally, in May 1897, the review *Cosmopolis* published his most challenging and enigmatic work, *Un coup de dés.*

After Verlaine's death in January 1896, Mallarmé was elected "Prince of Poets," a triumph reinforced in March of the following year when a group of young poets offered him an album of poems written in his honor. But when he died of a glottal spasm, on 9 September 1898, he left a hasty note for his wife and daughter urging them to burn all his accumulated notes: "There is no literary heritage here, my poor children," he announced. Despite the beauty of his published poems and of the still incomplete *Hérodiade,* Mallarmé felt he had fallen short of the goal he had set himself. How could it be otherwise, when his ideals had always been so high: he once wrote: "I would give the magnificent vespers of Dream and their virgin gold for a quatrain destined for a tomb or a sweet, provided it was a *success*" (52).

Mallarmé's letters offer particularly revealing insights into the formation and evolution of those artistic ideals in terms both of theory and of practice. Indeed, he himself acknowledged the interplay of creative and critical skills in a letter to Lefébure of 1867: "I've created my work only by *elimination,* and any truth I acquired resulted uniquely from the loss of an impression which, having sparkled, burnt itself out and allowed me, thanks to the shadows thus created, to advance more deeply into the sensation of the absolute shadows" (49). The elimination of facility, of the outpourings of inspired lyricism, is a theme constantly repeated, from the early concern at Des Essarts' "brilliant but empty" (12) pages in which he takes "a handful of stars from the Milky Way to scatter them over the paper and lets them form unforeseen constellations at random" (15), through the more ambivalent reaction to Zola's *Une page d'amour*—"as you close the book you have the conviction that it was written at the speed at which you read it, or rather that you've had a profound and limpid vision, and that's all" (80)—to the gently expressed reservation in response to Vielé-Griffin's *Les Cygnes:* "my only criticism would concern an occasional word which has leapt into place rather too easily, if I didn't fear that careful research would interrupt you!" (109). That careful research, that implacable banishment of lyrical flourishes, points to the powerful influence of Mallarmé's two great masters, Baudelaire and Poe. A letter to Cazalis in 1864 with its insistence that every word in a poem must be chosen in view of the total effect reveals the extent to which Mallarmé adhered to Poe's "strict ideas," at least in so far as they are conveyed by Baudelaire in his famous series of introductions to the American writer. Nor was this a momentary response: in 1876, admittedly in a letter to the woman who inspired Poe's "To Helen," he insisted: "however foreign I may be, Poe is so intimately linked to my mind that if ever I write anything of worth, I'll owe it to him" (75). Five years later, writing to the publisher Rouveyre, he elaborates both on the cult dedicated to Poe and the extent to which this, in turn, is an act of devotion to the memory of Baudelaire, "that extraordinary and pure genius" (164, cf. 91 and 51). The need for independence and the conviction that he had "cut free" from Baudelaire (48), therefore, in no way limited his awareness of what he owed the poet of *Les Fleurs du mal.* Other predecessors are also saluted in the correspondence, among them Banville ("whom I adore more and more" (51)) and Gautier, whose "miraculously balanced" sentences so perfectly render "the soul that dwells in beauty" (19).

That Mallarmé distinguished between a writer's social and his literary persona is made clear in his sharp rejection of Taine's image of the artist:

> what I criticize in Taine is the way he claims an artist is merely a man raised to his greatest possible power, whereas I believe that it is perfectly possible to have a human temperament utterly distinct from one's literary temperament. [. . .] I consider Taine sees only impression as a source of works of art and doesn't place enough value on reflection. It's in front of the paper that the artist *creates himself.* (30)

The belief in the individual's ability to conquer natural tendencies in favor of a deliberately chosen artistic ideal underlies much of his response to works sent him by friends. Here, in comments both urging and displaying the value of suggestion over statement, Mallarmé carefully metes out encouragement while indicating areas needing further thought, refusing to pontificate as master but also frequently unwilling to sidestep areas of difference.[1] Although the older Mallarmé is able to render his criticisms all but invisible to the naked eye, his early letters often point very clearly to weaknesses discerned. To convince Cazalis, for instance, that the rhythm of his sentences in *Armonia* is sometimes rather breathless, Mallarmé finds the following remarkable formula:

> the supreme art, in this case, consists in revealing, through an impeccable possession of all the faculties, that one is in ecstasy, without having shown how one reached those summits. Well, often your short phrases lift up their arms, take a deep breath and seem from time to time to take flight. Make them soar. (19)

Similarly, having indicated what he admires in Lefébure's poems, Mallarmé feels free to add a lively reproach: "love is too much the aim of your poems and this extremely colorless word is often repeated in a way which rather dulls the rest. If it isn't sharpened by a strange condiment such as lechery, ecstasy, illness, or asceticism, such an ill-defined subject doesn't seem to me poetic" (30). More subtle is the suggestion that Verlaine's *Poèmes saturniens* might have benefited from having more time to mature: "your book is, indeed, in all its beauty and in the romantic meaning of the term, a first work and one which made me regret on many evenings the vanity which makes me want to offer my work only when it is complete and perfect" (45).

Describing his reactions to works sent, he sometimes indicates the way in which he read, sometimes suggests evasion of the need for comment. Bonaparte-Wyse's book, *Scattered Leaves*, reached Mallarmé only after having moldered in the lycée from which he had been granted a year's rest: "I haven't yet read it, but I've leafed through it and deflowered it by eye," Mallarmé punningly claims and adds: "You know the charm and greed the mind feels in wanting to be initiated into a text before reading it" (61). The arrival of Zola's *Son Excellence Eugène Rougon* provided Mallarmé with the opportunity to

1. For a valuable study of Mallarmé's thank-you letters, see A. Fairlie, "'Entre les lignes': Mallarmé's art of allusion in his thank-you letters," in *Baudelaire, Mallarmé, Valéry,* ed. M. Bowie, A. Fairlie, and A. Finch (Cambridge: The University Press, 1982), pp. 181–201.

discuss two different ways of reading, one where the book is devoured at a sitting, the other where it is read and studied over several days, the latter being designated the "modern way" (73). And Huysmans' *A rebours* provokes a further refinement on this exploration of modes of reading: "you know that after one has been reading, one meditates and, almost always, a different book takes the place of the one just finished, even in the case of a book one admires" (95).

Turning to advantage the unavoidable and increasingly time-consuming task of acknowledging works sent to him, Mallarmé uses his thank-you letters both to explore the possibilities of language and to examine aesthetic issues. The artful slipperiness of his style is evident in the comparison he draws between *Eugène Rougon* and earlier Zola novels:

> a book whose special aesthetics are in absolute harmony with whatever mode of reading its readers may adopt is a masterpiece; and that's why, although I prefer, perhaps because I'm a poet (and wrongly) certain more tangibly magnificent aspects of *La Curée* and *La Faute de l'abbé Mouret*, I consider your latest creation as the most perfect expression of the point of view that you will always have the honor of having understood and revealed in the art of our times. (73)

Equally subtle is the indication that he would prefer Zola to leave space for the reader to muse rather than supply all the details: "everything is said and the poem is contained, in its entirety, in the book as in the reader's mind, without any gap whatsoever through which the reader can enter the text and idly daydream in distraction" (80). How often does he indicate an area he finds less than satisfactory, that is, less than perfect, then claim that this is merely a personal, perhaps wrong-headed, judgment which would be better discussed in a quiet conversation where critic and writer toast their toes in front of the fire and wreathe themselves in tobacco smoke. "We'll discuss this next time we have a chat" (81), "we'd need to talk" (147), "we'll talk of this" (82), "we'll talk about *Sagesse* at leisure" (90), "what conversations I foresee for winter's evenings this year" (102).

Letter paper itself often opens up a space for just such quiet conversation, where Mallarmé teases out aesthetic questions or responds to contemporary debates. The different demands of verse and prose are touched on in an early comment to Cazalis: "if you were to publish a volume of verse, I'd be worried; but, in your work in prose, those unfinished lines, with their harmonies and their rhymes, will merely provide so many wing beats for the mind as it seeks to soar yet higher" (30). The arrival of Heredia's *Trophées* prompts an evaluation of the sonnet, admired for forging into a concise form "those very rare magic moments which in the finest poems remain merely disparate" (169) while Vielé-Griffin's experimental verse elicits the wonderfully suggestive description of the poet creating "flights of entire stanzas on the tip of their mute 'e'" (109). The distinction between genuine experimentation and subservience to passing fads is neatly pointed to in a response to Verhaeren's *Les Soirs:* "it's in you that the renewal of poetry best operates and you do it without having anything to do with the farces of the moment" (113). The contemporary development of free verse offers a case in point. Kahn's use of *vers libre* incites a carefully worded comment revealing not only that Mallarmé was fully aware of the importance of this "unparalleled adventure" but also that he himself continued to value the safeguards and demands of traditional verse forms: "what a delicious liberation! for take good note that I don't consider you as having put your finger on a new form faced with which the old form must withdraw" (111). Arnold Goffin's prose poetry sparked off a far more ambiguous response, hedged around with conditions and undermined by the potential ambivalence of "modern" and "clear":

if Poetry is something situated between music and literature, and if there is, as we can sense nowadays, a rival tabernacle to rhymed verse where Poetry can be housed in a very modern way, or in a way which is completely variegated and mobile, it's certainly not the novel, strictly speaking—that error will pass away—but what you are doing with the book, a subtle series of prose poems, clear and transient. (114)

Mallarmé's repeated emphasis on the value of concision and compression, counterbalanced though it is by his admiration for longer but firmly articulated poems, indicates that the novel form is further removed from his own natural interests than either poetry or the theater.[2] *Jane Eyre,* for instance, is singled out for its "strange intensity of passion" yet Mallarmé adds the rider "but it's so long" (34), just as he describes Zola's *L'Assommoir* as a "fat" book (77). Other doubts are also evident from his remarks. As Alison Fairlie points out,[3] his letter to Paul Bourget shows how deeply he questioned the possibility of

2. On Mallarmé and the theater, see H. Block, *Mallarmé and the Symbolist Drama* (Detroit: Wayne State University Press, 1963), and J. C. Ireson, "Towards a Symbolist Theater," *Studies in French Literature,* ed. J. C. Ireson, I. D. McFarlane, and Garnet Rees (Manchester: The University Press, 1968), pp. 135–56.
3. A. Fairlie, "'Entre les lignes,'" p. 193.

representation and therefore how uneasy he felt about realist and naturalist fiction:

> if putting people into a book has any meaning, then reducing them to the state of thought is the true means, in accordance with the way in which we read, and truly lofty, of communicating with them: and how well after all it evokes their true image! for literature is always concerned with making an act of intellectuality about everything in life. (134)

This point was put more forcibly in reply to an inquiry made by the journalist Jules Huret, when Mallarmé, while expressing admiration for Zola's extraordinary descriptive and organizational gifts, added: "But literature has a more intellectual aspect than that: objects exist, we do not have to create them; all we have to do is to grasp the connections; and it is the threads of those connections which create verse and orchestras."[4] Nevertheless, his letters reveal a lifelong fascination with what his contemporaries were achieving with the novel.[5]

His comments focus on problems inherent to the genre. The borderlines between the novel and history (73) on the one hand and poetry on the other (162) are tellingly traced, while the question of dialogue frequently surfaces. While disturbed by the artificiality of certain dialogues in *Eugène Rougon,* he expresses sympathetic interest in the "admirable linguistic experiment" of *L'Assommoir,* which attempts to capture the idiom of working-class people (77). Composition, too, is highlighted: Zola's poetic backdrops of Paris and its changing sky in *Une page d'amour* are admired for themselves but Mallarmé quietly tests the weakness of the link binding description and narrative together, and Cladel is taken gently to task for not ensuring that all the facts in his tale accord with its underlying moral concept (81). His doubts concerning the mimetic novel may not have prevented a strong sense of admiration and sympathy for Flaubert and Zola, but one feels that Mallarmé is more at home with the poetic novels of Louÿs and Rodenbach. Louÿs' *Aphrodite* he describes as "delicate and ample, without those heavy foundations which normally, in novels, testify to the power of the work; every time you turn the page the wing-beat is present, dazzling and light" (203). The presence of that wing-beat, of the powerful incitement to the imagination, is attested to in Rodenbach's *Le Carillonneur* when Mallarmé admires "the

4. *Œuvres complètes* (Paris: Gallimard, 1945), p. 871.
5. For a detailed study of this aspect, see B. Swift, "Mallarmé and the Novel," in *Modern Miscellany,* ed. T. E. Lawrenson, F. E. Sutcliffe, and G. F. A. Gadoffre (Manchester: The University Press, 1969), pp. 254–75.

vast flights of the whole, the powerful blows which reverberate throughout the work," a work which he describes as being "of the soul's richest metal" (212).

Responses to contemporary paintings and musical performances further illuminate Mallarmé's tastes. A close friend of Berthe Morisot and Whistler, painted by Renoir and working in conjunction with Manet, Mallarmé was very much in tune with the impressionist painters and warmly sympathetic to their vision of art. The role he played in encouraging Sara Sigourney Rice to accept Manet's collaboration on the work she produced in homage to Poe, and his letter to Mirbeau on behalf of Gauguin, as well as his work in arranging the exhibition of Berthe Morisot's paintings after her death all show his willingness to give his time and energy to friends in the world of art. But perhaps the clearest indication the correspondence provides concerning his response to pictorial art occurs in his thank-you letter for Odilon Redon's homage to Goya. In a series of richly evocative appreciations, which draw much of their force from their resonance and their extraordinary concision, Mallarmé reveals how far his reaction to these enigmatic lithographs depends on an assimilation between them and his own mental landscape, setting up between the two minds a "highly mysterious sympathy" (100). Redon's drawings do seem to have given visual form to certain images Mallarmé, "in the depths of [his] soul" had of himself: the "delicious mad hermit," "the strange magician," the "obstinate seeker after a mystery he knows does not exist."[6]

The letters also shed further light on his love of music, conveyed in several of his articles and poems, particularly the tributes to Wagner and the frequently raised question of the relationship between poetry and music.[7] Léopold Dauphin, recipient of some of Mallarmé's warmest letters, found his request for Mallarmé's response to an organ concert rewarded by a description which in tone and vocabulary offers a foretaste of the reverie on Wagner published two years later. Qualifying his appreciation with claims that it could be expressed "only in a poem or a book" and that he himself listens "like an incorrigible poet," he produces this evocative summary:

> above all it's the rise of a star of shadow, contemplated at last with joy and terror by a mind that the absolute fills with despair; the shapeless pounding of waves of darkness which, by a

6. This is studied in more detail in P. Florence, *Mallarmé, Manet, Redon* (Cambridge: The University Press, 1986).

7. See L. J. Austin, "Mallarmé on music and letters" in *Poetic Principles and Practice* (Cambridge: The University Press, 1987).

miracle analyzed at length, happen to break and beat, here and there, on cliffs pure of all existence, rising up with all the height of their absence. (96)

And there is a boyish sense of delight when his comments on music in *Variations* elicit an admiring letter from no less a person than Vincent d'Indy (204, 205). Nevertheless, Mallarmé, while indicating music as a treasure trove for poets, remains convinced that the two arts are separate, marching in parallel (128), and he refuses to countenance suggestions that music might be the superior form. René Ghil's verse experiments for instance are granted "enormous interest" but criticized because "in this act of just restitution, which we must perform, in which everything is taken back from music, its rhythms which are merely those of reason, and its very coloring which is that of our passions evoked by reverie, you let the old dogma of poetry fade away somewhat" (101). A letter to Edmund Gosse contains his most forthright statement on the subject while at the same time insisting that there is nothing new in what he is doing, "poets throughout the ages [having] never done anything else":

> I create Music and give that name not to the music one can extract by the euphonious juxaposition of words, this primary condition is self-evident; but the beyond, which is magically produced by certain dispositions of the word; where the word, moreover, is merely a means of material communication with the reader, like the notes of the piano. Truly, between the lines and above the glance, that communication is achieved in all purity, without the intervention of the catgut strings and the pistons of the orchestra. (168)

Between the lines: like his published work, Mallarmé's letters constantly stimulate meditation and exploration, probing the central aesthetic questions, quietly teasing out moral and philosophical problems, conveying both encouragement and warning in phrases pregnant with meaning and occasionally slippery with irony. One particularly striking aspect is the contrasting voices displayed. Letters to Geneviève and to his wife are playful, childlike, without a hint of pomposity and revealing an intense joy in simple pleasures. To depict them as condescending, as Sartre[8] does, fails to respond to the mature Mallarmé's combination of intense intellectual questioning and lively humor. To Méry Laurent he wrote in tones of deep tenderness, where

8. *Mallarmé: la lucidité et sa face d'ombre* (Paris: Gallimard, 1986).

frank pleasure in her beauty and gentleness is finely balanced by teasing at her tendency to vanity. Again and again in his letters, Mallarmé indicates in images and phrases borrowing nothing from convention the quality of his friendship for his correspondent: "a letter between the two of us is a banal melody which we allow to wander at will, while our two souls, which understand each other wonderfully well, create a natural and divine continuo for its vulgarity" (37); "I write you so many letters in my imagination as I walk about on my own [...] that not only do I think it utterly unnecessary to write to you, but I'd even be afraid that by placing between us the reality of the post [...] I might make your ghost fade away" (46); "truly there is a country in which we must meet very often, but as our two Reveries may cross one another in such a way that the diaphanous natures of both feel no shiver of recognition, [...] let's return to our writing desks" (55); "you know I'm a little hungry to see you; and if you're occasionally absent from the shores of your beautiful lake, it's because you're no longer there but have popped up, unbeknownst to you, on the banks of the river here" (132).

What these letters reveal is the multifaceted nature of Mallarmé's personality: a gentle family man capable of erotic passion but refusing to let it dominate his life; a poet determined not to sacrifice his high standards for the sake of popularity and exasperated by the demands made on his time by the profession he carried out merely to earn a living, and yet willing to devote himself completely to friends in need; a man who enjoyed the company of others but who also valued solitary days watching the leaves change color at Valvins.

Above all, these are letters which, against the backdrop of the intellectual and artistic life of the second half of the nineteenth century in France, trace the development of a sensitive and intelligent individual, one of France's finest poets, a mind accustomed to dream, and a man of wit, charm, and great warmth.

Selected Letters of Stéphane Mallarmé

1   Childhood and Youth

*After the death of their mother and their father's remarriage, Sté-
phane and his sister Maria were cared for by their maternal grandparents
in Passy, on the outskirts of Paris. From 1850 to 1856 Stéphane attended
schools in Passy, but in 1856 he became a boarder at the lycée at Sens,
where his father lived. The following three letters to Maria give some idea
of his childhood personality. Maria died on 31 August 1857.*

1   MARIA MALLARMÉ

11 October 1854

I'm writing this brief note as I promised you I would last Monday
when I went back to school. I couldn't write before because I didn't
have time and even now I'm doing it at the same time as I'm writing
my algebra exercises. On Sunday I got a red star, which pleased
Grandma and Aunt. The abbé is still unwell.

Yesterday I wrote a letter to Father; if you haven't written to him
since you went back to school you mustn't forget to write to him
straight away. I've had a letter from Uncle Victor telling me that Eu-
doxie has arrived and that she was seasick despite the mint and lemon
pastilles. [. . .][1] she was in bed because of that seasickness, while the
people who were taking her were on the bridge. He was very worried
about her and took a small boat from the port to the ship, where he
found her in that state.

Farewell, dear little sister, be very good, I kiss you with all my
heart. My letter isn't very carefully written but as I explained at the
beginning, I almost don't have time to write it.

2   MARIA MALLARMÉ

undated

Now the holidays are coming, we'll see each other again soon, it's
perhaps the prospect of my stay at Passy,[2] when you'll be able to tell
me everything you want to, that prevents you from sending me a little
letter.

1. The letter has been torn at the bottom of the page and a few lines are missing.
Uncle Victor was the brother of Numa, Mallarmé's father. Eudoxie is his daughter.
2. Where his grandparents lived.

3

I think that by now Father must have sent you a letter I wrote you at the beginning of the month and which he forgot to post for three weeks. That's one for a start, then there was another which dates more or less from the baptism of the imperial Baby;[3] so that's two that you haven't replied to, little rascal. For a while I thought, as I hadn't had any letters from you, that you'd become a nun, and that during the days before and after your vows, you'd been meditating, and that made me wait patiently. Grandma disillusioned me, but told me you'd been very good, which reassured me a little. For I said to myself that the behavior of little sisters isn't something you take into account (when they are little sisters, for they don't need a brother to assume that title). [. . .]

3   MARIA MALLARMÉ

22 April 1856

I'd have liked to have written you a long letter, but I've only a few minutes before I go out and I'm devoting them to you. I arrived here in time to go to bed on Tuesday evening. This is what the dormitory is like. There are a lot of beds, and beside each bed is a little night table, very low, which we use for chairs and for storing our toiletries.

In the middle of the pupils' beds there's the monitor's bed and in the middle of the dormitory a sink where we wash each morning. In each study room there are about thirty pupils, and the president's chair is at one end. The play grounds are extremely small. This morning we went to mass. The chapel is very pretty and looks like a church, only we're perched on pews which are much too high and then we have to kneel on the floor. We have the same uniform as Henri Robert, one for Sundays and one for everyday. Today I'm going out with a pupil from my class to whom Father entrusted me for the first moments. I'm going straightaway, without going to the day house, to a country estate Father owns near Villeneuve-l'Archevêque, that's about 8 leagues from here. Talking about archbishops or rather archbishoprics,[4] I went there with auntie on Monday to see M. Chaveaux. While I was there I had a bad migraine and vomited.

By 1858 Mallarmé was already beginning to fill exercise books with poems and prose poems and in 1860 he compiled a personal anthology of

3. Eugène, the Prince Imperial.
4. "Archevêque" means archbishop.

favorite poems. It was at this stage, too, that he began translating the poems of Edgar Allan Poe. After passing the baccalauréat in November 1860, he began work at the Records Office at Sens, much against his will. Since his grandfather was his legal guardian, Mallarmé needed his permission to become a teacher of English, a career he felt would leave him time for writing.

4   M. DESMOLINS

17 January 1862

My heart was really in everything I said to you on your birthday, on Saint Stephen's day and on New Year's Day. I wanted to pluck up my courage and try to persevere in the Records Office.[5] But honestly, the work is absolutely hateful to me.

When I left high school, I said I wanted to enter the teaching profession. That was the course most suited to my temperament. The Records Office, unless you really enjoy it, doesn't just devour your time, it devours your individuality as well. Whereas with teaching, the more a teacher works and learns, the more intellectual value he acquires as a man.

And among the chairs that lead furthest must be counted the chair of foreign languages.

There's an examination in Paris every year: I would take it this year solely to see exactly what's involved and then I'd present myself seriously next year, in English.

Once you've passed the exam, you're appointed a teacher with a fixed salary of 2,000 francs, leaving aside supplementary payments or money earned from coaching. In the Records Office, I wouldn't be earning 1,600 francs for another 5 years and then only provided I earned them in some village. Father is about to retire and 5 years is a long time to wait, when you have expenses and you're not earning anything.

As a teacher, I'd prepare my B.A., just so that I could do a doctoral thesis. Doing a thesis on a foreign writer would be as much a recreation as a piece of work. Once you have your doctorate, the future opens up for you. With a few rudiments of Italian and Spanish, you can get appointed as a professor of foreign literature in a University department.

You can see that teaching offers just as brilliant a future as the summits of the Civil Service. If you don't achieve success, at least

5. Mallarmé had begun work in this office on 26 December 1860.

5

you're at peace, which is also one of the great charms of the Records Office, indeed, the only charm it has for me.

According to a young man I know,[6] who is 24 and who last year was an English teacher at the high school and who is now at Saint Cyr,[7] with 5,000 francs in salary or from coaching, there is at this moment, now that the Minister no longer wants those old English puppets who used to be the laughing stock of their pupils, there is, as I was saying, a real future for young French teachers who have a gift for literature.

I've been thinking this over for 8 or 10 days. You may have received, or if not you will soon receive, a letter from Mother[8] on this topic. We spoke about it very seriously as a family; think carefully about it and bear in mind this fact in particular, given that our means are about to be reduced by Father's imminent retirement, that I'd be a financial burden for only 18 months instead of 4 or 5 years.

I beg you, my dear Grandpa, (but why should I beg you when I know how warmly interested in me you are) talk this over with Grandma, you have experience of life, and it's up to you to guide me.

Before saying farewell, I'll tell you that Father has obtained his leave and a replacement, that he is neither better nor worse and that we don't know what weather to hope for, since humidity and mild weather relax his nerves and leave him melancholy and heavy, while cold, bracing weather excites him beyond measure.

Farewell, I hug you with all my heart, as well as my dear Grandma. My good wishes to my aunts and cousins.

5   M. Desmolins

31 January 1862

After reading the letter you wrote yesterday, I felt within me a great sense of sadness. It gave the impression that you were saying to me: "I'm allowing you to do this, *but* if you do it you'll disappoint me and I won't be pleased with you." Which seemed worse to me than if you'd said: "I forbid you." That *but* tortured me.

Mother reassured me by saying that what was clear from your letter as well as that of my dear grandma was that, without giving me the slightest encouragement, you were leaving me free to choose.

So I spoke to an English teacher from Sens, a man already mature

6. Emmanuel Des Essarts.
7. The military academy.
8. The reference here is to Mallarmé's stepmother.

6

and who, so it seems, has an excellent method. He would come five times a week, that is, every day except for Thursday,[9] and his lessons would last an hour. He would give me lots of homework, correct the translations into English himself, and would give me a fair copy for the translations into French so that I could correct them myself. In that way we wouldn't waste time and could spend it instead on practical lessons, on grammar and on conversation. It'll be an expense, I know that, but I'll be the one who pays for it.

My superintendent has sworn to me that there's no reason to resign and so, just in case there are great mysterious circumstances that I haven't foreseen, I'd have a door open in the Records Office until June, when I have my first exam. As for your saying to me, my dear good Grandpa, in addition to your excellent advice and your serious remarks, that if I'm left to my own devices, I won't work enough, that could well be true for work which didn't please me, such as the work I'm undertaking for the Records Office, if, for instance, I were to work without a superintendent. And is it true that I'd be left to my own devices? I'll have my teacher just as I had a superintendent and I'll work for 8 or 9 hours instead of for 2 or 3. Finally, dear Grandpa, I'll keep you up to date with all my studies, and with my progress. To do so, I'll write to you in English, and often, and you won't have to answer me. I'll do my utmost in all possible ways to make myself worthy of the freedom you're giving me, and I've made a packet of the three letters you and Grandma have written on that serious subject so that I can reread them often, and take heart from them, seeing that I'm the only one responsible for my own future. Rest assured that my work and, one day, my success, will make you abandon the regret you feel at the moment, when you think, just as my poor mother, whose place you've taken, could have thought about my future, and you'll never have to repent the decision I've taken. All that I'm telling you here, I'm also saying to my dear Grandma, to whom I owe, just as much as to you, my love and my gratitude.

On 11 May 1862 Emmanuel Des Essarts, whom Mallarmé had met towards the end of 1861, invited him on an outing to Fontainebleau, where he met Henri Cazalis, Ettie and Isabelle Yapp, Nina Gaillard, and Henri Regnault. These friendships were to play an important role in Mallarmé's life over the next decade or so. It was also during this outing that Cazalis fell in love with Ettie Yapp.

9. The traditional day off in nineteenth-century French schools.

24 May 1862

I arrived at Emmanuel's[10] place yesterday. He instantly assumed a tragic countenance and cried out: "What's this I hear? You've published a book and haven't even shown me the cover! You give Cazalis a copy and don't even offer me one. I can guess why: I know what a cynic you are. This book of yours is designed to replace certain packs of cards prohibited by modesty and by the police, and bear in mind that there's no difference between those two." Terrified, I denied everything. He showed me your letter and, indeed, there it was in black and white: "What's really firing me up is Stéphane's book."

Sad and desolate at wreaking such havoc in your soul, I was almost on the point of admitting the paternity of some obscene poem or other, written in my sleep, when I remembered *Hugo's book*.[11]

Since then I've thought about you often, you dear lucky man. When I woke up this morning, your image came into my mind through the curtains with the first ray of sunlight. I took two cups of tea in the garden in your honor and came upstairs again to write to you.

Neither Emmanuel nor I laughed, of course we didn't;[12] but we each interpeted your letter in our own way. Emmanuel frowned and I smiled. What that Olympian frown indicated, I think you already know, for you must have received the letter which he immediately devised and declamed to me in a voice of thunder. What my smile indicated, you shall now hear.

I'll tell you that I believe love is serious and true only when it has been consecrated by the passage of time, which makes many an entablature collapse on the heads of its caryatids. So, for the moment, although you spew forth fire and flame, I'll think of your passion as a flirt. But that doesn't diminish it at all in my thoughts. Happiness consists of flirts as well as love affairs: so, I'll say what I'll always say to a friend whom I see on the point of tasting new impressions— "Drink as deep as you can, you're happy only when mad, that's to say, tipsy." Man is born curious and must remain so forever. You should never let a chance pass you by. That's the only way of *living*. In that way, a heart which is extremely full-blown can experience a virginal love and a virginal heart can learn what it is to be blasé. *Learn* and

---

10. Emmanuel Des Essarts, a friend of both Mallarmé and Cazalis.

11. Crossed out under this phrase is "Les Châtiments," a work banned by the police as Hugo was in exile.

12. Cazalis had just confessed to Mallarmé that he was in love with Ettie Yapp, a young English girl.

enjoy, that's the whole secret. By enjoy, I mean morally for some and for those for whom that's impossible, physically. So, love Ettie, and let the current take you as it will.

The fact is that English girls are adorable. That sweet golden hair, those drops of water from Lake Geneva, set in candor, which they're pleased to call their eyes, like other women; their figures, which are so Grecian in their harmony: not a pretentious wasp's waist, but the figure of an angel who has just folded her wings under her blouse!

So, love Ettie, and let the current take you where it will. Ah! what a charming memory I have of our delightful outing.[13] Alas! it seems such a long time ago already, and it's beginning to fade. If Henri[14] hadn't crushed them underfoot, the strawberries would combine with the lips to give a shade of purplish pink and thus everything would already be mingled together in a series of half-shades. The town of Sens is so gloomy that everything that passes through it turns gray!

Oh! those wild races from rock to rock! the carriage in which all 10 of us travelled! the oaks! the periwinkles! the sun in our eyes and in our hearts, even though it wasn't shining in the sky! and the song we shouted at the tops of our voices! *All is over,*[15] as Byron says, Ettie will translate that for you.

You tell me I pleased the ladies, and that delights me. Mlle Nina[16] has asked me for some poetry, I'm sending her some lines, a Louis XV sonnet.[17] You've asked me for a sonnet; I'm sending you two. Choose the one you want and the other will be for Henri. He has to have something to remember me by. I want something of his: he can sketch or draft something for me when he has time. Isn't he charming! I'll write to him soon. Be sure to tell him to consider my poem only as a souvenir; otherwise it would be fatuity not friendship on my part. I'm Pylades, not Trissotin. I wanted him to understand clearly my intention of removing a foot from each line.

Emmanuel tells me it would be good to send "Le Guignon" to Mmes Y. Give it them for me with all my good wishes and many many thanks for their kind welcome. The other poem is for Mlle Gaillard. With the same recommendation. I really don't know if I'll be able to go to Meudon. There are two devilish horns which only too often stick out of my wallet. Rest assured that if I can, I will. As

13. Mallarmé and some friends, including Cazalis and Ettie Yapp, had gone on a long and happy walk in the Forest of Fontainebleau on 11 May.
14. Henri Regnault, a friend of Cazalis.
15. In English in the original. The quotation is from "To Emma."
16. Nina Gaillard, a close friend of many young poets of the Parnassian school.
17. Probably "*Placet.*"

for the Black Forest, that will depend on the editor Emmanuel is meeting for our volume of *Contes étranges*.[18] You know we're working on it together, like brothers. If the editor pays for it straightaway, that will decide matters and we'll go and drown ourselves in the lakes of cherry brandy. Farewell.

Lose yourself as best you can in the paradise of your folly—and for as long as possible.

To you and Henri with all my heart.

P.S. Another word about my poems. Tell Mme Y. when you give her "Le Guignon" that I read it so badly the other day that I thought it would be polite to send it to her on *cream-laid paper* (ask Ettie the meaning of those three words, too).[19]

Tell Mlle Nina that this sonnet is offered to her only until I've something more serious to write in her album.

7   HENRI CAZALIS

4 June 1862

I'm briefly interrupting my article on Leconte de Lisle,[20] dear friend, to write you twenty lines. And first of all, do you know you're still a madman? It makes me jealous.

Alas! You know how delighted I was at Fontainebleau, which will give you an indication of how much Chaville would enchant me. But, you poor scatterbrain, I'm tied down: and it's not even, as in your case, a gold thread of Ettie's hair that binds me!

I think it's more likely torn from Harpagon's red wig. Let me explain. My poor father has been very ill for a long time, and as he no longer has much notion of the cost of money and would give me 1,000 francs as willingly as 10 cents, a certain sense of propriety prevents me from asking him for anything, for whatever purpose. . . .

Moreover, the purse is in my stepmother's desk, and she's a relatively young woman[21] who has never understood what a young man is like and has only one word on her lips: the horrible word Economy! Well, as I live in constant fear of seeing her spit out that red mouse, I hardly ever speak to her. That's what family life is like for me. Emmanuel, moreover, may already have told you about it.

I can tell you that if I said I needed long walks and fresh air, she

18. This seems only to have been a short-lived project.
19. In English in the text.
20. This article has not yet been found.
21. On 27 October 1848 Mallarmé's father had married his second wife, Anne Mathieu, born on 6 March 1829.

wouldn't fail to reply: "There are paths in the garden, and as far as fresh air is concerned, we in Sens breathe the healthiest air possible" It's partly to escape this mean and stifling domestic life that I'm going to spread my wings and go as far as London this January. Here I live a strange kind of existence: every one considers me a wastrel and honors me as if I had three mistresses, but I never have a cent in my pocket and don't even sleep with the maid. I'm a gilded bohemian.

So, please don't count on me at all for Sunday; if I had any tears left, I'd cry about it! You'll do your best to give my excuses, won't you? And, too, I give you my thanks, my adorable friend, for your brotherly offer. Two reasons prevent me from accepting: the first is that I'd need between thirty and forty francs, the second is that even if you had them, I'd not be able to pay you back. But you will think of me, won't you? Fancy having to say that happiness is sometimes contained in the glitter of two gold coins! Often it's in even less.

Forgive me, you butterfly through whose wing the sun shines, forgive this gloomy letter and these stupid details, but shouldn't friends tell each other everything?

Did you receive my poems? Since you're good enough to want to keep them all, I'm sending you, to accompany your own sonnet, a poor little sonnet hatched these last few days, all sad and ugly.

Emmanuel may have told you of a curious sterility that the Spring had installed in me. After three months of impotence, I've at last shaken it off, and my first sonnet is devoted to describing it, by which I mean cursing it. It's a fairly new type of poetry, in which the material effects on the blood and the nerves are analyzed and combined with the moral effects, those of the mind and the soul. It could be called *Springtime Spleen*.[22] When the combination is successfully harmonized and the work neither too physical nor too spiritual, it can really stand for something.[23]

You may well laugh at my mania for sonnets—but no, for you yourself have written some delightful ones—but for me it's a great poem in miniature: the quatrains and tercets seem to me to be songs in themselves, and sometimes I spend entire days balancing the different sections, so that the complete work is harmonious and comes close to Beauty. [...]

Towards the end of June Mallarmé fell in love with a German woman, Marie Gerhard, who was working as a governess for a local fam-

22. The sonnet in question is "Vere Novo," later called "Renouveau."
23. There follows a copy of "Vere Novo."

ily. On 8 November she and Mallarmé set off together for London, where Mallarmé intended to spend a year learning English as part of his plan to enter the teaching profession. The year 1862 also saw his first publications in journals, not only of poems but also of his early artistic credo, "Hérésies artistiques."

8   MARIE GERHARD

26 June 1862

The German Lady is none other than me, as you've guessed, and I alone wrote that letter. Forgive me for this trick: yesterday and the day before, unwittingly and unwillingly, you played some fairly pretty tricks on me. The day before yesterday I thought you were English, and had written, in the best English I knew, the most beautiful letter you could dream of. On leaving you I realized my mistake and was forced to tear it all to pieces. That's the first thing. Now for the second, which is also funny. Knowing that you were to return to the island, I walked up and down prudently for an hour or two, and to avoid attracting attention, I drew the church steeple in an album, glancing more often in the direction from which I hoped you'd come than in that of the steeple—and in my whole life I've never touched a pencil! But enough of laughter.

You must have seen from the fact that I have often waited at the school gate and from the way I looked at you on Sunday in the Cathedral, that you haven't failed to make a serious impression on me. If you've understood that, then that's already an achievement, but it's nothing compared with the truth. For the last three months I've loved you violently and for several days now I've idolized you even more wildly. Will you accept my love?

Be charming enough to answer me before burning this letter: if you consent to letting me love you, I'll be mad with joy; if you refuse, I'll still be happy to suffer for you and through you.

You can see that I must have a reply, and you will give me one, won't you? Tomorrow? For I prefer even the sorrow of a refusal to my old hope, which, because it has lasted so long, is very close to despair. Moreover, whether you love me or not, you won't be able to prevent me loving you with all my heart, in a melancholy way.

Farewell, my angel, believe in me: rest assured that everything you've just read is written by a man of honor, a man of feeling, and forgive me for adoring you. Moreover, who's guilty of my love? It's you, my charming girl, and it's on those eyes that I place in advance a kiss that is full of hope—those eyes that will smile at me tomorrow, won't they?

Forever yours.

9   HENRI CAZALIS

4–5 August 1862

Mio povero, you ask why I don't write to you and whether I'm angry with you. How naive you are. I haven't written to you because for several days pen and ink have become singularly odious to me. I don't know why. The fact is that for a fortnight I've been running round like a madman and my room fills me such horror I go there only to fling myself into my armchair and dream.

You know that I'm clumsy and that I've snared myself in a trap I laid in a grassy tussock of the domain of love. This is what has happened. I'd noticed a young girl who is fairly pretty, distinguished, sad. She is German, and a governess in a rich local family. That happened some six weeks ago. She attracted me, I don't know how, and I began a determined courtship. Refusals, flights, fears, and blushes on her part: tenacity on mine. Well, a few days ago she softened and I've begun to enter her life. Like all governesses and tutors, who are always living out of their station in life, she has a melancholy charm which worked its effect on me, with the result that I fell somewhat in love with her.

When I saw what had happened, I tried to struggle, foreseeing innumerable problems: her position, which I could destroy, for she depends entirely on her good behaviour; the spying that goes on in small towns; time lost. The struggle only sharpens my longings.

She's unhappy here, and bored. I'm unhappy and bored. From our two melancholies we could perhaps make a single happiness. It wouldn't be surprising if she began to love me a little; it's certain that I've already become part of her life. This may be an act of folly I'm committing. But no, I'll be less lonely on holiday.

I needn't tell you that even if I have to resort to highway robbery, I'll see you in Paris this vacation. I'll probably spend a week with you and a week at Versailles. What lovely walks we'll go on in the evenings, and how charming it's all going to be. In the meanwhile I have you here. Thank you for sending yourself to me: I open my album twenty times a day to see you. Of course I've put you beside Ettie. Oh, my poor friend, how I pity you! What sad evenings you must pass after all the stunning events of the last months! How lonely you must be!

13

But also, how wonderful it is to be able to tell oneself in all certainty: "Someone over the sea loves me! Even if there's a terrifying storm, even if everything is raging, that gentle swallow will always send her thoughts to me, serene and calm, through all the uproar!" How consoling that must be.

Something else makes me pity you, too, and that's dealing with stamped paper all day and every day, and writing on it . . . I've been through that and I know what it's like. It's true that you're doing it for her sake.

You want to know when I'll go to London. I still don't know, but in all likelihood, it will be in December or at the beginning of January. So we'll go together! You'll have to know English—no, don't study it beforehand: *she* will teach you and it will seem to you like the warbling of birds.

Farewell dear friend. Signor Emmanuel shakes you by one hand and I by the other. My love to you.

Read me if you can. If you can't, guess.

10   HENRI CAZALIS

4 December 1862

Oh, my poor friend! I've wept so much since yesterday that it's made me ill, and my poor Marie has no tears left. Yesterday, I came home after seeing Katie, who is feeling a little unwell. Ettie and her mother were at a photographer's. When I kissed Marie on returning she was very sad.[24] I asked her why she was sad, and realized that she had reflected at length during my absence. "I must leave," she told me gently. Imagine what the poor child must have suffered, in reaching such a decision—she lives for me alone!

Was it in thinking of herself that she reached that decision? Was it the result of remembering her poor mother who particularly loved her and who last year as she lay dying entrusted to her her younger sisters? Or did she tell herself that her father, whom she adores, would reject her and blush for her if he knew she was with me? Or perhaps she thought of her own life which I'm daily destroying, of her honor which I erase hour by hour, when she is so chaste and good and would never have suspected in the past that love was bringing her to such a pass?

No, my friend, no, she's doing it for me, this is yet another sacrifice

24. Mallarmé had been living with Marie without having married her, and was trying to keep the fact from his friends the Yapps and from his own family. Katie is Ettie Yapp's sister.

she's making for me as she has made all the others. She can see I'm poor—the notary isn't keeping his word to me—and that life is hard. She's distressed to see that I'm depriving myself of everything. She can see that her presence prevents me from inviting people who could be useful to me, and that I'm forced to hide from them. She has guessed—and this is the truth—that my mother has been told everything now and she is afraid to harm my relationship with my family.

So she said to herself: "I'm not needed here. After having sacrificed everything to him, I'm going to sacrifice even the happiness I have in being with him, my life!" And nothing can change her resolution. She is more courageous than I am. I sob and cry unceasingly. She tries to remain firm while she's in my sight so as not to cause me more pain, and then she goes outside to cry. I really don't dare, although I already feel half dead with grief, to dissuade her. That would be selfishness, Henri. Who knows? Perhaps she has not lost anything yet. Her father is still in ignorance, as are the people who know her. There is still somewhere where she can hold her head high and that's something she wouldn't be able to do later. I sob at the mere thought of not feeling her beside me any more, and yet, it seems to me that duty orders me to let her leave before it's too late. How horrible! I have to be my own executioner!

Oh, my dear friend, I cry and I cry as I write all this to you! I've been crying since this morning; I don't have a moment's respite, as soon as I set eyes on her, I burst into tears.

It's terrifying to think of what she's enduring in her heart to remain unshaken in her resolve despite my tears and my kisses. Her pallor tells me she has struggled horribly with herself. Poor Marie. Dear friend, she has taken devotion and self-sacrifice to its absolute limits. She is doing more than killing herself for me. She is great, she is holy; I should speak of her only on my knees.

It's I who am killing the poor child. She was born in a town in Germany. Her childhood was gentle, calm, and pious. She left her homeland at an early age. Despite that isolation, she always respected duty. She is candor itself. Then her mother died. She found herself even more alone, in a *foreign* land (I'm beginning to understand the painful meaning of that word). There, a young man loved her. For a long time, although her noble heart was pounding, she fled him. She wanted to leave. *Out of the goodness of her heart,* so as not to upset me, she stayed. She loved me as no one has loved. She sacrificed everything to me in order to follow me! What have I done to this good, serene angel? I have made her into the woman of whom it will be said: "She lived with her lover!" How I despise myself! What a monster I am! I should have foreseen this! Yes, that's what I've done! And even if we leave that aside, what is to become of her? She would have returned to Camberg, have made a good marriage and been happy! I weep, because I'm an assassin ... for she'll die of grief, little by little. And even if she survives, her life will be poisoned by this memory. For her, everything is sad, there is no happiness. My image will pursue her everywhere. Yet again, *I've destroyed her existence!*

And yet, my poor Henri, when I go over this whole catastrophic story in my memory, I don't see at what precise moment I was guilty. Once we loved each other, separation was impossible. The fault was no more committed the day I spoke to her of London than the day before or the day after. It was inevitable that she would say "Yes," and for me to have left without taking her would have been to kill both of us, or rather, it would have been impossible. Poor child! Not to love any more! For her heart is broken and she will no longer have the strength to love. She'll never marry because she wouldn't want to marry without love. And what's more, she's too noble to deceive a husband by allowing him to believe in a virginity she no longer possesses.

Love excuses everything. She considers herself chaste and pure at this moment (and she is), although she has given herself to me. But later, when I'm no longer there—I know her—she'll despise herself. She'll feel she's lost something which can never be given back. Oh, what a future I have prepared for her!

And what shall I do? Advise me, dear brother. After she's sacrificed everything for me, surely it's cowardice to abandon her like this, all alone—with remorse, perhaps—to let her destroy her whole life like this! And from another point of view, in sacrificing myself as she has sacrificed herself for me, that's to say by declaring open war on my family, I'm not sacrificing myself alone. My father and grandfather wouldn't survive something they wouldn't understand. Am I the master of their lives?

Oh, tell me how I can sacrifice just myself to her! The very thought of her departure makes me shudder. Oh, my Henri, am I to accompany her to London bridge and let the poor child take the ship that brought her here a month ago? And am *I* to stay here and watch her leave? Can you think of it? And when I returned home, there would be nothing more, ever again.

Friday, 11 A.M.

I left you yesterday to go to dinner. After dinner, I no longer had the strength to survive the evening. Marie was exhausted, too. We went to bed. The poor child didn't close an eye the entire night. When I fell asleep she took the opportunity to cry. Her sobs woke me several times. Once she was saying: "Nothing left, nothing left." That phrase sums up her whole future. She is already dead. Another time she was saying that she wouldn't live very long because, since she was crying incessantly and feeling such a disgust for life, she would gradually lose all her strength until the final day came. That's true, dear friend, people can die like that. Remember she's German. "I'll contract tuberculosis," she was saying. And she will. She spoke to me about you. She told me she'd be afraid of seeing you because you'd remind her too much of me. And what's more, she wouldn't dare to see you because you'd despise her. I had the devil of a job to convince her that you would venerate her and that what could attract the scorn of certain people was precisely what you see as her sacrifice, which only made you honor her all the more. "My Stéphane, for your sake I lost what I most valued in all the world," she said to me this morning, "and that's my honor. As long as I'm with you and you love me, it seems to me completely normal that I gave you everything, but one day, when I'm on my own, I'll really miss it and I'll hate myself!" The poor angelic child.

Where had I got to yesterday evening, Henri? Oh, yes, I was telling you about her departure. I was going to say to you: "See, I'm still crying as I watch her." You saw Ettie leave, but that was for a fixed time. *Our* separation is *forever*. What's more, although you loved Ettie then as deeply as you can love, she hadn't, as a result of that shared existence which unites two people forever, become as deep a part of your existence. Losing her would have been like losing a dream, for she is a dream in your eyes. But for me to lose Marie is to lose half of my life, the better half. That communal existence which makes one breathe the same air as the beloved—how often, when she slept, have I breathed in the warm breath of her mouth—eat the same meals as her, that life which means that each knows the number of the other's clothes and that both write with the same pen, that life binds you so closely that one sees husbands who, having been perfectly indifferent to their wives, finding them insipid or even hating them, mourn in all sincerity and grieve to the point of going mad when they lose those wives. It's something you can understand only when you've experienced it for yourself. I would not have believed it a few months ago. What! Am I never again to see her moving around me, will she never again wake me in the morning, will I never again kiss her goodnight before falling asleep, will I have the heart to eat when the meal has not been served by her? And what is to become of this dear little household we'd created? Henri, Henri! We're already talking of the future and that distresses me. When one knows one has to think of the thousands of things that accompany a departure, one is already half-way to being separated. Don't you think I'm right?

That's how things are when a dear creature leaves. And now the dear creature is irreplaceable, she's my blood, my soul, my entire life, Marie. You know her. Forever. . . . My mind's wandering and I'm rambling on. Let me do that in my grief. I'm crying so much as I write to you that everything I see is red. And to say that nothing can be done about it! I could rebel against my family, but they have against me a weapon which is the law, for I'm not yet 21. And then there's my poor grandfather who's very ill. I've just received a good letter from him. What still hurts me when I think of it and what tortures her is that my family must be cursing her. My mother has heard her described, by my enemies at Sens, as an astute, clever, educated person who is much older than I. With descriptions like that she's going to think that I've been tricked by a hussy! If I were to weep in front of her, she would pity me as a poor dupe. She would do everything against Marie,—whose only crime is to have loved me too deeply! Oh, poor soul, too loyal and too good! Those whom I love, even Emmanuel himself, told me her kisses were, or could be, motivated by self-interest! What did she get by loving me? She has lost everything, and she may perhaps lose her very life! How horrible it all is.

Yes, she is noble, yes, she is pure, yes, she is virtuous. She is more than an angel, she's a saint. The poor exiled soul gave to the man she loved everything she had and fed my heart with the best of her being. I respect her as I respect my dead sister.

Even those who don't attribute to her the intentions I've just mentioned consider her as a vulgar mistress, an adventuress! No, she has not been my mistress. She has been my guardian angel and she ought to be my wife.

Just listen to how noble and delicate she is. Not only has she never reproached me but she even said to me sometimes when I looked at her with sorrow in my eyes: "Do you think I love you less? Even if you destroyed me irrevocably, I'd never reproach you with anything, not even in my private thoughts." She's never said a word to me of those imprudent conversations when I spoke to her of marriage. The poor soul smiled sorrowfully, but deep down she didn't believe it. Yesterday, the day before yesterday, this morning, she could have said to me: "But you told me we'd marry, if you could, one day." And, although I spoke to her about it only after our voyage to London had been agreed on, so it can't have been a consideration in her decision, she could have said a word or two about it, and she chose to keep quiet. I even saw from the expression in her eyes and on her face that she didn't think of it for a moment. Oh, how great and beautiful that is! No one will ever know all the treasures in her heart.

In the past, on leaving her, I would have said: "I'm leaving happiness aside and happiness is rare enough on this earth for one to neglect it when one happens upon it." Today, I say: "Head bowed and knowing what I'm doing, I enter the domain of sorrow." I no longer hold out any hopes for anything. And I'll suffer remorse! I took her when she was young, candid, and trusting. I took everything excellent she possessed and I took it for myself, for she has made me a better man, dear friend. And here I am leaving her broken and with nothing before her.

She won't dare return to Camberg, for her father would guess something had happened when he saw her grief. She's going to find a position with strangers. There she will have to *work*. You know how possible that is when one is suffering. She will be all alone in the world. There'll be no one to pity or understand her. And having to begin anew that sad governess's life as if nothing had happened since she gave it up. It's too much for her: she is very strong, but she has too much heart and will never be able to bear such a fate. [. . .]

Marie returned to France on 9 January, came back to London on 10 February, went to Brussels on 4 March. Towards the end of March Mallarmé returned to France, to be with his fatally ill father, who died on 12 April. At the end of the month he went back to London with Marie. They were married on 10 August.

11   HENRI CAZALIS

27 April 1863

For ages I've had an envelope with your name prancing over it in a tempting fashion. Were it not for the sad preoccupations of the funeral ceremony, I would have loved to have told you by other means than a banal circular that we had suffered a great loss.[25] It's true that my poor father had been on his deathbed for four years, or five—but there is a vast difference between a dead man and a dying man!

I spent about two weeks at Sens—slightly less, perhaps. Then I went to fetch Marie in Belgium, and now, after a pilgrimage to Ant-

25. Mallarmé's father had died on 12 April.

werp, we're back in London again, the country of the false Rubens paintings. As soon as I've found out how to go about it, we'll get married. We're in a strange position—the only thing we lack is a knowledge of the formalities. So it has come, my good Henri, that day which, in your brotherly solicitude, you so feared. Yes, it's close enough for me to see clearly what lies beyond. Over the last two months I've lived much more than in the past, and perhaps I'm a little more mature.

This is how the future looks to me. If I married Marie to make myself happy, I'd be a madman. Besides, can happiness be found on earth? And should one seek it, *seriously,* anywhere but in dreams? That's not the real aim of life: the real aim is duty. Duty, whether you call it art, struggle, or whatever. I don't hide from myself the fact that I'll sometimes have horrendous struggles—and great disillusionments which will later become sources of torment. I'm not hiding anything from myself. Only I want to look at everything with an unwavering glance and call a little on that willpower whose name I've never known.

No, I'm marrying Marie solely because she couldn't live without me and I would have poisoned her limpid existence. So if I suffer in the future, you who alone receive these deep and intimate outpourings from my heart, don't say to me: "You were wrong, despite my wise recommendations." Say rather: "You are accomplishing through your sufferings the high goal you set for your life: take heart and don't fall short."

But I don't want to talk to you any longer about these sad predictions, or I'll end by believing in them already. Henri, I'm not acting for myself, but for her alone. You are the only person in the world who knows I'm making a sacrifice: in front of my other friends, I'll put on a show of believing that I see this union as a means of building my own happiness—so that Marie will seem greater in their eyes.

Burn my letters; you alone will see into the depths of my heart. But I'm talking of myself all the time. Do tell me about yourself, about yourself alone for a change, and at length.

I've seen Ettie, my dear Henri, once when I was in Paris. I spoke a lot about you: I told her that it was my dream to return to London via Strasbourg.[26] And she thanked me with her loving eyes of days gone by for mentioning your name so frequently. And your poor heart? How are your wounds? Henri, will you ever recover? *Tell your-*

26. Since March, largely to avoid Ettie Yapp, Cazalis had been living in Strasbourg.

self you won't, and don't speculate on the passing of time. Time does
enough on its own, alas! My poor hopeless friend! You have wonder-
ful memories, it's true. But memories make martyrs of us.

Farewell, dear Henri, let's never forget each other. Wherever we
may be. I feel we're so far apart now. Marie loves you and embraces
you as I do.

12   HENRI CAZALIS

3 June 1863

Don't be surprised to see this envelope written in pencil. Yesterday
we went on a wonderful boat trip through the enchanted woods of
Richmond and we wanted to moor the boat for a few moments to
inscribe a good letter for you in the trunk of some birch or other as it
leaned over the dark green water. But the current pulled us on. For a
long time now the current has been pulling me along from day to day
and I've no idea how I'm living. I love you so much I don't write to
you. First, if I did write I'd have too much to tell you, and then, too,
there's no point, for you know my heart better than I do myself.

Marie would smile if she saw me write that expression: "I've too
much to tell you"; for ten times an evening, I pretend to misinterpret
the slightest of her actions and cry out: "I'll tell Cazalis!" She does
the same to me. You are the supreme Judge. So, my Cazalogre,[27] you'll
forgive my silence—as I forgive you for being better than me. You
mention Switzerland. There's so much blue in that country, apart
from the sky—and Marie's eyes which would follow me—that that
dream is one of those whose manes I most caress and on whose backs
I ride with the most joy.

But, judge! Can I go to a country I don't know without having
anything certain to go to? Would that be wise? What would become
of us there, if we ran out of supplies? If I thought of Switzerland
solely for its virginal glaciers and its snow which is as much a flower
as are the lilies, I'd set off without a penny in my purse and with our
two minds full of stars. I'd fly there as an Artist.

That way I'd be sure of not being disenchanted. But as I only want
to make of it a bank in which to capitalize on the mines of my
thought, I'd be afraid of disillusionment. I'm already too familiar with
such disillusionment.

But still, I'm grateful to you Henri, for having thought of me

27. Mallarmé here invents a word based on a combination of Cazalis' name and
that of a fairy-tale monster.

straightaway. And rest assured that I won't go into any office—I believe I have that much pride. The life of a teacher in a high school is simple, modest, and calm. We'll be peaceful there. I'm working on it.

Nevertheless, I'd rather copy out deeds for an attorney-at-law than articles written with the aim of earning a few hundred-sou pieces. I think Emmanuel is greatly harming himself by abandoning himself to his great facility: he perpetrates all too easily that kind of brilliant but empty page. He doesn't distinguish clearly enough between the Real and the Ideal. A modern poet has even gone so far as to lament that "Action was not the sister of Dream"[28] and Emmanuel is one who shares that regret. Dear Lord, if it were otherwise, if the Dream were thus debased and deflowered, where would we retreat to, we unlucky ones whom the earth repels and for whom the Dream alone offers refuge? Henri, my friend, seek your sustenance from the Ideal. Earthly happiness is ignoble—you have to have hands full of calluses if you're to pick it up. Saying "I'm happy!" amounts to saying "I'm a coward"—and more often "I'm a fool." For you have to avoid seeing above that ceiling of happiness the sky of the Ideal, or else you have to close your eyes deliberately. I've written a little poem on this subject which I've called "Les Fenêtres" and I'm sending it to you: and another called "L'Assaut"[29] which is as vague and frail as a reverie. From a head of hair which gave birth in my mind to the idea of a flag, my heart, seized with military ardor, leaps through hideous landscapes to lay siege to Hope's stronghold, in order to plant on it this standard of fine gold. But my mad heart realises after this brief moment of folly, that Hope is merely a kind of veiled and sterile specter. I'm including with these poems those you asked me for. I'd like you to have most of my poems. I'll include some in each of my letters. Dear Henri, send me those very fine prose poems that the good Emmanuel told me about. I want you to. You tell me you've met noble souls, elevated and sympathetic souls. Lucky man! I greatly envy you, for I'm so alone here. I have no one to whom I can talk about Art, poets, and the Ideal. I don't know any serious young artists in London.

Shake your friends' hands, whom I shall love because they are your friends, on behalf of a bohemian spirit forever disgusted with the place in which he has pitched camp and who would like to find repose in their calm and lofty conversations.

Farewell, dear Henri. Yes, life on earth does smell of cooking.

Marie and I embrace you. We'll let you know our wedding day, which won't be far off.

28. Baudelaire, in "Le Reniement de Saint Pierre."
29. This poem, retitled "Le Château de l'Espérance," was not published until after the poet's death.

24 July 1863

Forgive me for this long silence. I've been ill, and now I have an enormous amount of work to do to prepare for my exams. Ill, but not dangerously so, only in a rather irritating way. London's sun is not that gay sun of Paris which brings out along the boulevards a vast array of charming verdure in the form of beer tables and whose light is full of gaiety. Here the rays seem to have taken on some of the pallor of the poor hospital walls where they have fallen asleep and whose sickly plaster they have warmed. The unhealthy air is full of all the exhalations of poverty, a poverty putrefied by the heavy heat, and, for the poor, summer is merely that season when vermin, warmed up, flourish in greatest numbers in their rags. I hate London when there are no fogs: in its mists, it is a town without peer.

All this may be mere homesickness, and I'm already breathing in the air of Paris where I'll return at the beginning of next month. Yes, it's homesickness, since the English girls, those angels of the kitchen who dream in the rays of light reflected by their pans, without imagining that Astarte's star ever existed,—oh, do you know Poe's lines:

And I said—"She is warmer than Dian:
She rolls through an ether of sighs—
She revels in a region of sighs:
She has seen that the tears are not dry on
These cheeks, where the worm never dies,
And has come past the stars of the Lion,
To point us the path to the skies—
To the Lethean peace of the skies—
Come up, in despite of the Lion,
To shine on us with her bright eyes—
Come up through the lair of the Lion,
With love in her luminous eyes"[30]

and finally the English men, like the rooms of the *Grand Hotel,* strike me as being all alike. I mean the English of London, my Henri.

Till now I've told you more about Astarte than about myself. My illness was an eruption and since then I've been completely yellow— as yellow as a lemon, as yellow as a coward. Yellow blood, yellow eyes, yellow face—and yellow thoughts. Is it boredom? Is it impoverishment of the blood?

The truth is that I can't write poetry, my head being too heavy and ill, and it's with the greatest of difficulty that I'm preparing for my

30. From Poe's poem "Ulalume."

exam—and yet it's Romeo and Juliet! So allow me not to write you any poetry today, for it makes me ill and when I compare it with my present wan thoughts, I blush. Pray that I may get better—in body and soul.

Alas! Why do doctors charge for their services, why aren't they public servants forbidden to accept the lowest salary? Moreover, in a well-constituted country shouldn't there be merchants whom the government would pay so much a year to let their shops be pillaged throughout the year without demanding a cent? That's what true reform would be—that's what progress would be. And until we've reached that point, we won't have taken a step in the right direction.

You know that all my political illusions[31] have faded away, one by one, and if I now run up the red flag, it's because I hate knaves and detest force. Henri, you'll come to see that nothing is true, unchanging, great, and holy apart from Art. All vain political disputes pass away, for they have nothing of the Absolute about them.

"There is no truth other than eternity, unique and mournful,
Oh, Brahma, everything is but the dream of a dream . . ."[32]

Nevertheless, yesterday I went to a popular meeting in support of Poland.[33] What struck me above all, was that all these workers applauded frenetically whenever they were addressed as *gentlemen*. I don't like workers: they are vain. For whom, therefore, would we create a Republic? For the bourgeoisie? Look at them *en masse,* in the gardens and the streets. They are hideous, and it's quite plain that they have no soul. For the aristocracy? By that I mean the nobility and the poets? As long as the former have money and the latter have beautiful statues, everything will be fine.

Henri, don't you think that the man who made the Venus de Milo is greater than the one who saves a race, and wouldn't it be preferable that Poland should fall rather than see that eternal marble hymn to Beauty lying in pieces?

How I chatter on, for an invalid, and I was forgetting to tell you that my good, sweet Marie, who cries all day to see me ill, thanks you with all her German heart for the forget-me-nots you sent her: she had picked some on the charming banks of the Thames at Richmond, in one of those little patches of shade and green water where Ophelia must have drowned—but the stupid maid swept them away. Had it not been for that, the exchange would have been charming. [. . .]

31. Until then, Mallarmé had shared Cazalis's liberal opinions.
32. From Leconte de Lisle's poem "La Vision de Brahma."
33. 1863 had seen a rebellion in Poland against Russian authority, which was rapidly crushed.

24

2 Teaching in the Provinces

At the end of August the young couple returned to France and in November Mallarmé was appointed to a teaching post in Tournon. From Tournon he made two visits to Avignon, one in July and one in August. Through Des Essarts, who was teaching there, he met members of the Félibrige, the group of writers and activists who were attempting to reinstate Provençal as a literary language.

14   ALBERT COLLIGNON

Tournon, [Saturday] 12 December 1863

I received your dear *Revue,*[1] to which I had been looking forward with much impatience. This first number is dazzling: how many beloved names there are and how many fine things!

Everything will go marvellously well, have no doubts about that. Such a fine collection, published in the Latin Quarter, at such a price, *can only* prosper. I'll help you with all my feeble strength. Count on my propaganda, particularly in London. The advertisement I promised you in the *Gazette des étrangers*[2] appeared there two days after my departure. Armand Renaud hasn't written to me, and I don't know if the advertisement he was going to hatch out in the *Revue contemporaine* isn't very late. Look into that.

I'm sorry I'm not in surroundings where I could be of more use to you; but here, I've no desire to know anyone. The inhabitants of the grim village to which I've been exiled live in too close an intimacy with pigs for me not to hold them in horror. The pig is the spirit of the house here as elsewhere the cat is.

I haven't even found anywhere to live which wasn't a pigsty. I'm still at the hotel and won't be in my own home for another two days. Not having touched my trunks, I haven't been able to translate for you the three unpublished poems of Edgar Poe we'd decided on. In the meanwhile I'll send you a very short *terza rima*. Could you put it in your second number?[3]

Farewell, I'm leaving you since I suffer terribly from rheumatisms

---

1. The *Revue nouvelle,* which Collignon edited, had just begun to appear.
2. This appeared on 4 December 1863.
3. Whatever this was, it wasn't published in the *Revue nouvelle.*

brought on by this horrible hole of Tournon and have been in bed for several days. I shake your hand.

15   HENRI CAZALIS

January 1864

I'm at last sending you the poem "L'Azur" that you seemed so eager to own. I have worked on it these last few days, and I won't hide from you the fact that it cost me infinite trouble. Even before taking up my pen I had to conquer a moment of perfect clarity by laying low my distressing impotence. It gave me a lot of trouble, because in banishing a thousand lyrical flourishes and fine lines which constantly haunt my brain, I wanted to remain implacably within my subject. I swear to you that there's not a single word which hasn't cost me several hours of research, and the first word, which contains the first idea, not only helps create the general *effect* of the poem, but also serves to prepare the last word.

The *effect produced,* without a dissonance, without a fioritura, even an adorable one, for that distracts—this is what I am seeking. I'm convinced, having read these lines to myself, perhaps two hundred times, that I've achieved it. There now remains the other side that has to be considered, the aesthetic side. Is it beautiful? Does it contain a reflection of the Beautiful? Here, it would be immodest of me to talk, so it's up to you to decide, Henri. It's a long way from these theories of composition to the way in which our glorious Emmanuel takes a handful of stars from the Milky Way to scatter them over the paper and lets them form unforeseen constellations at random! And how his enthusiastic soul, intoxicated with inspiration, would recoil in horror, faced with my way of working! He typifies the lyric poet in all his admirable outpourings. Nevertheless, the further I go, the more faithful I'll be to the strict ideas I've inherited from my great master, Edgar Poe.

The unparalleled poem "The Raven" was created in this way. And the reader's soul takes pleasure exactly as the poet wanted it to . . . So follow my thought through my poem and see if that is what you feel as you read me. To open on a broader scale and to deepen the whole, I myself do not appear in the first verse. The azure tortures the impotent in general. In the second verse, the reader begins to suspect, because of my flight before the possessive sky, that I suffer from this cruel malady. In this verse I also prepare, by means of a piece of boastful blaspheming, *And what haggard night,* the strange idea of invoking the mists. The prayer to "the beloved tedium" confirms my powerlessness. In the third verse, I'm as frenzied as the man who has seen his relentless vow come to fruition.

The fourth begins by the sort of grotesque exclamation one expects from a schoolboy who's been set free: "The sky is dead!" And suddenly, armed with this admirable certainty, I implore Matter. That's precisely what gives joy to the Impotent. Weary of the ill that gnaws at me, I want to savor the common happiness of the herd, and await an unsung death ... I say "I want." But my enemy is a specter, the dead sky haunts me, and I hear it singing in the azure bells. It passes by, indolent and all-conquering, without soiling itself on the mists, and, quite simply, it pierces me through and through. At this I cry out, full of pride and failing to see in this a just punishment for my cowardice, that I am suffering an *immense agony*. Again I seek to flee, but I feel I am wrong and admit that *I am haunted*. That entire poignant revelation was needed to motivate the sincere and bizarre cry of the conclusion, *the azure* ... You can see that for those who, like Emmanuel and yourself, seek in a poem something other than the music of the lines, it contains a real drama. And it was terribly difficult to combine, in a precise harmony, the dramatic element, which is hostile to the concept of pure and subjective poetry, and the serene, calm lines essential to Beauty.

You'll tell me I've gone to a lot of trouble for lines which are very little worthy of it. I know it's true. That, nevertheless, obliged me to tell you how I judge and conceive of a poem. Remove from these lines all allusion to myself, and all that concerns my poetry, and read these pages, coldly, as the formless and very badly written draft of an article on art. Write.

16   HENRI CAZALIS

[c. 7 January 1864]

I'm adding to my poems and instructions for using them[4] a word about your strange letter, the last one you wrote. As for the other one, it was charming and I'm awaiting a luminous hour next week to reply to it.

Yes, we are indeed married.[5] The proof of this is that the choir boy, who was six years old, signed his name in a big register in the

4. This letter may have been included with the preceding one.
5. Cazalis had asserted that the marriage ceremony carried out in London would not be valid in France.

chapel—and that we love each other. But yes. Let's talk seriously. The mayor at Sens is a lawyer, well versed in law. My grandfather took advice from many lawyers and all recited the same lesson. And, too, the French consul in London, who knows the drill in such matters, has assured me that the ceremony is sufficient. So calm down and remember that if I ever bring a little faun into the world, it'll be legitimate.

Please go immediately to a translator. I'm including with this letter the five francs you mentioned to me. Send it all to Mme Mallarmé at Les Gaillons, in Sens.

—Emmanuel, who has just written to me, tells me he's spent several hours with you. Lucky Emmanuel!—I was able to decipher in his mysterious scrawl, which will make me go blind one of these days, the information that you had read him some marvellous prose poems. I considered that epithet insolently inferior to the subject. Was it Sperata?[6] His enthusiasm in that case neither surprises nor astonishes me. Is it a new work? In that case, I want, d'you hear me, I want you to go to bed at 2 A.M. tomorrow morning, and by the day after tomorrow I want you to have copied them all for me.

Marie says you are a wretch for frightening her, for your last letter, in which you spoke of our marriage being a mere figment of the imagination, horrified her.

P.S. Take one of your prose poems to the *Revue nouvelle,* next door to you (14 rue Jacob): they exactly fit its brief. It's a review which reconciles art and poetry—even the most dream-like and otherworldly.

17   HENRI CAZALIS

Tournon, [23 March] 1864

You complain of our silence! First, I'll explain that it's been a long time since I've written to anyone. Then I'll tell you that your name is so often—always!—on our lips that I consider it almost unnecessary to weary my feeble brain, rummaging about in it for an hour to extract banalities you already know.

I haven't written for a long time because I was in a state of utter dejection. You say you were bored at Strasbourg, which is a great city, a friend to thought. Ah! my friend, I'll tell you that here one sinks into the very depths of despondency. Nothing happens: you turn

6. This poem, inspired by Cazalis's love for Ettie Yapp, appears in his collection *Vita tristis.*

28

around and around in a narrow circle like the brainless horses of fairground circuses, accompanied by the most god-awful music! If there were no law courts, I'd set fire to the ignoble houses I see irrevocably from my window, at every hour of the day, stupid and mindless; and at certain moments how I'd put a bullet into the stupefied skulls of those miserable neighbors who do the same thing day after day and whose irksome lives offer, to my tear-filled eyes, the horrendous spectacle of immobility, that fount of boredom. It wouldn't be so bad if it were the sun's immobility! Yes, I feel I'm collapsing in on myself day by day, each day discouragement dominates my mind and the lethargy is killing me. When I emerge from this, I'll be stupefied, annulled. I feel like banging my head against the walls to wake myself up.

Look, the provinces are good and healthy only to exuberant people, those who are active and full of good health. People like that enliven everything around them and are supported, if they weaken, by a noble willpower. For instance, our Emmanuel.

But the passive soul, ill, weakened, and powerless, when excited at every moment by contact with Paris and finding new strength in the great bath of the multitude—can do great things, but dies in the provinces, in a miserable village which doesn't even offer distractions for the body.

You'll tell me there are two of us. No, there's only one of us. Marie weeps when I weep and is bored when I'm fed up. She is my angelic and paradisiacal shadow, but her gentle nature couldn't transform her into my Lady Macbeth.

So please understand my silence: every month I've about twenty letters to write or thirty. I put them off every day; they represent so many wounds I have to reopen. Leaving aside the fact that a letter makes me look on my pen with repugnance and so I don't take it up for several days afterward, even for my literary compositions . . .

In the morning, I get up relatively strong and happy, then I go into a decline and towards dinner all my strength is worn out. I go to bed at seven.

You won't understand that. But I'm the one who's suffering from it. Don't give me those bits of advice that you can give with your strong and often invincible soul, I need to be healed first. *Sursum corda* would be a perfectly ridiculous expression to shout at me. Above all, don't bear me any ill will if I don't write to you more often. Writing a single letter makes me unhappy for a whole week—before and after.

Before writing this letter to you I waited for Emmanuel to visit us. He came to see us recently and will tell you about it: what an adorable day! I'm so weak in the head that his marvellous joy and his noisy friendship, at the time of his visit, literally made me ill one entire evening. I had an unbearable bout of neuralgia.

Farewell, my good Henri, each of us loves you wholeheartedly. Marie is a little unwell and weak.

P.S. I'm sending you some lines I've written, "Les Fleurs" ["The Flowers"], which I don't think you've read—and a wonderful sonnet—one of the most beautiful I know, by one of my old and intimate friends, Lefébure. Greetings to Armand Renaud.

18 ALBERT COLLIGNON

11 April 1864

You must think I'm dead, and, to tell the truth, I can only admit you're right to do so, since I myself have shared that view for a long time now. Nevertheless, couldn't you have thrown the latest numbers of your beloved *Revue* on my tomb in the same way one places funeral wreaths and sometimes even—remember Heine's monument—visiting cards? If by chance you agree to fulfill this pious act, I'd ask you to send to the house I used to inhabit during my lifetime, the numbers for 15 March, 1 April, and 15 April.

I'm joking, but, alas! I'm wrong to do so. Yet I do indeed feel dead: tedium has become in my case a mental illness and my lifeless impotence makes the lightest work painful to me. I cannot tell you how my pen, abandoned on my dust-covered table, seems a terrible weight to pick up again—even to write to you.

My friend and living antithesis, Emmanuel Des Essarts,—who is protected from sorrow by prodigious activity and whom solitude, far from allowing him to sink irremediably, fortifies—gave you some poems by me. I can no longer write any. Today I'm sending you some prose poems, inspired by writers you love.[7] Could you publish them soon? I'd like them to be published almost immediately, so that the one describing Baudelaire won't be in the same issue as an article I'm planning to write (will you have space for it?) on spleen in Paris and on the Master's work.[8] When you've also published all my poems, I'll send you three translations of short poems by E. Poe, the only ones that have not yet been translated. But I'd prefer to have something—

7. The reference is to a first draft of "Symphonie littéraire," in which Mallarmé pays tribute to Gautier, Banville, and Baudelaire.

8. Collignon did not publish the prose poems. The article Mallarmé mentions has not been found.

in prose or in verse—that was original before publishing these copies of an inimitable poet.

Will you reply? Perhaps not, but that won't prevent me from being entirely devoted to you and to the *Revue*.

19   HENRI CAZALIS

25 April 1864

Forgive me for not writing to you sooner: you know I'm weak. I really have to struggle to force myself to lay hands on a pen. Writing reopens a wound and I can find respite only by sleeping incessantly. Otherwise, if I open my eyes, I hate myself for doing nothing and yet I feel I lack the strength to do anything. But I hope that Glatigny[9] will resuscitate me. He's soon going to come and stay with us for a month. What happy walks we'll go on!

Marie also looks forward to this distraction impatiently, for she is very low and as nervous as can be, or more precisely enervated. She's been unwell for a fortnight and all the signs are that before next year there'll be a little poet between us. She hardly exists and everything disgusts her. You can imagine how little that lifts my spirits.[10] I tremble at the idea of being a father—what if there were going to be an imbecile in my life—or an ugly duckling! What horrors!

I was expecting a great deal from Victor Hugo's book *William Shakespeare*. But all it did was unsettle me, not revive me. There are pages which are marvellously sculpted, but what a lot of horrors! Among others, that shameful chapter: "The Beautiful as Servant of Truth," in which, among other deathless infamies, one can read the following: "empty the tub of the public's dirty washing, Polyhymnia, roll up your sleeves and settle down to the dirty work, why not?" Happy Venus de Milo, since you have no arms, such a blasphemous remark can't be addressed to you! And, too, why take as the eternal model of Art unconscious Nature, and say: "Let us be dirty!" just because the ocean foams? Isn't that the height of absurdity? Nature has many deserts: art has only Parthenons.

Now don't tell Vacquerie all that.[11] You put your finger on the often limited nature of that honest chap, who is admirable as a tragic dramatist but a very poor lyric poet.

9. Bohemian and poet.
10. Mallarmé was, however, to become a devoted father.
11. Vacquerie was an admiring disciple of Hugo and acted as his representative in Paris during Hugo's exile.

Let's speak of you. I love *Armonia* infinitely, when one reads it one feels rocked by all the waves of the blue. It's a rising tide of azure. Your dream is a brother of perfume and music: your language, free of bones and even of *contours,* is just material enough to be human. Just as the female saints painted by Flandrin have only enough of womanhood to let them live on this earth.[12]

Nevertheless I have one little observation to make. I consider your sentences too short, and their harmony is at times a little breathless. My remarks here apply to the artist and in no way to the dreamer who, in you, is completely superior. Théophile Gautier's sentences—which imbeciles judge to be plastic—but which I consider miraculously balanced, have a correctness of touch which is justice itself and they offer the perfect model of the soul that dwells in beauty and the less serene one which explores the furthest depths and the seventh heaven of mysticism, *used by Balzac,* in *Séraphita*—that's what you need to make your dream appear, in the eyes of the few artists, even more immaterial.

The supreme art, in this case, consists in revealing, through an impeccable possession of all the faculties, that one is in ecstasy, without having shown how one reached those summits. Well, often your short phrases lift up their arms to the Ideal, take a deep breath and seem from time to time to take flight. Make them soar.

Will you understand me? What I want to tell you is so intimate, so veiled, so vague, that I fear I've occasionally been too precise. Forgive me. And allow me to finish with a recipe that I've invented and that I use. "You must always remove the beginning and end of what you write. No overture and no finale." Do you think me mad? I'll explain to you one day that my madness lies elsewhere. For this morning all I need do is embrace you with all my heart. My Marie also embraces you and I let her do so.

P.S. Ask Emmanuel for an *Introduction* to *Three Prose Poems* and the *Poem to Banville* I sent him. The thought of recopying all that fills me with horror. The first and second poems are on Gautier and Baudelaire.

20   ALBERT COLLIGNON

26 June 1864

I learned definitely yesterday through a letter of announcement sent to me by your editor, M. Gosselin, that the *Revue* no longer exists.

---

12. Flandrin, who had died in March 1864, was a leading religious painter.

I cannot tell you how deeply that saddens me: that charming collection, the only one in Paris, apart from *L'Artiste,* which was not hostile to Poetry and the arts, attracted, as you know, all my sympathy and my fervent good wishes. If you remember, I was even to some extent present at its baptism.

It will be a great regret to me to have been one of its collaborators only on the cover,[13] for I find in it all the names I love. But I can't blame myself for any negligence.

That glittering dream is now merely a memory for you, but such a memory is glorious, and you must feel, my dear sir, something other than melancholy when you look at that dear collection of beautiful and noble things to which you gave asylum. In our time, Maecenas would be a director of a review, if he wanted to remain worthy of his name. And you will say: "As long as I could, I welcomed the Muse in her buskins and wounded feet, I stretched out my hand to that modern source of inspiration, Freedom; and a few months of hospitality are an entire lifetime."

Farewell, dear sir, or rather, au revoir, for I plan to come to Paris in two months' time and I hope that you will allow me to continue to feel the intense sympathy that you aroused in me in the days of hope when I saw you, and that you'll let me see you again.

P.S. If you still have the *Three Prose Poems* I sent you some six weeks ago, I'd be very obliged to you to return them to me, as I have only an incomplete draft of them.

21   ARMAND RENAUD

27 June [1864]

It's been a long time since we've heard anything of one another. What are you doing? And, to get all my questions over at once, didn't you put on a play at Versailles?[14] I think Emmanuel told me. And you haven't told me anything about it! That's bad—But no, it's good and you're right. The absent, as a punishment for their ridiculous absence, must be regarded as dead; and I bear you no grudge.

Another question: did the article I wrote on the dear *Caprices du boudoir*[15] appear in *L'Artiste?* Did Houssaye[16] mention it to you afterwards?

13. Mallarmé's name appears on the back of the numbers for April and May as one of the contributors.
14. Probably *Les Gloires de la Paix,* a cantata performed by the Vaudeville Theater company on 15 August 1864.
15. A collection of poems by Renaud.
16. Editor of the prestigious art review, *L'Artiste.*

33

I've just finished an article on *Les Flèches d'or:*[17] it's marvellous what beautiful things there are in this book, written at the whim of inspiration! The lines have a lyrical fullness that delights me. Only one thing really made me very indignant: that was to see neither your name nor that of Des Essarts among the list of young poets he quotes in his preface and which he evidently wants to be complete.

And I still have an article to write on *Philomela!*[18] These three articles will certainly be the ones I've found most charming to write, since behind the poet I could see the friend.

I've written little poetry since the lines I sent to Cazalis, but I have written a few prose poems (from which I detach this last one for you)[19] and a *Literary Symphony* in which Gautier, Baudelaire, and Banville act as motifs. I'll send you that in the vacation.

For we are going to see you soon. Didn't you tell me you counted on visiting Marseille this year? If you still plan to do so, let me know; we'll agree on dates and I won't leave Tournon until you've spent at least a week here. It'll be more or less just the two of us, far from the dust and din. Will it be in August?

One thing, alas!, will poison my holiday. You know that my wife has promised me for this autumn a cradle complete with a baby; well she can't go to Paris without risking her life or that of the baby and as she doesn't know anyone hereabouts she'll be obliged to stay at Tournon. That will be a bitter pill for me. I'll stay with her as much as possible, but I can't, without running the risk of spiritual decay, stay the whole time—I need men, Parisian women, music, and paintings. I'm already three-quarters stupefied.

P.S. Have you seen a performance of the *Fourberies de Nérine?*[20] It's adorable! What do you think of the *William Shakespeare* written by the master of all of us?[21] There are some very fine things—but some very poor ones as well: among others the chapter entitled "The Beautiful as Servant of Truth"—"The Usefulness of Art" etc.

Recently, I saw from my window a wretched pauper child singing all alone in the streets an insolent song; the very high notes forced the child to lift its head in a curious way which struck me for a long time. At one stage I had the horrible thought that its head wanted to leave the body and would one day really be removed from the rest of that

17. This article has not been discovered. The work is by Glatigny.
18. A collection of poems by Mendès published in 1863.
19. "Pauvre enfant pâle" ("Poor pale child") was sent with this letter.
20. A play by Banville.
21. Victor Hugo.

scrawny body by the knife of justice and that evening I wrote the prose poem I'm sending you now.[22]

22   HENRI CAZALIS

July 1864

I was beginning to despair of you, and wondered whether it was an excess of happiness or of bitterness that made you forget to write to me. Dear Henri, if my shade were not one of those that bring bad luck, I'd tell you it accompanies you in all your sad peregrinations on the pavements of Paris. Ah yes! it's hard for a poet and a noble heart when he comes across a wooden board painted black which allows donkeys to earn 2,000 francs. Perhaps even harder than you now think. And what an absurd life compared with a free career[23] which would send you away from Paris momentarily, that's true, but which couldn't fail to bring back a talent such as yours. And then, what of the future? Is there a future in all this pen-pushing, is there a retreat?[24] The Town Hall would be best thing, because it's clear and defined and because Armand Renaud and those of my friends who work there are basically very content there. For that, you have to try the exam and attempt to get yourself sponsored. I know that everything is done there by sponsors and then it's very easy. Helped by a young Pole, a nephew of Haussmann,[25] you'd force open the great bronze door and pass victoriously under the great statue of Henry the Fourth on horseback. . . . How I know that route, so often have I been to see Armand Renaud who slept or wrote poetry, two equally divine things, on his empty desk.

At last we're going to see each other and make up the time lost last year! And we won't have to write, for I abhor letters (except for those I receive). You know a letter irritates me to such an extent that for two days I can't work any more—that is, when it doesn't break me completely. At heart it's so banal. One spends one life thinking adorable things about one's friends, and then, one fine day, you have to take up your pen for an hour to scribble down to them the first inanities that come to mind. So don't talk to me any more about letters and long silences, you tyrant! During the silences we love each other and everything's perfect.

22. "Pauvre Enfant pâle" ("Poor Pale Child").
23. Teaching.
24. For a fortnight Cazalis had been searching for a legal office which would employ him from 10 to 4 and pay him from 1,500 to 2,000 francs straightaway.
25. A government minister.

35

Alas, my poor Henri, we won't all see each other: my poor Marie will not be able to travel at that moment without putting two lives at risk. She's condemned to remain in exile in this miserable Tournon: she's already in tears about it, the poor girl.

As for me, I'll sacrifice to her half my holidays, but my brain is so ill that I'd become an idiot—and I'm not joking—if I didn't breathe in a little better air. I need men, Parisian women friends, paintings, music. I thirst for poets. First I'll go and see Soulary in Lyon for a bit, then Glatigny at Vichy—where he strolls about with the musician Debillement—Coquelin and Gustave Flaubert, and finally Cazalis in Paris. For you are a tremendous poet, my friend. You couldn't guess what a deep impression I felt on reading the poems you gave me. You alone, together with Edgar Poe and Baudelaire, were capable of that poem which, like certain glances from a woman's eyes, contains worlds of thoughts and sensations. That's what Emmanuel should take as a model his whole life long.

He never did anything which struck and moved me as much. Everything is marvellously arranged to create the desired effect and despite such artistry the tableau remains simple and alive. I'm mad about those lines because they sum up my entire aesthetics and yet I've never achieved such an effect. You could have knocked me over with a feather when I read them.

You mentioned the *little plant*. I want it to be a woman. She will be born in autumn. Add to that she *was born* in my saddest hours of tedium this springtime. I'm very much afraid that she may be, like her father, a splenetic and miserable creature. I take my Marie out walking in the sun and make her life as little unhappy as my nasty character allows me.

Poor Marie, she blushed when I read her the passage in your letter which mentioned her, and said: "That wicked Cazalis!"[26]

Alas, she has no friend here—there is indeed one charming woman here, one of the rare women I've seen in my life, but she only comes a few days each month and stays in the neighborhood.[27] I'd guessed what she was like from the energetic way in which I saw her stroke an admirable cat, one day (when she does come, she's our neighbor).

As for the rest, they're an infamous herd of cows who resemble

26. In a letter of early July Cazalis had written: "How I should like to be like you and to be able to lean over my wife's breast and hear something coming to life. How deep and truly divine is this mystery of life! And the mystery of woman!" (*Documents Mallarmé*, 6:217).

27. Mme Seignobos, the mother of one of Mallarmé's pupils.

women only in so far as they lack what is necessary to be a man. They repel us.

I dare not talk to you of your beloved immediately after mentioning them, for that would sully her: I need a transition, and I find it in the person of Louise L.[28] I belive her to be as you describe, but Emmanuel is mad about her. You know that for him she is the wittiest of women, the one who lets him talk the longest. That's how it comes about that he is often happy with provincial tarts who would have made me throw up.

I won't talk to you about Ettie, because you know that everything I would say about her is in my heart and I'd be afraid to sin in telling you any more than: *Love her.* Farewell.

23   HENRI CAZALIS

[2 August 1864]

I am not equal with your grief to be in a position to write to you.[29] Forgive me for not speaking of it, for you know that I suffer as you do.

Listen, what I suggested to you is possible, although your whole life long you've been pitiless in regard to my prayers. You need a change, even if only for two weeks. So come from 15 August until the first days of September. If you don't do it for your own sake, do it to some extent for Marie's sake, since the poor girl can't leave Tournon this vacation. And for my sake, for I'm now in one of my saddest times of drought and arid impotence.

I'm including with this letter the 100 francs you need. So you can't make the eternal financial objection.

This is what my holiday will be like: since Marie can't travel now, I'll sacrifice to her about a month. The prize-giving is on the 8th. On the 9th, I'm off to Vichy and will return on the 15th for Marie's feast-day. While I'm away, she'll have been to spend a few days at Vienne with the wife of a colleague,[30] and will meet me in Lyon. I'm stopping in Lyon to meet Soulary and then I'll return. We'll stay at Tournon together until 5 September. That's when we'll have you. Think of the good it will do Marie to have you here, and since she can't go to Paris, she'll see Paris come to her, for truly you're almost all Paris to

28. Louise Ledieu, a close friend of Nina Gaillard.
29. The cause of this grief is not known. A letter from Cazalis to Mallarmé seems to be missing.
30. Mme Fournel, who was German and whose husband taught German at Mallarmé's school in Tournon.

her. And, too, our home will be less distasteful to us when you have lived here. (If you come we'll go and see Aubanel, in Avignon, and Mistral, too.)

On 5 September, we'll leave. Marie is going to stay with a charming friend in the area, whom I think I mentioned to you, where she'll spend a good two weeks, and I'll go to Paris with you. I'll stay at Sens until the 10th, and near Sens, with my poor friend Lefébure,[31] until the 15th. I'll go to Versailles until the 20th. I'll reach Paris on the 20th, and will spend the last week of September and the first of October there.

Add to that the fact that during the 18 days I'll have there, I have to find the means of spending three days, which, with the time for traveling, makes six in all, in London which I *want* to visit.

You can see that I won't be spending much time in Paris. Yet another reason for you to come here. And what's more, I can't wait such a long time to see you!

Don't ask me to devote the first half of my holidays to Paris. That would deprive Marie of her few chances to stroll in the area and amuse herself a little. Moreover, I couldn't bring myself to return to Tournon in the middle of my vacation unless I were forcibly called back by the college bell. I'd be too unhappy during those last weeks. By delaying the voyage, I'll at least have some hope before me.

Farewell, my brother, I embrace you. Once again, forgive me for not mingling your great grief with the banality of my plans. One is all too much a comedian when one writes and I want to pity you sincerely, my hand in yours. I'm revolted by the thought of the rhetorical devices I'd have to summon up. What's more, I'm ill *in the head* and couldn't do it. And why should I stupidly drag out those words: "I suffer as you do"?

Come, and we'll talk.

p.s. What you tell me about Glatigny is *absurd*.[32] He is very fond of me, constantly sends me his papers, his book etc. He doesn't need money, having more than I do myself now. He even wants to put me up. I detect behind those few lines of yours the curses of Emmanuel who lent him 7 francs in two weeks, three years ago and who hasn't stopped lamenting their loss. Moreover, the dear lad, who doesn't like admitting or recognizing superiority—the most one can expect is that he'll admit having rivals—has always cast a baleful eye on the talents of Glatigny and Catulle.[33] He begrudges them their color, which he'll

31. Lefébure's grandfather had just commited suicide.
32. The letter in which Cazalis accuses Glatigny is missing.
33. Catulle Mendès.

never have. I'm saying all this with no ulterior motive. You know I love Emmanuel like a ... son. But as a poet I prefer the others.

Answer me straightaway, since Marie has a few arrangements to make for her voyage to Vienne. She'd like to see everything clearly beforehand. So I'll hear from you on Thursday morning.[34]

24   HENRI CAZALIS

Tournon Sunday evening

The sad black letter[35] we received yesterday explained your silence. Alas! poor friend, yet another bereavement brings you sorrow and all that was your childhood disappears at a stroke! We pity you from the bottom of our hearts, for I know that cold loneliness arising from the departure of those loved ones who presided over our first years of life.

But let's remove momentarily from our horizon those funereal birds, and fix our gaze together on the pale blue of autumn which in these days suits our thoughts.

What are you doing? Are you working on medicine already, without neglecting to put the final touches on your literary jewels, those blue jewels which fall, in pearls, with an adorable gurgling sound, like water from a fountain, under the moonbeams?

As for me, I'm resolutely back at my work. I've at last begun my *Hérodiade*. With a sense of terror, for I'm inventing a language which must of necessity burst forth from a very new poetics, which I could define in these few words: *paint, not the object, but the effect it produces.*

Therefore the lines in such a poem mustn't be composed of words; but of intentions, and all the words must fade before the sensation. I don't know if you can guess my meaning, but I hope you'll approve of me when I have succeeded. For *I want*—for the first time in my life—to succeed. I would never touch my pen again if I were floored.

You can imagine that these efforts, to which I'm very unaccustomed, weary me and wear me out, to the point where I can only rarely allow myself to shake your hand in a letter.

Alas! The baby is going to interrupt me. I've already had one interruption through the presence of our friend—towards whom, even, the imp of the perverse pushed me into being very sharp, I don't know why—. Then it was one of those gray, gloomy days when
The drowned poet dreams of obscene lines.
I even wrote some, but I won't send them to you because the nocturnal

34. Cazalis replied that as his mother had fallen gravely ill, he couldn't accept Mallarme's invitation.
35. Cazalis had just lost his mother.

emissions of a poet should only be milky ways and mine is merely a horrible stain.

Farewell, my Henri, it's impossible for me to make by brain give birth to two consecutive ideas today. But I embrace you, which is worth more. Marie accepts my suggestion that she do likewise. I believe she'll be *a little mother* within a fortnight; I'll let you know immediately.

3   Herodiade and the Faun

On 19 November 1864 Geneviève Mallarmé was born. By this time Mallarmé was at work on his long poem Hérodiade. *Although he often returned to it, this poem was to remain uncompleted when he died.*

25   HENRI CAZALIS

[20 November 1864]

Just a word, for a distressing number of envelopes lies on my table and horrifies me. Our little Geneviève has arrived, last evening at 8 o'clock. Marie suffered for a long time, but there's nothing to fear now. Those two little girls are marvellously well. If only you could see the smaller of them, with her big blue eyes and her long black hair! She is delightful, tall and beautiful, *for her age.*

You can imagine how happy we are: Marie is charming in her role as mother, with her white bonnet. I'm about to begin my role in lulling the baby to sleep.

P.S. Now my work is interrupted, for I'm going to be in charge of the household for some time. You'll come and see it when it's finished, won't you, and kiss the baby who by then will be able to smile at you. Thanks for your letter: I like your poetry. How are you? Your news about Nina is bizarre.[1]

26   THÉODORE AUBANEL

27 November 1864

I knew you'd share our joy. Thank you for being happy. It'll soon be my turn to shake your hand and wish you a charming paternity. Don't be jealous for long.

In the meantime, let's talk of us. My wife is heading as prudently as possible towards recovery. She gives me cause to predict a happy outcome, while nevertheless horrifying me, by displaying the appetite of a young wolf. Her daughter, moreover, imitates her, and seems to want to make up for lost time, for during her first days she saddened us by her sleepiness and her obstinate refusal to suckle. So I have cause to hope that all will go well.

1. Cazalis had told Mallarmé of Nina's marriage to the journalist Callias.

Emmanuel tells me you read him an admirable play:[2] when will I hear it? You really ought to come on New Year's Day, or New Year's Eve, or the day after, if it isn't too cold, and spend a day with us.

As for myself, I haven't yet gone back to my work: with her cries that wicked baby has put to flight Hérodiade with her hair as cold as gold, her heavy robes, her sterility. Nevertheless, I have hopes that the baby won't be too stupid, for when I pronounce the name of Legouvé[3] she cries, and splits her sides laughing when I describe with comic gestures Emmanuel Des Essarts—just as she smiles when I talk to her about you.

Farewell, my good Théodore: my wife wakes up just long enough to beg me to mention her to you and to tell you not to forget to mention to Mme Aubanel that she loves her from afar and predicts that before long she'll have a second Théodore.

If there could be two of them, that is.

27   Joseph Roumanille

[December 1864]

For a long time I've had here an image of myself that I'd planned to send you, and would you believe that I've waited until the New Year to give it to you, not because I consider myself worthy to be offered as a New Year's gift, but, lazily, because I was counting on writing to you at the same time and wanted to spare myself the fatigue of a letter. Now you know all about my lazy calculations, let me shake you by the hand, both you and Madame Roumanille, on behalf of my wife and myself and wish you a happy, happy New Year. As you are the elder, and indeed the father, I'll ask you to convey my good wishes for the coming year to the dear Félibres from Avignon to whom time, and forty-odd envelopes scattered over my desk demanding *copy,* prevent me writing individually.

I haven't written any poetry, all this time, but I have had a little daughter, in beautiful rhythm, whose eyes are a blue I couldn't put into my rhymes, and whose hair already unfurls with the movement of your great Provençal poems. This poem, unfortunately, deprives me of the others and even if I had the strength to write some, I believe her cries would drive away the nine Muses, as well as the muse you have beside you, were she not accustomed to similar melodies. Since we're talking of the mother, may I ask if your lovely little daughter is still well? I'd already like to see her playing with Geneviève.

2. Probably Aubanel's play *Lou Pan dou Pecat,* published in 1873.
3. A highly traditional poet and dramatist.

I see I've spoken very little of you. Are you working? If you are, all the better for us. If not, *you,* at least, can rest serenely and insist on your rest being respected, for you've harvested enough corn in the wheatfield of the skies.

P.S. If, by any chance, you still have a *card* with you on it, or when you find one, slip yourself into an envelope and send yourself to me. I'm *interested.*

28   HENRI CAZALIS

[15 January 1865]

I've spent a sad and rainy Sunday answering several letters I had on my table, so that I could free my week which is devoted to work. And now all that hasty correspondence has gone, I want to chat a little with you before dinner. First, I'll thank you personally for a very great happiness you've given me, which is that of hearing my Marie at this very moment rocking our little Geneviève, who is destined to wear two long plaits down her back, to some delicious German songs, as white as the moon and as comical as you. Marie's eyes were damp when she received that lovely book of music and pictures, as she realized that someone in the world thought about her. She offers you a sisterly kiss, will you accept it?

Unfortunately, I don't rejoice in all the charm that floats around a cradle. Understand me. As I said to Armand Renaud the other day, I'm too much of a poet and too much in love with poetry alone to enjoy, when I can't work, an inner happiness which seems to take the place of the other, that great pleasure the Muse gives. And on top of that I'm too impotent, my brain's too weak to be able unceasingly, like others who make me envious, to give myself to that one occupation which is worthy of a man, Poetry. (I'm putting this in a very confused way, as the little darling, who is a bit ill tonight, is tearing my ears apart with her screams.) Where was I?

Nevertheless, I've been working for the last week. I have settled down seriously to my tragedy of *Hérodiade:* but how sad it is not to be exclusively a man of letters! At every moment, my most beautiful flights or rare moments of inspiration, which cannot be recovered, are interrupted by the hideous work of the teacher, and when I return, with papers stuck to my behind and cut-out men on my coat, I'm so weary I can't rest.—It wouldn't be so bad if I'd chosen an easy work: but it's typical of me, sterile and crepuscular as I am, to choose a terrifying subject, in which the sensations, when they're intense, are taken to the point of atrocity, and when they're vague, have the strange appearance of a mystery. And my Verse sometimes hurts and wounds as if it were made of iron! Moreover, in this work I have found a singular and intimate means of depicting and noting very fleeting impressions. Add to that, to make it more terrifying, that all these *impressions* follow one another as in a symphony and that I sometimes spend entire days wondering if that impression can accompany this one, what is the relationship between them, and what is their effect. . . . You can guess that I don't write many lines in a week.—But why should I tell you about a Dream which may never come to fruition, and a work which I may tear up one day, because it was well beyond my poor capabilities. What's more, now my head is too bruised by the cries of the child to continue the incoherent laments and these projects. Let's change the subject. What's the weather like? *How are you, my dear Milky Way,* do you follow me?[4] Are *you* working?—Oh, how impatient I am for summer to come, for you promised me, didn't you, you really promised me that you'd come and visit us. [. . .]

Ask Armand Renaud for the poems I scribbled out for him, and whose cruelty he felt perfectly, although the description is entirely plastic and external: that was the aim I set myself. I'm sending them, with two others I have in my head, to the *Satirical Parnassus* Malassis is publishing. They'll go under the name *Obscene Pictures.*[5]

29   HENRI CAZALIS

[January 1865?]

I had planned to devote my evening to work, so, despite the cruel migraine which deprives me of that happiness, I can't resolve to go to bed without touching my pen. That's why I'm scrawling a few lines for you.

I'm sad. A black and glacial wind prevents me from walking and I don't know what to do in the house when my poor brain makes work impossible. Then I'm disgusted with myself. I recoil before mirrors, seeing my face debased and dull, and cry when I feel myself to be empty and can't get a word down on my implacably white paper.

To be an old man, finished, at 23, when all those I love live in light and flowers, at the age of masterpieces! And not even to have the

---

4. Perhaps, as Lloyd Austin suggests, an allusion to Cazalis's venereal disease, but Mallarmé does use this term in relation to inspiration, so he may be referring to Cazalis's poetry (compare letter 24, for instance).

5. Only one poem by Mallarmé appeared in this collection and then with a title he hadn't given it: "Rosy Lips."

resource of an early death, which could have made you all believe that I was really something and that if nothing of me remains, the fault lies solely with the Fate that carried me off!

It's true that everything has conspired to annihilate me. As my head was weak, I needed all possible stimulation, that of friends whose voices fire me, that of paintings, of music, noise and life. If there was one thing on earth I should have fled, it was solitude, which enlivens only the strong. Well, I'm doomed to an exceptional solitude, in ugly countryside, where I don't even have the companionship of Nature.

When I don't go out for two weeks, my life takes place in the college, which is opposite us, and in our house, which I know in all its sorrow. I never open my mouth to speak to a man. Can you understand what that means? You'll tell me I have Marie: Marie, however, is myself and I see myself reflected in her German eyes. Moreover she herself vegetates as I do. My Geneviève is charming to kiss for ten minutes, but after that?

I have never known willpower, but for some time I've *wanted* to learn how to care for and revive my miserable body (I have so little liveliness that my lips hang down and my head, unable to lift itself, leans on my shoulder or falls on my breast). Well, when after a day of waiting and thirsting, there comes the holy hour of Jacob, when I wrestle with the Ideal, I haven't the strength to put two words together. And the next day it will be exactly the same!

It poisons my life. After such humiliations, I don't have enough peace of mind to look at Marie and Geneviève with a happy heart. Even my friends, all of you, I consider as judges.

But these complaints are wearisome, even for you. I'll make an end to them. But don't bear me a grudge, that's all I ask. A great genius, an austere thinker, a scholar would find my solitude stimulating: but a poor poet who is nothing more than a poet—by which I mean an instrument which resounds under the fingers of various sensations— is mute when he lives in a milieu where nothing moves him, then his strings slacken and he gathers dust and oblivion.

You told me about the basalt caves. There will be in the first days of August, since I won't be free until then, an admirable excursion to make in the Ardèche.[6] I've often planned it, but lack of money nailed me to the ground. We'd leave from Tournon, to visit our friend in the area who'd stuff us with letters for the Ardèche people who'd guide us: from its very beautiful mountains we'd reach the Gerbier-des-Joncs,[7] the source of the Loire, then your caves, then the astonishing

6. The region in which Tournon is situated.
7. A curious volcanic plug in the Massif central.

45

wonder of the Pont-d'Arc,[8] which you can see in *Picturesque France,* on the quays, then the famous ruin of Rochemaure, which is uniquely grandiose, and finally that aerie of eagles and bishops, Viviers. We'd go back up the Rhône then, in a steamboat, until we get to my flat and meager Tournon. It'd be a rather expensive trip, but in no way vulgar and hackneyed, and it would present us simultaneously with several of the great beauty spots of France.

And what happy days we'd have, the two of us! On my own, I feel such distaste that I would never do it.—Promise me you'll come. And your book? When will we have it? The day it comes will be one of the great joys of my life—but alas, it won't resuscitate me!

Farewell. We embrace you, all three of us. Marie is very weary; Geneviève has flu, poor little soul, and cries all night long.

30   EUGÈNE LEFÉBURE

[February 1865]

I've thought a great deal about you these last few days, from my bed, to which I've been consigned by a foul cough, complicated by a vulgar and dirty nuisance. I was almost on the point of writing to you when I received your letter. I'll begin by answering you, so that we can chat a little and I can tell you how much I appreciated your poems.

How did you come to suffer such sorrow?[9] Was your wife imprudent, did she tire herself? A violent gesture, a badly performed movement, are sometimes all it takes to cause such misfortunes. At least I can see you're no longer in torment and that your dear invalid can walk from her bed to her armchair. I'm reassured. But all the same, be careful to avoid any complications. . . .

Here everyone is well apart from me. My Marie however is still weak and, with her German obstinacy, didn't agree to stay in bed long enough after the birth of Geneviève, and she occasionally suffers as a result. *My daughter* is a marvellous doll who delights all the old biddies of the neighborhood. She is highly intelligent and declares, at the top of her lungs, that she will definitely not read M. Legouvé's *Deux Reines.*

Les Elévations[10] strikes me as detestable. The thought is loose, it slackens into clichés, and as for the form, I see words, words, some-

8. A natural bridge carved by the Ardèche river into the rock.
9. Lefébure's wife had suffered a miscarriage: she herself was to die shortly afterward.
10. Des Essarts' book had appeared at the beginning of 1865.

times included merely at random, "sinister" capable of being replaced by "lugubrious," "lugubrious" by "tragic," without changing the sense of the line. Reading it doesn't give one any new sensation at all. The rhythm is very cleverly managed, which is what makes up for so much grayness and chatter, but what of that? You'll tell me I'm treating a friend badly. No, Des Essarts is one of the few whom I greatly love: but through a great misfortune, I can't bear his poetry, which runs counter to all I think of this art.

To give you heart after these sickening pages, I'm sending you a play in prose for which theater would be too banal a medium, but which will appear to you in all its divine beauty, if you read it in the solitary light of your lamp: it's *Elën,* by my friend Villiers de L'Isle-Adam.

The idea is as grandiose as Goethe would have imagined it, it's the eternal story of Man and Woman. The characters in it are beyond compare, from Samuel Wissler, that great philosopher who takes the trouble to have genius when he speaks, and is not the ceremonial great man invented for such plays, to the fatal Elën. And Tanuccio, as perfidious as the Italian moon, and Mme de Walburg: "the obscure pride of her glance never reveals the lugubrious feast of her heart"—an astonishing sentence!—and that human lover, Andréas de Rozenthal!

You'll find in it some remarkable scenes, I don't know any more beautiful than that of the memory of hours of love deepened by opium drunk by mistake, in the second scene of act three. And as for the last scenes, they're equal to that of the graveyard in *Hamlet.*

I'm not saying anything about the style. You'll feel a sensation at each of his words, as one does in reading Baudelaire. There isn't a syllable which has not been weighed in a night of reverie. Moreover, Villiers de L'Isle-Adam has been preparing this for three years.

In a word, the thought, the feeling of art, the voluptuous desires of the mind (even the most blasé) have a magnificent festival in this work. Taste the precious drops of this flask one by one.

I'm awaiting your response with real impatience.

Thanks for the detail you gave me about *Hérodiade,* but I won't use it. The most beautiful page of my work will be that which contains only the divine word *Hérodiade.* What inspiration I've had I owe to this name, and I believe that if my heroine had been called Salomé, I would have invented this dark word, as red as an open pomegranate, *Hérodiade.* Moreover, I want to make of her purely a creature of dream, with absolutely no link with history. You understand me. I'm not even invoking all the paintings of Da Vinci's pupils and all the Florentines who have had this mistress and named her as I do.

But will I ever write my tragedy? My poor brain is incapable of any application and resembles the gutters when the doorkeepers have been sweeping, I'm a coward, or perhaps a poor idiot whose light has been snuffed out and who occasionally finds a gleam but can't shine through a whole 800 lines.

Thanks again for your articles by Taine, which I haven't read. What I criticize in Taine is the way he claims an artist is merely man raised to his greatest possible power, whereas I believe that it is perfectly possible to have a human temperament utterly distinct from one's literary temperament. That makes me judge him differently from you: I consider that Taine sees only impression as a source of works of art and doesn't place enough value on reflection. It's in front of the paper that the artist *creates himself*. For instance, he doesn't believe that an artist can change his style utterly, and that's wrong, I've observed it in myself. As a child, when I was at school, I used to write stories 20 pages long, and was renowned for never knowing when to stop. And since then, isn't it true that I'm quite the opposite, exaggerating rather my love of concision? I used to be violently prolix and enthusiastically diffuse, writing everything as it came to me, of course, believing that effusiveness was what constituted good style. What can be more different from the schoolboy of yesteryear, who was true and impulsive, than today's man of letters, who is repelled by anything said without having been *arranged*.

But let's talk of you. What wonderful hours I spent yesterday with your poems in my hand, breathing in the soft perfume of slightly faded roses that emanated from them, feeling within myself the trembling of the yellow poplars and, from time to time, those atrocious wounds which are like swords suddenly plunged into one's spine and broken there and which fade away before one's fury has risen to one's eyes.

For instance, the last line of that unparalleled poem called "A ma fenêtre":

Irritated desire writhes like a serpent.

Or this one:

Oh, dear God! Death has come into my breast.

You know them.

[...][11] My God, how truly you are my brother! I believe you'd feel a particular sympathy for Villiers; he, Mendès, and you, among the young poets, form my spiritual family.

11. Mallarmé gives here a list of his favorite poems from the collection.

Now a reproach. Love is too much the aim of your poems and this extremely colorless word is often repeated in a way which rather dulls the rest. If it isn't sharpened by a strange condiment[12] such as lechery, ecstasy, illness, or asceticism, such an ill-defined subject doesn't seem to me poetic. I myself would be incapable of pronouncing the word without a smile, in poetry. Perhaps the word is too well-worn? No, I think the truth is that love, simple love, is too natural a feeling to provide a sensation for the dulled senses of poets who read verse; and if you talk to them of it, it's as if you wanted to offer the deep fresh water of a spring to the palates of old drunkards enflamed by brandy, palates that a match would set ablaze. I'm very cruel, my friend, to say this to you beside your "little Chinese angel" who would certainly tear my eyes out with her painted nails, if she were to read me: don't be angry with me; what has particularly set me against that word which I can't write or pronounce without experiencing a disagreeable sensation, is the stupidity with which 5 or 6 jokers, Des Essarts included, have declared themselves the priests of this fat boy, who's as red and chubby-cheeked as a butcher's lad and whom they call Eros, casting each other looks of martyrs in ecstasy each time they perform his easy rites and mount the women they have seduced as if they were going to the stake! In a word, they say that that is all-important, whereas the truth is that Love is only one of thousands of feelings that lay siege to our souls, and mustn't take the place of fear, remorse, tedium, hatred and sadness.

But I'd have done much better to have devoted all this paper to the analysis of the rare sensations your poems provide, poems which I believe I've written myself, so closely do they resemble me.

Farewell, my good friend, try to come and spare me the desolate work of such long letters, for I've always so many things to tell you. In the meantime, take good care of the woman who would tear me apart with her crimson claws, and we hope that your first missive will be smiling with good news. My wife squeezes your wife's hands with all her heart and Geneviève smiles at her, which is all she can do. You know whether and how much I love you.

p.s. Are you still doing English? I used to think Lord Chesterfield nothing more than a perfect gentleman, but as empty as a Massillon[13] from the point of view of his letters. I'll send you your poems back, wrapped up with the Taine, as soon as I've copied them and read Taine. Meanwhile I'm sending you Arnim's very lively *Voyage to the*

12. Baudelaire's influence can be clearly seen in the choice of this word.
13. French preacher, 1663–1742.

Pyrenees, which I like, and Schlemyl, which I don't like, apart from the rolled-up shadow.[14]

31   HENRI CAZALIS

[February 1865]
I received your fine poems which I like wholeheartedly. They're as distressing as everything that exists, but shouldn't they be? How often we've already reread them, Marie and I!

I'm not distinguishing between those in verse and those in prose, because your verse, when all's said and done, is your winged prose, just more rhythmical and more caressed with assonance. To some extent, it's a random dream, and doesn't give that impression of deep study one finds in modern poets. There's not the shadow of a criticism in that remark.

If you were to publish a volume of verse, I'd be worried; but, in your work in prose, those unfinished lines, with their harmonies and their rhymes, will merely provide so many wing-beats for the mind as it seeks to soar yet higher!

But what beautiful things there are in them! That distress you feel at the hour when dreams and the pillow must be left and you must enter the cold day which holds no secret and whose monotonous emptiness you know in advance!—"The Poor," so lovely because it is nothing other than a cry of a soul in love with Beauty, a soul which suffers at the sight of an evil so marked with ugliness—but it doesn't conclude, stopping when the torrent of tears has been shed!—The sad herd of women in the hospital, laughing, laughing! Man alone, in all creation, my .friend, is stupid enough to laugh.—Everything, in a word.

I had a good chat about you with that monkey, Emmanuel, whom I surprised the other day in Avignon. He told me he owed 6 francs to a tailor, 24 sous to a grocer. What's distressing is that he owes his housekeeper 2 francs 50, and times are hard, and he's desolate at not having visited me on New Year's Day. After which this poet read me poems I considered very fine, if you accept his somewhat slack style and his rather diffuse thought.

My pen is writing on its own at the moment, I'm so gloomy I can't think and yet, tonight, while the fat-bellied lawyers dance like bottles on water, at the Sub-Prefect's Ball which I'm avoiding, I want to begin an important scene of *Hérodiade*. Pity me.

14. Arnim is the famous German Romantic writer; the reference to Schlemyl alludes to the story by Chamisso of the man who lost his shadow.

Geneviève, who is already laughing, her mother who is amusing herself downstairs with her, and I all embrace you from afar for your fine poems.

᠅᠉ *At the beginning of the summer Mallarmé began work on his poem* L'Après-midi d'un faune, *which was to go through several versions before being published in 1876.*

32   HENRI CAZALIS
[Late June?] 1865

I don't know where to begin in telling you how delighted I am with your book, its sobs of seraphic violins, its shivers of feathers and stars, in a word, its paradise of azure and its milky way of tears. As I don't want to turn my letter into an article (that's what I'm planning to do for both *Vita tristis* and Villiers de L'Isle-Adam's *Elën,* two of the most beautiful prose poems I know here below), I'll limit myself to giving you a kiss. May my lips be feminine! But no, for they would bleed, wounded by the flute I'm blowing with fury, for I've been at work for ten days now.

I've abandoned *Hérodiade* for the cruel winters: that solitary work had sterilized me and in the interval I'm rhyming an heroic interlude, whose hero is a Faun.

The poem contains a very lofty and beautiful idea, but the lines are terribly difficult to create, for I'm making it absolutely scenic, not just "capable of being staged" but "demanding the stage." And yet I want to retain all the poetry of my lyric works, my verse itself, which I'm adapting for the theater. When you come, I think you'll be happy: the thought of the last scene makes me sob, the conception is vast and the lines finely wrought. I won't tell you anything more and only mentioned it to get it off my chest. I'll add that I'm hoping to present it to the Théâtre Français in August.

But you and you alone are the soul of my day. Marie and I, in front of Geneviève who kissed the book, are reading *Vita tristis.* How proud I am to see my name on one of those beautiful, chaste pages.

Do you realize that the volume is deliciously coquettish? Oh! I'd like to write you hundreds of letters, for what can be written in one article has no limits when it's transformed to the expansion of a conversation, even one written from a distance! But how we'll talk about this dear book when you are at Tournon! I'll have read it many times by then, I've already read it twice and I haven't missed a word. So you will come toward the end of July, won't you? Fly until then.

Forgive this letter *for being nothing but a squeeze of the hand* and don't be angry with me if (Geneviève is growing and Marie too, I think) I write little, because my *Faun* grasps me by the hair and won't leave me for a minute.

33   HENRI CAZALIS

[July 1865]

No. I'm not angry with you for the disenchantment I felt on reading your news that you're putting off your visit until next year: for I never believed for a minute, seriously, that you'd come. Nevertheless, I liked deluding myself with that promise as one likes deluding oneself with harmonious words.

But the important thing is that I should see you and I will.

I plan to stay at Tournon until 25 August, more or less, to complete my Interlude, for you know that, unfortunately, I work with great difficulty.

After that, I'm planning to spend a few days at Sens and at Versailles: you'd see Geneviève and Marie, my too little German girls, en route. They would probably return to Sens and I would devote the month of September to Paris. Those are my dreams. Provided that I can bring my story of the Faun to a worthy end!

You've no idea how hard it is to work away unrelentingly at this poetry, which I want to be very new and very beautiful, although it's theatrical (above all I want it even more rhythmical than lyric poetry, because it must delight the ear when performed on stage); you've no idea how difficult it is, sometimes impossible, to pursue one's thought lucidly, in this southern heat, sometimes burning, sometimes stifling, but always conquering the animal in us. Add to that the distressing complication of classes which cut into my day and shatter my brain, for I command little respect and I'm even sometimes worsted by paper darts and catcalls. But, with the help of willpower and jugs of coffee, I'm determined to win.

What you tell me about the appreciations of your aunt and her court distresses me, although it causes me no surprise, so deeply do I feel that art is for artists alone. If you only knew how it hurts me to water down my thought and weaken it to make it instantly intelligible to a room of indifferent spectators!

Nonetheless, I believe you'll get more out of prose than verse. You are already master of your prose. But if you only knew what nights of desperation and what days of reverie have to be sacrificed to succeed in writing original poetry (something I've never achieved up till now), and poetry which is worthy, in its supreme mysteries, of delighting the soul of a poet! And what study of the sounds and color of words, the music and painting through which your thought must pass, however beautiful it may be, if it is to become poetry!

But I don't want to spend any more time in pedantry: moreover, you'll of course pardon this outburst and, what's more, the platitude of the rest of my letter, when I tell you that I'm scribbling this down in front of a class of idiots who torment me—for I've sworn to myself that there will be no piece of paper unconnected with my poem on my desk at home until I've completely finished it all.

So my correspondence is abandoned for a month. You won't tyrannize me too much, will you?

Farewell, the three of us embrace you, without bearing you any grudge, you man of promises.

34   EUGÈNE LEFÉBURE

[July 1865]

I'm reluctant to write you a brief reply on a sheet of letter paper, because that would make it a letter, and I've forbidden myself all correspondence for this month, as much to avoid breaking the thread of a reverie as out of hatred for any task not related to the one which is currently fascinating me. I've been, for the last fortnight, and will be for some time to come, fully engaged in composing a piece for the theater. I bet that surprises you! I, who was little more than a shade, am actually giving life! Indeed I am giving life. By dint of studying I even believe I've discovered a new dramatic verse form, in that the rhythm is modelled exactly on the gestures, without excluding a form of poetry which has both weight and effects, something which in itself is little known. My subject is drawn from antiquity and is a symbol. You'll be going from surprise to surprise, but how much I long to show it to you when you come! If I've finished it. There are only 400 lines, but you know what that means for me. I'm planning on taking it to the *Comédie française*.

So you really are coming then! Yes, my dear friend, Tournon is indeed on the way to Eaux-Bonnes and even if it were not, we'd make sure it was. But the route through Lyon, Sète, and Toulouse is the only one you could take. From Sète, one can even go directly to Bordeaux. What a special pleasure it will be! But why must that pleasure be saddened and veiled with melancholy through the sufferings of your dear wife? A few sisterly kisses from my Marie for a week—for you'll give us a week, at least, won't you?—may perhaps cure her. But no, that can't be, for your own have been powerless to do so!

Your poetry is very fine. When I forget that it is addressed to me,

53

I admire the sonnet. As for the "Mot du printemps," that's you all over, and, to my great pleasure, I'm there too, so closely are we brothers. So you feel the spurs of the Lady who does not lightly abandon her former prey! May she wound you, if from your wounds flow crimson and rubies. Man is made to bleed. I take pleasure in being one of your tormentors!

Farewell my good friend, excuse the voluntary banality of my letter (I don't want to *cut into myself*). We'll make up for it in endless talk when we see each other! Marie embraces your wife[15] and Geneviève puts her foot in her mouth to salute you. For my part, I send my love.

P.S. Seized with remorse on rereading your letter and my own, I scribble down these belated words:

There is an immense talent in English literature, but Taine's theory, which is humiliating for the artist, seems to me highly debatable. What's more, he is wonderfully sensitive to the soul of poetry, but he does not understand *the beauty of the verse,* which constitutes at least half of the art.

I can't afford to buy the *Histoires grotesques ou sérieuses*[16] and what's more I'm not reading at present. I've had a copy of Shelley since my days at College, and consider him one of the greatest poets I know.

Where in the devil were you able to find Banville's *Améthystes* (you know they are merely studies in rhythm)? I've been looking for it in vain for ages.

I have a copy of *Jane Eyre* and will give it to you when you come. There is in it a strange intensity of passion, but it's so long! I'll make you read one of the most beautiful novels I know: *Un prêtre marié,* by that brilliant Catholic, Jules Barbey d'Aurevilly.

Hérodiade, which was a solitary work, had left me sterile. I'm keeping it for the cruel winters. In my *Faune* (for my hero is a faun) I'm abandoning myself to summer outbursts which I didn't know I was capable of, and at the same time I'm exploring the possibilities of verse, which is very difficult because of the action!

What I told you about the line from Sète to Bordeaux and then, halfway between them, to the Pyrenees, isn't a mere project, it's the truth.

Farewell, once more, I'd go on chattering like this until you arrived.

15. On 5 July, Lefébure wrote to tell Mallarmé that he had lost his wife on the day this letter arrived.

16. Baudelaire's translation of various tales by Poe, entitled *Histoires grotesques et sérieuses,* was published in 1865.

54

Monday morning [16 October 1865]

Thank you for your kind letter, I'd wanted to write first, but the upheaval of moving house interposed itself between me and my intention. Now, I have a room worthy of you and I'm impatiently looking forward to the instant when I can offer it to you. It's stark, with a chest, Henri III chairs in Cordovan leather, and a tapestry of Louis XIII, a contemporary clock worked by weights, an old lace thrown over the bed, and simply, together with the portrait of Hugo, portraits of friends who deserve to be here: you above all. But what I like is that when you open the curtain on the one window you see the Rhône, calm and enclosed, as if it were a lake on a painted backdrop. Here I live in the midst of nature and can see both sunrise and sunset, and I participate in autumn, not that of the leaves with their reds and yellows, but that of fogs and melancholy water.

In a word, I no longer think I'm at Tournon.

Dear friend, this description is not in vain, for I know we all like to imagine in their homes those who dwell in our thoughts, and I also know you think about me.

Now, let's talk about you. Alas, I have bad news. Rouvière[17] is on his deathbed, has been for months, and will be taken from us by his diabetes. It would therefore have been uselessly cruel to go and arouse his enthusiasm for your admirable play, and all my friends dissuaded me from doing so. Let's wait and see what happens.

But you're already working on the next one. I've reread your letter in vain to discover if you finally chose your medieval subject.[18] So come, once you've finished the first draft, on one of those fine winter days and we'll talk about it: for I myself would like to come and see you at Easter.

My *Faune* poem gave infinite pleasure, but Banville and Coquelin considered it didn't contain the essential plot the public demands and assured me that it would be of interest only to poets.[19]

I'm putting this subject away in a drawer for a few months, to revise it freely later on, and then, after the departure of my wife's sister, who came to give her a surprise, and of my friend Lefébure who is to spend a few weeks with me, I'll begin *Hérodiade,* no longer as a tragedy but as a poem, (for the same reasons) and above all be-

17. The famous actor was to die on 20 October 1865.

18. Aubanel replied that his new drama was modern but exotic.

19. Mallarmé had hoped to have his play about the faun performed at the Comédie française. As a result of this rejection he transformed it into a poem in the more traditional sense.

cause I'll thus gain the attitude, the clothes, the décor, and the furnishings, not to mention the mystery.

To that end, I'm going to make my rebellious temperament accept the habit of working at night, for the skinflints who pay me at the college have laid waste my finest hours and I no longer have my mornings free, and as a result not even my evenings for I have to be up by 7 to give a class. Well, God will repay them in another world and will give me recompense.

So now Emmanuel is far away from you,[20] separated not only by distance which is nothing, but even more by life, the routine and necessity which always prevent us from returning to the spots we have loved. It saddens me, for he was my sole apparition in this solitude. Still, you seem closer to me and I'm happy to think that it's for you alone that I'll go down the Rhône, dear neighbor.

What a lot of pages, especially as I write only on half pages, for letters weary me and sometimes empty me to the point where I'm prevented from working. Tell the good dear Brunets that we shake their hands throughout this letter: Geneviève is a real little woman and is madly in love with both me and a magnificent Punch I brought her. She speaks a mixture of French and German, walks with a support and soon will be able to wander about on her own. She hugs Jean de la Croix:[21] on our behalf, too.

I'm happy with each of these firstborn children, doubly so in thinking that you will soon have one too.

My wife, delighted at Madame Aubanel's delicious note, hugs her and I lay my respects at her feet—and my friendship, for she'll certainly allow that.

🥀 *Mallarmé's grandfather died in December 1865.*

36   THÉODORE AUBANEL

Tournon, Sunday 31 December 1865

I've delayed replying to your letter because I've only just got back and my mind is still shivering with a senile incoherence, incapable of stringing two words together, I was so cold on my journey. And yet, as a terrible torment(!) I had to fill more than forty envelopes with New Year's greetings, crouched over the flames in the chimney place.

You can imagine my horror at the moment of anything resembling

20. Des Essarts had been appointed to the lycée at Moulins.
21. Aubanel's son, born in 1865.

a letter and you'll forgive me for these unconnected words and the brevity of this letter, which I'm writing on small-format paper less in order to tell you few things than to dupe myself into thinking that it's not an addition to my missives. It will always be big enough to let you guess all my good wishes which you already know!

Thank you, my good friend, for the fine and charming welcome you gave my dear Lefébure and I'm happy that the two of you instantly felt a mutual sympathy, for you are two beings I adore.

Lefébure, beneath his modest timidity, hides treasures. I'll read you his poems and you'll see that he was my initiator. The sad thing is that his health won't allow him to work as intensely as is necessary for a profound originality in our Poetry.

Thanks again with all my heart! The project of a reunion between the three of us which you tell me about in your letter is a delicious dream I'll do my utmost to bring to fruition.—Until that moment I want to work without a break. Unfortunately the death of my poor grandfather made me lose a rich vein of my reverie. But I hope to find it again. And you? Tell me about your nights.

Farewell, my good friend, receive my wishes for a beautiful and happy year. Marie joins me and we beg you to share those wishes with Madame Aubanel. Geneviève, who can walk alone and has twelve teeth! doesn't that make you jealous! dispenses her finest kisses to the dear Jean de la Croix,[22] whom we too embrace.

37   AUGUSTE VILLIERS DE L'ISLE-ADAM
Tournon, 31 December 1865
A letter between the two of us is a banal melody which we allow to wander at will, while our two souls, which understand each other wonderfully well, create a natural and divine continuo for its vulgarity. Moreover I believe that we have the gift of being unable to join two words together except when we write a Poem: add to that the fact that since this morning I've been filling forty envelopes with copy for charming beings whom I met in the past and who loved me, and whom I'm not cruel enough to forget. But I'm not in tune with them and can offer them only empty words. This weariness, together with the hatred of writing when it is not for Art, will excuse me, won't it, since I'm making this concession to reality, feeling you always so near me and present in my solitude, that I'd like you to receive a sheet of paper from me on New Year's day.

22. See note 21.

Are you working, my good friend, in your exile? Be sure and tell me that. For my part I've really had every possible problem since my return to Tournon, my time chopped into pieces by the college, a boring visit lasting a month made to my wife by one of her sisters whom I don't like, and, a fortnight ago, when I was dreaming admirably of my entire poem of *Hérodiade,* I was interrupted by the death of a grandfather which summoned me back to Versailles. But I'm going to get back to work again, with joy! I have the plan of my work, and its poetical theory which will be the following: "to create the strangest impressions, certainly, but without letting the reader forget for a single minute the enjoyment given him by the beauty of the poem." In a word, the subject of my work is Beauty and its ostensible subject is merely a pretext for approaching Beauty. That, I believe, is the clue to Poetry.

I'm sending you a fairly accurate indication of the lines, in a little poem[23] composed after a night of work, to which I acclimatized my spirit in memory of you. The poet, terrified, when the wicked dawn appears, at the funereal progeny which caused him such intoxication during the illuminated night, and seeing it deprived of life, feels the need to take it to his wife who will resuscitate it.

My sheet of paper is full, that's as good a reason as any not to write to you throughout the night, I shake your hands with all my heart and wish you a beautiful and great year.

38   THÉODORE AUBANEL

[3 January 1866]

Alas, my dear Théodore, everything conspires to deprive us of the pleasure of seeing each other. First, a footling reason which is that there is so little money in the house that I dare not lay a finger on the little purse we're going to have to deplete throughout the month in part-payments for those of our suppliers who are good souls and deserve it. Moreover, I'm very tired after my sad and freezing journey[24] and I need to rest by the fireside, and I needn't add that Marie would be sad, having spent the Christmas period alone, if I abandoned her during my holidays over New Year, which in any case finish this evening. This is the most serious reason in my eyes. My earlier trip, so abrupt!, tore me out of my Dream, and I couldn't get back to work again. I was fortunate enough last night to have my Poem return in all its nakedness and I want to try the work this evening. It is so hard

23. The reference is to "Je t'apporte l'enfant."
24. Mallarmé had been to Versailles for the funeral of his grandfather.

for me to isolate myself enough from life to feel, effortlessly, the extraterrestrial impressions, the necessarily harmonious impressions I want to convey, so I study myself with a prudence that resembles a form of mania.

I'm very sorry about this hitch in our plans, it would have been so good to see you again and so pleasant to hear the outline of your play. That's what causes me most distress, for as far as seeing you is concerned, I'm sufficiently fond of you and your image is clear enough in my mind for me to be able to summon you up at will. But believe in yourself and follow your thought unswervingly until Easter; I promise I'll visit you then and there would be less risk at that stage of my misinterpreting lots of things which are at present only vague inklings in your mind, wonderfully comprehensible to you as poet, but too frail and shimmering to be subjected to an outsider's gaze.

Thank you, my dear friend, for the charming hospitality you prepared. Farewell, Marie embraces Mme Aubanel, and Geneviève (who talks in German!) embraces Jean de la Croix. As for us, we love each other.

🎝 *From the Spring of 1866 Mallarmé went through months of depression and spiritual crisis, from which he drew the basis of new aesthetic principles. 12 May saw the publication of 10 of his poems in the anthology* Le Parnasse contemporain.

39   HENRI CAZALIS

[28? April 1866]

You have to admit that you've abused, and in a curiously mischevious way, a word I let slip in a smile, and which of course was belied by the letter I wrote you on New Year's Day and which you let go by without even shaking my hand.[25] For my part, I've been waiting ever since. So now I have three months' worth of events to tell you about, in very broad outline. But that's a terrifying prospect! I've spent them furiously working on *Hérodiade,* my lamp can bear witness to that! I've written the musical overture, which is still almost completely in draft stage, but I can say in all modesty that it will create an unparalleled effect and that in comparison with these lines, the dramatic scene you know is like a mere vulgar scrawl compared with a canvas

25. An allusion to the letter in which Mallarmé had said he was so immersed in *Hérodiade* that he didn't want anything to distract him. Cazalis pretended he had interpreted this to mean that Mallarmé didn't want to receive any letters.

by Leonardo da Vinci. I'm going to need another three or four winters to complete this work, but then I will at last have achieved my dream, written a Poem worthy of Poe and unsurpassed even by his own poems. If I speak to you with such certainty, I who am the eternal victim of discouragement, it must be that I can glimpse true splendors!

Unfortunately, in the course of quarrying out the lines to this extent, I've come across two abysses, which fill me with despair. One is the Void, which I've reached without any knowledge of Buddhism, and I'm still too distraught to be able to believe even in my poetry and get back to work, which this crushing awareness has made me abandon.

Yes, *I know,* we are merely empty forms of matter, but we are indeed sublime in having invented God and our soul. So sublime, my friend, that I want to gaze upon matter, fully conscious that it exists, and yet launching itself madly into Dream, despite its knowledge that Dream has no existence, extolling the Soul and all the divine impressions of that kind which have collected within us from the beginning of time and proclaiming, in the face of the Void which is truth, these glorious lies!

That's the plan of my lyrical volume and that might also be its title: *The Glory of the Lie* or *The Glorious Lie.* I shall sing it as one in despair!

If I live long enough! For the other void I've discovered is that of my chest. I really am not very well, and cannot breathe deeply, or with the pleasure of physical well-being. But we won't talk of that. The only thing that saddens me is the thought that, if it's my destiny to live for only a few more years, I have to waste so much time in earning a living, and so many hours, which I no longer have, ought to be devoted to Art!

Truly, what poetic impressions I would have, if I were not obliged to cut up all my days, tied without respite to the most stupid and wearying of careers, for only if I wished to distress you would I tell you how much I'm shattered by my classes, full of uproar and flying stones. I come back from them in a state of stupefaction. And that's why I've had to accept the cruel resort of working by night.

As for the present, I'm resting (although I'm taking no part in spring, which seems to me millions of leagues away from my windows) and fleeing the beloved torture of *Hérodiade,* I'm going back to my *Faune* on 1 May. For I've conceived of it as a true summer task!

I'll only interrupt that to correct my poems for the *Parnasse* collection, the proofs for which I'm hoping to receive in the near future. If they don't forget me altogether. What you tell me about the first revisions fills me with distress.[26] But they can't all be bad, or that would be an indication of decline. I myself think they reveal a real superiority now over their earlier forms, and, with the exception of one or two, which are not definitive, I consider them excellent. My conscience prevents me changing anything. I would have liked Catulle[27] to tell me which ones he doesn't like.

Farewell, my good Henri, don't be worried about certain passages in my letter, I won't work at night this summer, but will return to my beautiful blue mornings. And don't be unhappy at my sadness either, for it probably results from the grief I feel at Baudelaire's poor health. For two days I believed him to be dead (oh what days they were! I'm still crushed with our present grief).[28]

Marie, who is still pale and weak, stretches out her cold hand and Geneviève, a real little woman, who is walking and talking, and whom you'll devour with kisses, puts on her prettiest smile for you and offers you one of her curl-papers.

P.S. My regards to all, especially Henri Regnault.

If you want to see the Ardèche and Provence with me, hurry, for I'll probably scheme to get a post at Sens, the isolation is killing Marie who doesn't set eyes on a human being and Tournon has become hateful to me.

I realize I've let my pen wander without telling you anything of my enchanted journey. Lefébure removed the curtain which had always hidden from me the view of Nice and I fell madly in love with the Mediterranean. Oh, my friend, how divine that earthly sky is!

Your name was on our lips every two minutes, accompanied with the frankest bursts of laughter. You were the pink-striped clown of that wonderful fairy tale! Now don't take umbrage!

Lefébure is devastated by reverie, of course, but also by all the local swindlers who have descended on his villa. All he has is a pair of stockings that his housekeeper saved for him while he, unmoving, dreams of the others while imploring the police and Brahma, the source and end of all things!

I take it he has written to you. Farewell. Don't forget me.

---

26. Cazalis had written to say that Mendès considered Mallarmé overcorrected his poems.

27. Catulle Mendès, editor of the collection.

28. Baudelaire had suffered a severe stroke on 4 February 1866. He was to die on 31 August 1867.

[21? May 1866]

First let me tell you how much I like your poems![29] From the first to the last I adore them and recite those I didn't already know by heart in the half-light of my room, created by the closed shutters and the bouquets blooming on my old furniture. It's a good place for you, with your fervor and your lack of constraint!

But pardon me for a crime I've committed. I'm harming your glory. This is how:

For the last few days I've been gathering in all the issues containing my poems, in order to withdraw them from the hostile light of full day. You are not unaware that I have been the victim of a distressing surprise, for which I blame Fate and Absence, since it would cause me sorrow to blame Mendès for carelessness. Catulle, some months ago, wrote me a rapid note which *demanded for the printer* a certain number of my poems. At the time I was ill with *Hérodiade,* worn out by staying awake at night, impotent. I felt that none of the poems had really been conceived with the aim of Beauty, but rather as so many intuitive revelations of my temperament and the note it would sound, and that as a result I shouldn't alter them according to my current principles. Nevertheless, some were still too imperfect, even from the point of view of rhythm, to be published as they stood, so I devoted several nights to correcting them, but I was conquered by fatigue and on Mendès's pressing and pointless injunction to hurry, I sent them in that state. However I begged him, on the day when they were to have appeared, to send them to me for a few instants, to remove those corrections which appeared to be bad, retain the good ones, and in a word revise everything in the mental calm which must of necessity have succeeded, one day or another, the illness my brain was suffering from. Since then I wrote to him twice more on the same subject, and one final time to M. Ricard.[30] But all that was in vain.

You know what happened as a result of this, and I'm deeply hurt by it. Some poems, it's true, are wonderfully corrected, but others are weighed down with temporary alterations, in a word, detestable, when they could have been passable if the old version had been retained, or exquisite if they had received new corrections, *corrections which I have before me on my desk* and which I swear to you are perfectly beautiful.

29. Cazalis and Mallarmé shared between them the eleventh volume of *Le Parnasse contemporain.*
30. Co-editor of the collection.

That pierced me to the heart, for you know I have no desire for publicity, accepting it only on condition that I publish works which can assure for me a reputation of perfection.

Well, let's speak no more of this dreadful business. These poems will reappear one day in my book, beautiful enough to make everyone forget that they were taken by surprise and exhibited in the secret of their prestigious preparation. Nevertheless, no criticism can be levelled at "Les Fenêtres," "Les Fleurs," "L'Azur," "Soupir," "Vere novo," and one or two other poems—apart from the typing errors (poor punctuation and absence of essential capitals) which add to their ugliness.

That makes almost four pages. Don't mock them, and if you pity my exile and my sorrow, dear friend, don't neglect to tell everyone who has cast eyes on our number of the review. I beg you!

I'm in the process of noting down the basis for a book on *The Beautiful. My spirit is moving in the Eternal and has experienced several intimations of it,* if one can talk in such a way of the Immutable. I'm resting from that by writing three poems which are short, but which will be without parallel, all three glorifying Beauty, and from them in turn I seek repose through an equal number of extraordinary prose poems. That's my summer.

Since I'm doing my best to wangle a post at Sens, although I have very little hope of doing so, I can't risk a trip to Paris from which the need to move might perhaps recall me to Tournon, and take me back from there to Sens, which would be exorbitant.

So I'm hoping to spend a month on holiday at the waters near Allevard in the Alps, which may perhaps cure the weariness I feel in my chest. In that solitude, I'll probably finish the *Faune* and continue my aesthetic studies which will lead to the greatest work written on Poetry.

Oh, my dear Henri, what a joy it would be if we were to be sent to Sens! How life would change! We'd almost be together. Even better than that, because I could be both with you and alone.

What you tell me about Sperata[31] is full of divine and sad reverie. Yes, I can understand your fine modesty which, after loving the maiden, cannot love the woman. Nonetheless, I believe the two of you would find happiness.

Serious marriage is too primitive, you're absolutely right in that,

31. Cazalis called Ettie Yapp "Sperata" in his book of poems, *Vita tristis.* He explained to Mallarmé why he couldn't bring himself to marry her: "I cannot love the woman in her, since I have too deeply loved the maiden."

but why don't you look on it as a means of having a home, that's to say a little peace, and a "tea-maker," to quote De Quincey?[32] You see it too much in terms of the lingam fiction.[33] It's true that solitary life is very fine and also very tempting. I think I would prefer it, but having married, I'll stay that way.

Farewell, my friend, my mornings are so full of work that I can write only in moments of rest, by which I mean writing stupidly as I have throughout this letter—and then not for long. If I have devoted this single page to your heart it is because my own heart is content to beat in unison, and because the other subject was the first to come to mind, as you can guess. As for your theory of philosophy, it makes Geneviève smile. I myself admire it. Truly, given those two hearts I was talking about a moment ago, there are not two minds on earth more disunited and I'd even say, unquestionably, more antipathetic than our two.

p.s. I was forgetting. Another word, still about *Parnassus*. I sent X. de Ricard six very fine poems by Lefébure.[34] He hasn't said a word about them. I'm worried. I beg you, Henri, don't let them be forgotten. Their absence would be an injustice and would of course pain our good friend who would not understand it. Can we count on you?

Emmanuel's poems are charming, particularly the first two sonnets, which I love infinitely. It's true that they are, as ever, variations on well-known impressions, but they are delightful and very successful as variants. Don't you agree?

Do you know I'm furious with you? You, Sir, have stolen from me the last line of "Les Fenêtres" ["The Windows"], its movement and its situation, in the last line of "A la nature" ["To Nature"]. I can hear your guffaws from here. . . .

Notwithstanding that, let's embrace one another.

41   HENRI CAZALIS

Tournon, Friday evening [13 July 1866]

I'd asked Lefébure, who's just left us, to speak to you at length about me—to tell you about our hours of conversation and the way in which your name floated incessantly about us. But, despite a hothouse warmth which makes my pencil fall from my fingers, I want to

32. In his *Confessions of an English Opium Eater.*
33. A reference to Indian rites of adoration of the phallus.
34. These appeared in the fourteenth volume of *Le Parnasse contemporain.*

communicate with you more directly, and I'm taking advantage of the fact that I have to send a note to Lefébure who, since he didn't leave his address with me, will collect it at your place, when he comes to shake your hand.

Don't ask any more of me, my good Henri. Imagine that I'm away on a voyage and that, in such heat, the ink has dried up in the inns. In truth I am on a voyage, but in unknown lands and if, to flee torrid reality, I take delight in evoking images of cold, I'll tell you that for a month I've been in the purest glaciers of Aesthetics—and that after having found the Void, I've found Beauty—and you can't imagine in what lucid altitudes I'm venturing. The result will be a dear poem on which I'm working, and, this winter (or another) *Hérodiade,* in which I placed my whole being without realizing it, whence my doubts and my discomfort, and to which I've at last found the key, which will strengthen me and make my work easier.

Where? For Lefébure will tell you that I'm plotting to go to Sens but that in any case they no longer want me here. That's another reason why I can't write to you, for, in addition to my poems and the lycée, I have a whole series of horrible official and diplomatic letters to write, and in summer, too.

Farewell, good Henri, ask Lefébure about all the rest. He'll talk to you about Marie and Geneviève, who is a real little John the Baptist with her light eyes, and love me despite my silence which you'll understand.

P.S. Another word.

It seems, my Henri, that I'm not yet summoned to dinner so let's chat a little. I won't see you this vacation as I don't have enough money to risk that journey before the possible voyage to Sens. Ah! what a dear dream! If we were at Sens, how we'd see you, dear Cockatoo of the Infinite, brightly colored with your own hue!

Don't bear a grudge against me but write to me! Tell me about Ettie, whether your meeting really happened or was merely a dream. More than all other women I'd like her as your wife; what remains to be decided is whether one should have a wife or not? An utterly personal question. The answer for me, for example, is yes, because I need a carpet spread by her between the earth and my naked feet, but not perhaps for you who can trample the sand with an athlete's foot. Farewell, once more, more handshakes, for you again, and for Henri Regnault and Armand Renaud. It's sad we won't see each other again in September. But even if I had the money I couldn't do so since I've too much work.

Tournon, Monday evening [16 July 1866]

I'm scribbling a little note for you in pencil, so as not to seem to put a letter between us, and to allow us to chat more intimately.

We much regretted the mishap which deprived us of your company. Lefébure, who was charmed that you liked his poems, has left, asking me to return your handshake. For my part, I've worked harder this summer than in my entire life and I can say that I've worked *for* my entire life. I've laid the foundations of a magnificent work. Every man has within him a Secret, many die without having found it and won't find it because, since they are dead, neither it nor them will have any further existence. I have died and been born again with the gem-encrusted key to my final spiritual casket. It's up to me now to open it in the absence of all extraneous impressions and its mystery will emerge into a very beautiful sky. I'll need twenty years during which I'll remain cloistered within myself, renouncing all publicity other than readings to friends. I'm working on everything at once, or rather I mean that everything is so well ordered in my mind that, as a sensation reaches me now, it is transformed and automatically places itself in the right book or the right poem. When a poem is ripe, it will drop free. You can see that I'm imitating the laws of nature.

Don't, however, take as a model of my Dream the disjointed nature of the images on these pages, I'm working too hard, within myself, not to let myself go when I'm with friends. And then, like children who seek to hide something and babble to put off the confession, I've a bit of bad news for you and I lack the courage to start with it.

Here it is: they no longer want me at Tournon: the headmaster wants to replace the teachers of English and German by a teacher who speaks several languages and I'm a victim of this economy measure.

Warned in advance and having the opportunity to go to Rodez or Albi (nothing to choose between them), I had to request the residence of my choice. Avignon, unfortunately, is impossible, for the teacher called Honorius is still going strong, as I know. I was forced to set my heart on Sens, the town where my stepmother lives and where the incumbent teacher is leaving. That was the great point, for had a colleague I wanted to replace refused, I could have been thrown into worse Tournons, if such things exist. We'll be a long way from each other, unfortunately, but at least when you come to Paris I'll stop you for a week on your way and as I'll be slightly better paid (having moreover even more work) I can almost promise you that

I'll visit Avignon every year. What a delight it will be from such a distance!

As for these vacations, I'm planning to spend them locally, during the second half working, perhaps in the company of Villiers, who is to visit me at Tournon—and in the first half we must find a way of seeing each other. We'll have such a lot of things to say to each other—about what we've done and about our future separation!

Meanwhile, farewell, my good friend, forgive my long silence, you know I think of you every day. Marie embraces Madame Théodore, and Geneviève hugs Jean de la Croix, which doesn't exclude diagonal kisses—nor mine to your dear son, nor my compliments to his mother.

43   THÉDORE AUBANEL

[28 July 1866]

I couldn't find a minute to explain the enigmatic phrase in my letter and I don't like to remain cryptic for friends like you, although I'm happy to be so when I want to force others to think of me.

(It seems I forgot to light the lamp? the one from which I hanged myself in days gone by.)[35] All I wanted to tell you was that I'd just established the foundations of my entire work, after having found the key to myself, the keystone or center key if you prefer, to avoid mixing the metaphors—the center of myself, in which I dwell like a sacred spider, on the main threads that I've already spun from my mind and which will enable me to weave *at the joins* wonderful lace, which I envisage, and which already exists within the heart of Beauty.

... That I foresee that it will take me twenty years for the five books which will make up my complete work and that I'll wait, reading the fragments I write only to friends like you—and I'll consider glory as an outworn folly. What is a relative immortality, which often relies on the minds of imbeciles, compared with the joy of contemplating eternity and experiencing it, alive, within oneself?

I'll talk to you about all this and I'll show you a few specimen drafts if I can go to Avignon after having read your Play.

Meanwhile I love you with all my heart: Marie and I and Geneviève love Madame Aubanel and embrace Jean de la Croix. As for Grivolas I'm not hugging him. Terrify this wretch with the recital of how you'll perpetrate on him his own crimes and be the Incarnation of Remorse.

35. The allusion is to Mallarmé's poem "Le Guignon."

In October Mallarmé was appointed to the lycée at Besançon. The change of residence did little to aleviate his depression, although his friendship with a growing number of poets offered some consolation.

44   FRANÇOIS COPPÉE

5 December 1866

More than ever, a few minutes ago, I was crushed by the Provinces. I was grieving, head in hands, when trumpets, blaring out at my windows, pierced me and shook from my eyes an old tear, caused by many ordinary hours, by problems which have no connection with Anguish, by stupidity. Your dear volume appeared on my desk and I'm taking advantage of its charming invitation to leave my torpor behind me through a conversation with its poet, and to let myself give way to my emotions beside the friend I feel I have in you. Don't you think I'm right?

I'm no longer at Tournon, but at Besançon, ancient town of wars and religion, a dark city, a prisoner. I've been here a month. Perhaps I'll come to congratulate myself on this. So far, I've suffered a great deal, barely recovered from the problems of such a long-distance move, the setting up of our home and the countless *visits* I had to pay on fools, to avoid alienating myself on the first day from the bosses who watch over me as if I were a shady character. (I'll tell you before too long about how I had to leave Tournon.) My God, what torments one has to undergo to earn a living! And one does not even earn it! What tasks our Society inflicts on poets! You know all this, dear friend, and that's why I can complain to you.

And what's more I'm suffering in my home! As yet I have only half an apartment, and will come to life only when I have my own room, where I can be alone surrounded by my thought, the windows bulging with my inner Dreams like the drawers of precious stones in a rich piece of furniture, and the hangings falling in their familiar folds. I would like, even just to write you this letter, to create a few lines of poetry in the temporary corridor I live in, just as one burns a scent jar, or alternatively wait a year, by which time my solitude will have had time to recompose itself within these walls. Oh, the old mirror of Silence has broken!

These lines must be as disorderly as my decor. Moreover, your book is still too closely linked with my life and I'm too much of a pleasure-lover (especially in the discomfort of my present life) to turn a source of intimate happiness into an article. Do I even need to tell you that it is *a work entirely after my own heart.* "Le Lys" is one of the most magnificent moments Poetry has granted me. The same is true of "Ferrum est quod amant." I believe that that is the real *you:* a purity so clear that all the other emotions the poem might arouse (such as depth or richness), far from arising separately in the spirit, add their own weight to that purity, which is clear-cut, unique, and has nothing radiating around it, so to speak, as there is in poets whose thoughts miss the point. Neither does anything seep out into the framework, but everything is set into a sharp contour, cut off exactly where it ceases to exist. (I believe there is no other poetry these days). Chance doesn't enter into any line and that is the great thing. Several of us have achieved this, and I believe that when lines are so perfectly de-limited, what we should aim for above all, in a poem, is that the words—which are already sufficiently individual not to receive exter-nal impressions—*reflect upon each other to the point of appearing not to have their own color anymore, but to be merely transitions within an entire gamut.* Although there is no space between them, and although they touch each other wonderfully, I feel that sometimes *your words live a little too much as individuals, like the stones in a mosaic of jewels.* Since I'm playing the pedant, I'll tell you I'm less fond of your great pieces than of your short ones, because in the former you have a little of Hugo's tone, which doesn't seem to belong to you. (But I assume you must have done them as studies?) Your real brotherhood would be with Mendès, if you were not perfectly Coppée, whose lines, from a distance, appear to me like a cameo figure with its name written on a sword blade, yielding as a blade does.

Forgive me for speaking badly and vaguely to you. In an evening of discussion on any subject (and rather on anything other than your art for, I repeat, to my mind it's with the man that your lines fuse), we'd say so much more about all this! All the more so as I hate letters and scribble them as poorly as possible to disgust my friends. Never-theless, I won't ask you to shake anyone's hand on my behalf, because I'm hoping to spend this month of waiting in writing a New Year letter to each of our friends, and I've begun with yours. Just tell Vil-liers why I have been silent so long, and that my first pages will be for him. Since the name of Glazer[36] appears in your book, greet him for me, and say I remember him. (Tell Catulle I'm dead, that will calm his conscience.) Finally, I'm not forgetting you.

36. Coppée's collection *Reliquary* contains a poem dedicated to the Hungarian poet Glazer.

[December 1866]

Allow me to see in the exquisite thought that made you send me your volume, although you don't know me, not merely a sign of literary fellow-feeling, but also the wonderful presentiment of an unknown friendship.

You forestalled a vow I'd made to shake your hand, a vow taken after reading your poems in *Le Parnasse*. I thank you twice over—and more than that, for *Poèmes saturniens* have rescued me for several days from the stupidity inflicted on me by the upheaval of a removal, and they raised me from the shame of reality.

So when your book found me I was no longer at Tournon, but at Besançon, surrounded by upside-down paintings and broken furniture, and in the midst of visits which I had to make to get some peace from those on whom my fate and work depend. I feel so tired, since I don't yet have a room furnished with my thought but live in a corridor, that I'd prefer to engage in mortal combat rather than write a letter. I have the feeling that I'm crossing swords with an enemy, so painful is it for me to appear as I am at present. So allow me to leave my wit in its scabbard, covered with dust and spiderwebs, and don't resent the torpor of my expression.

To continue my sword fighter's comparisons—forgive me! (it's more than a month since I've made a comparison!), I'll tell you what a pleasure it was to see that from all the old forms, like well-worn favorites, that poets inherit from one another, you felt yourself obliged to forge a new, unsullied metal, fine blades for you alone, rather than continuing to rummage through all those worn-out embossings which lend a vague and old-fashioned air to things. You've now created your own arms, which you'll be free to explore in depth (they sometimes have a hint of that audacity which is suitable only in a first volume). But your book is, indeed, in all its beauty and in the romantic meaning of the term, a first work and one which made me regret on many evenings the vanity which makes me want to offer my work only when it is complete and perfect, and at a moment after which my gifts can only decline. And, moreover, I'd so like to give you in exchange for your offering something other than this miserable and banal letter to which I append my signature only in order to find yet another pretext for shaking your hand, wholeheartedly (and in *friendship*)—do you accept?—until we can have a good chat together, in better times,—and those times will be better, even if I were condemned to suffer forever my present state of stupidity, if only because I'll be seeing you! At present I'd only have the courage to recite to you all the lines I know by heart from the *Poèmes saturniens,* preferring, so far am I from my usual state, to cling to the delight they give me, rather than trying to explain it.

After this winter's work, you'll receive a real commentary, and until then you'll live in my neighborhood like all my absent friends.

46   ARMAND RENAUD

20 December 1866

I write you so many letters in my imagination as I walk about on my own—I chat with you mentally so often in my room, which your dear presence fills even more than your portrait which hangs on the wall, that not only do I think it utterly unnecessary to write to you, but I'd even be afraid that by placing between us the reality of the post and the time it takes for a letter to reach you, I might make your ghost fade away. Nevertheless, as you do indeed exist, so it seems, elsewhere, and may perhaps not guess how present you are in my thoughts, I've decided to take up paper, but not pen.[37] All the more so, dear friend, as I have to thank you with all my heart, for you are one of those over whom absence has no power, as I found out through the recommendations you were kind enough to make on my behalf to a leading figure in the Ministry of Education whom you know. I won't tell you how much we were touched by this—I prefer to strengthen the bonds between us even more by considering it perfectly natural!

So now we're here at Besançon, I can say, to some extent thanks to you. The great benefit up to now has been leaving Tournon, for, in financial terms, I'm more or less in the same situation and as for the time I owe the school, my days are horribly broken up, even on Thursdays[38] and Sundays. But I'll try to wangle my way out of that for I need long hours of reverie, which is an indispensable condition of my work. As a result of that condition, I'll beg you not to consider this note, written in the midst of the upheavals, dust, and ineptitude of moving house, as a real letter. *I haven't yet rediscovered myself spiritually.*—On the other matter, that of money, my move has utterly ruined me, and I could wish that that problem had not added itself to the preceding one, to hobble my winter's work. So I'd ask you to be kind enough to beg M. Lebourgeois (to whom, moreover, I plan to write a note of thanks) to add his support to the request I'm making

37. This letter is written in pencil.
38. Thursday was the traditional day off, with Sunday, in the French education system.

through official channels to the Ministry to allocate removal expenses. I'm attaching to this letter a copy of the one I've sent the Ministry. Please send it to him—*always providing that sending it won't cause you the slightest embarrassment,* my dear friend.

Even more than paper and time, I lack sufficient brains to talk to you about our Art. I've worked infinitely hard this summer, on myself first of all, creating, through the most beautiful synthesis, a world of which I am the God,—and on a Work which will result from that world, and will be, I hope, pure and magnificent. *Hérodiade,* which I'm not abandoning, but for the execution of which I'm allowing more time, will be one of the twisted, splendid, and Solomonlike columns of this Temple. I'm allowing twenty years to complete it, and the remainder of my life will be devoted to an Aesthetics of Poetry. Everything is in draft form, I've only to determine the place of certain internal poems, a place which is predestined and mathematical. My entire life has its *idea,* and all my minutes work towards creating it. I'm planning to publish everything together and to detach fragments of it only for my close friends, like you, my dear Armand. When will I send you the first of these? (I am, moreover, working on all of them at once.) Oh! If I had enough money to go to Paris for the next vacations, what good hours we would spend. But we really must see each other—even if it means your going to Switzerland to have a reason to come through Besançon. Farewell until then, my dear Armand, I wish you a year of peace, if not happiness, and send my love.

47   José-Maria de Heredia

7 March [1867]

Time passes with vertiginous speed, when one is possessed by an obsession, and now that I am working more than ever before, I am in that state.

Let's pretend, therefore, that I received news of your marriage only yesterday, and let me shake your hands warmly, like an old friend, for the two years that we've known each other are worth thousands of years, thanks to absence, for those who are absent accompany my life much more than if I were living in their earthly neighborhood.

Nevertheless, if I'd received your letter only yesterday, I'd still have, vibrating around my thoughts, a thousand delightful things to say to you, and a realm of happiness suggested to me by the announcement of your own happiness. But, egoist that I am, I took pleasure in it in hours of repose, or of mental exhaustion, when returning to mere reality would have seemed to me to be too cruel. I drank, to the point of intoxication, the charm your happiness caused me and found the means (as in all things, alas!) of profiting from it myself.

The result is that now I know only one thing, which is to shake your hand and tell you stupidly that I love you. But if my brain is worn out this evening, there still exists, deep inside me, an old heart whose presence I guess at, and which beats in harmony with the emotions of my hand. The vampire I am, which devours everything in order to make its own blood and color, and which will devour itself one day, has apparently not yet eaten this heart, and it's thanks to that last act of pity that we are not yet the Monster I predict and will become.

And yet, therefore, even if I were allowed to keep only one human sentiment, of all of them it would be the deep friendship I feel for my friends, alone and unadorned. But as that sentiment is at present still adorned with a thousand charming and feminine tremblings, I beg you to present all my respectful sympathy to the one who will be your wife.

Be kind enough, too, to offer my regards to your mother, whose character you allowed me to perceive one day.

Farewell, dear friend; for my part, I'm returning to my *mania,* which I can be induced to abandon only by something as great as the joy or grief of one of my friends, and I'm disappearing for a long time. When I see you again, it will be with something truly beautiful and glorious.

P.S. I don't know if you had heard, other than by the heading on this letter, that the room over which your *Hérodiade*—the photograph of the Titian[39]—now presides is in a house in Besançon, instead of a house at Tournon, as was the case a few months back—a circumstance which, it's true, is highly insignificant.

39. Heredia had given Mallarmé a reproduction of Titian's *Salomé.*

4   The Descent into the Void

48   HENRI CAZALIS

Friday 14 May 1867

I'm turning to good account the delightful emotion your letter caused me by writing in reply. You're right, what have we to say to each other? If we were together we'd give free rein to endless conversations as we wandered, hand in hand, along a broad avenue ending in a fountain, and the pleasure we'd have makes it all the more terrifying to face a sheet of white paper which seems to demand the lines dreamed of for so long, and which would contain only a few words of a friendship which has ended by becoming so much a part of us that we've forgotten it, as we forget the rest of ourselves, and that terror holds us back from committing what is almost a sacrilege!

I've just spent a terrifying year: my Thought has thought itself and reached a pure Concept. All that my being has suffered as a result during that long death cannot be told, but, fortunately, I am utterly dead, and the least pure region where my Spirit can venture is Eternity. My Spirit, that recluse accustomed to dwelling in its own Purity, is no longer darkened even by the reflection of Time.

Unfortunately, I've reached this point through a dreadful sensitivity, and it's high time I wrapped it in an outward indifference, which will replace my lost strength. After a final synthesis I have reached the stage of slowly acquiring that strength—you can see I am unable to distract myself. But this was even more the case a few months ago, firstly in my terrible struggle with that old and evil plumage, which is now, happily, vanquished: God. But as that struggle had taken place on his bony wing which, in death throes more vigorous than I would have suspected him capable of, had carried me into the Shadows, I fell, victorious, desperately and infinitely,—until at last I saw myself again in my Venetian mirror, such as I was when I forgot myself several months before.

I confess, moreover, but to you alone, that the torments inflicted by my triumph were so great, I still need to look at myself in that mirror in order to think and that if it were not in front of this desk on which I'm writing to you, I would become the Void once again. That will let you know that I am now impersonal and no longer the Stéphane that you knew,—but a capacity possessed by the spiritual Universe to see itself and develop itself, through what was once me.

My earthly being is so fragile that I can bear only those develop-
ments which are absolutely necessary if the Universe is to find, in me,
its own identity. Thus, at the hour of the Synthesis, I've just traced
out the work which will be the image of that development. Three
poems in verse, of which *Hérodiade* is the overture, but possessing a
purity which man has never yet achieved and may perhaps never
achieve in the future, for it is not impossible that I am merely the
plaything of an illusion, and that the human machine is not perfect
enough to reach such results. And four poems in prose, on the intel-
lectual concept of the Void.

It will take me ten years: will I have them?

My chest still causes me much trouble, not that it's been attacked,
but it's horribly delicate and kept that way by the Besançon climate,
which is dark, damp, and icy. In the vacation I want to leave this town
for the South, the Pyrenees, perhaps. I want to bury myself, until my
Work is completed, in some Tarbes[1] or other, if I can find a place
there. That's necessary, for a second winter in Besançon would kill
me. Unfortunately, I won't have the money to go to Paris, and I lead a
wretched existence here, where everything is expensive, even cutlets.
You must come and see me, therefore, or the chances are strong we
won't ever see each other again.

Lefébure is going to spend a month with us, why don't you do the
same? Your holidays begin early, I think, so do come.

To conclude the information about me, I'll tell you that Marie and
Geneviève are growing, and are astonishing rogues, which is less pain-
ful to me than in the past, for my nervous system has, so to speak,
overturned itself so that an absurdity now causes me the pain that the
children's cries used to inflict a year ago. If you only knew how grate-
ful we are for the Arithmetic of *Mademoiselle Lili!*[2] Forgive me, Henri,
for not expressing our gratitude earlier.

Now, let's talk about you. Your titles and your poetic projects fill
me with rapture. I have made a long enough descent into the Void to
speak with certainty. There is nothing but Beauty—and Beauty has
only one perfect expression, Poetry. All the rest is a lie—except for
those beings who derive their existence from the body, love, and that
love of the mind which is friendship.

I hope your queen of Sheba[3] and my *Hérodiade* will be friends.

1. A French town in the High Pyrenees.
2. A famous series of books for children, published under the pseudonym P. J.
Stahl.
3. Cazalis' poem "La Reine de Saba" ("The Queen of Sheba") was published in
April 1873. It later appeared in his collection *L'Illusion* of 1886.

Since you are lucky enough to be able to have both Poetry and love, then love: in you, Being and Idea will have found that paradise that unfortunate humanity hopes for only in death, through ignorance or laziness, and when you think of the Void to come, because you have achieved those two happinesses, you won't be sad but will even find it very natural. As for me, Poetry takes the place of love because it is in love with itself and the pleasure it takes in itself drops deliciously into my soul. But I confess that the Knowledge I have acquired, or rediscovered in the depths of the man I used to be, would not suffice and it wouldn't be without a real pang of anguish that I'd enter into the final disappearance, if I hadn't finished my work, which is *The Work*, the Great Work, as our ancestors the alchemists were wont to say.

So, although the Poet has his wife in Poetry, and his child in Poetry, adore Ettie, whom I myself love as a rare sister. Is she not linked with my entire childhood as you yourself are, Henri,—for before my first poems, which date from the days when I first knew you, we were nothing but the fetuses of our minds—and pretty much witches'-sabbath fetuses, if you remember.

Farewell. Geneviève and I embrace you and Marie embraces Ettie.

P.S. Recently I read a poem by Mistral which I hadn't read earlier but which struck me as really weak. Dierx's book is a fine development on Leconte de Lisle. Will he cut free from Leconte de Lisle as I have from Baudelaire?[4]

49.   EUGÈNE LEFÉBURE

[27] May 1867

How are you? Melancholy stork of the unmoving lakes, does your soul see itself appear in their mirror with a sense of deep boredom, a boredom which as it disturbs the pure and magical charm with its distorting dusk reminds you that it's your body which stands there, abandoned, on one leg while the other is tucked up, ill, in your feathers. Come back to the awareness of reality and listen to the deep, friendly voice of another old bird, simultaneously heron and raven, which swoops down beside you. May this entire picture not disappear for you, in the shivering and atrocious ripples of illness! Before letting ourselves give free rein to our murmurs, the true, reed-like conversation of birds, murmurs mingled with a vague stupor when we return to life from staring fixedly into the pond of dreams, the pond in which we only ever hook our own image, mindless of the silver scales of

4. Mistral's poem is *Calendau;* Dierx had just published *Les Lèvres closes.*

76

fish!, let's nevertheless ask ourselves how we are situated in that life! I reiterate my first question, dear brother: *How are you? And how well advanced is your convalescence?*

Tomorrow I'll send you two divine volumes of short stories by Madame Valmore:[5] *Huit Femmes [Eight Women]* Women like her! *Le Parnassiculet*[6]—horrible word!—has been sold out, but I'll be able to extract one from Des Essarts' terror, together with the *Nain jaune*[7] (and I'll send them to you). He must be hiding mysterious piles of them, thus robbing posterity of them. As for my lines jotted down in pencil, they're very weak—but my thought is still naked and so horribly sensitive—that I'm afraid of touching it. My heart is close to you—what remains of it! And there's so little left that I prefer to leave it in your keeping rather than use it, for I'm afraid of wearing it out. So it's my good old cat body which rubs itself against your armchair in the hope of extracting from it a few sparks. You understand me well enough, my friend, not to ask anything more from me.

Nor have I gleaned anything worthy of repeating to you in the review I make each Monday of the newspapers and magazines—apart from the fact that in the *Revue des deux mondes* of 15 May there was an article by Montégut, in the fine first four or five pages of which I felt and saw with emotion my book. He speaks of the modern Poet, of the *last,* who is in fact "a *critic* above all else." That's exactly what I observe in my own case—I've created my work only by *elimination,* and any truth I acquired resulted uniquely from the loss of an impression which, having sparkled, burnt itself out and allowed me, thanks to the shadows thus created, to advance more deeply in the sensation of the absolute shadows. Destruction was my Beatrice. And if I speak of *myself* in this way, it's because yesterday I finished the first draft of my work, perfectly delimited and imperishable, provided I myself do not perish. I contemplated it, with neither ecstasy nor terror, and, closing my eyes, *I realized that it existed.* The *Venus de Milo*— which I take pleasure in attributing to Phidias, to such an extent has the name of that great artist become generic in my mind—and Da Vinci's *Mona Lisa,* seem to me, and indeed *are,* the two great scintillations of beauty on this earth—and that Work, such as I dream it, is the third. Beauty, complete and unconscious, unique and unchanging,

5. Best known for her poetry, Marceline Desbordes-Valmore attracted the attention of Sainte-Beuve and Baudelaire and was included by Verlaine in his *Poètes maudits.*

6. A collection of parodic poems published in 1866 as a response to *Le Parnasse contemporain.*

7. A periodical in which there appeared an attack by Barbey d'Aurevilly on the poets who had collaborated on *Le Parnasse contemporain.*

or Phidias' *Venus,* Beauty whose heart has been devoured since Christianity by the Chimaera, painfully coming back to life with a smile filled with mystery, but a forced mystery, and which she *feels* is the condition of her being. Beauty, in a word, having through man's knowledge rediscovered the entire Universe in its *correlative phases,* having learnt all that knowledge has to offer, having remembered the secret horror which forced her to smile—in the time of Da Vinci, and to smile mysteriously—smiling mysteriously now but from happiness and with the eternal calm of the *Venus de Milo,* a calm rediscovered after knowing the idea of the mystery of which the Mona Lisa knew only the fatal sensation.

But I take no pride, my friend, in this result: rather, I'm saddened, for all that has been discovered not by the normal development of my faculties, but by the sinful and hasty road, a road which is satanic and *facile,* the road of self-destruction which has produced not strength but a sensibility which was doomed to lead me to that point. I myself have no merit and I'd go so far as to say that it is to avoid remorse (for having disobeyed the slow process of natural laws) that I like seeking refuge in impersonality—which seems to me to be a consecration. Nevertheless, *by probing into my heart of hearts,* I find the following belief: "I do not think that my brain will be snuffed out before I have accomplished my work, for, having had the strength needed to conceive it, and having now the strength to receive that conception (that is, to understand it), the likelihood is that my brain is eager to bring that work to fruition." But it is my body which is *totally* worn out. After several days of spiritual tension in an apartment, I am ice and reflect myself in the diamonds of that ice to the point of mortal agony; then, when I seek to revive myself in the terrestrial sun, it melts me— it shows me the profound disintegration of my physical being and I have the feeling that my exhaustion is *complete.* And yet I believe that if I can sustain myself by my willpower and that if I have luck on my side (and hitherto I've had no luck at all), that is, if there are no adverse circumstances, I shall finish my work. Above all I must, by leading an exceptionally careful life, prevent the disaster—which will inevitably begin with my chest. At present, the school and the absence of sun (I would need continual warmth) are destroying my lungs. At times I have the urge to go and live the life of a beggar in Africa! Once the work is completed, I don't care if I die; on the contrary, I'd need so much rest! But I must end now, as my letter is beginning, since my soul is spent, to turn to carnal and social complaints, which is disgusting. Till Friday.

I was forgetting to tell you what it was in Montégut's article that caused such emotion: the name of Phidias at the outset, and an invocation to Da Vinci, those two congenitors of my work, before he turned to speaking of the modern Poet!

[Added in pencil on other sheets of paper.]

Since, even through all the obstacles, circumstances and Stupidity—the circumstances and follies of life—the Idea always bursts forth with its exact and fatal word: woman, ignoble, vulgar woman finds the zenith of her preoccupation in all that renders the state of womanhood abject, passive, and sickly, a passive destruction just as our destruction is active, *her periods,* which she calls her "business"—just as man, so noble when he is merely a pure example of life, and so stupid when he develops that life in social necessities—finds the zenith of his preoccupation in those necessities, which he too calls "business." And both assert themselves through these trifles (which would be greatness if they managed to attain Beauty, when Woman, instead of Illness, becomes the courtesan Destruction, or Man, instead of Brain, becomes Spirit), they assert themselves, as I was saying, in their pride, through these trifles, and answer with that air of mystery—which has not been wiped away even in these times of sadness, so indelible a mark of Beauty is it—even of the Beauty of Stupidity—"I have my business," each meaning something very different behind their deceptive similarity, but both basically identical. If I were to write a cantata, that would be part of the chorus and would be divided into stanzas for men and stanzas for women.

Since we've reached these heights, let's go on and explore them, then we'll do our best to descend from them. This is what I heard my neighbor say this morning, as she pointed to the window on the opposite side of the street from her: "Gracious me! Madame Ramaniet ate asparagus yesterday." "How can you tell?" "From the pot she's put outside her window." Isn't that the provinces in a nutshell? Its curiosity, its preoccupations, and that ability to see clues in the most meaningless things—and such things, great gods! Fancy having to confess that mankind, by living one on top of the other, has reached such a pass!!—I'm not asking for the wild state, because we'd be obliged to make our own shoes and bread, while society permits us to entrust those tasks to slaves to whom we pay salaries, but I find intoxication in exceptional solitude, and apart from brothers, as you and I are, or cousins, like Catulle or Villiers, or fathers, like our masters whose sons we truly are—I'll always reject all company so that I can carry my symbol wherever I go and, in a room full of beautiful furniture just as in the countryside, I can feel myself to be a diamond which reflects everything, but which has no existence in itself, something to which you are always forced to return when you welcome men, even if only to put yourself on the defensive.

Every birth is a destruction, and all life, at every moment, the agony in which one brings back to life that which was lost, in order to experience that which before was a mystery to us.

I admit only one sort of fat woman; certain blond courtesans, in sunlight, especially wearing a black dress—women who seem to shine with all the life they have taken from men and who really give the impression that they have grown fat on our blood and thus, seen in their true light, represent happy and calm Destruction—beautiful personifications.

Otherwise, a woman must be as slender and slim as a libertine snake in her outfits.

I think that to be truly a man, to be nature capable of thought, one must think with one's entire body, which creates a full, harmonious thought, like those violin strings vibrating directly with their hollow wooden box. As thoughts are produced by the brain alone (which I so abused last summer and part of this winter), they now appear to me like airs played on the high part of the E-string without being strengthened by the box,—which pass through and disappear without *creating* themselves, without leaving a trace of themselves. Indeed, I no longer remember any of those sudden *ideas* I had last year. On Easter day, when I was suffering from an extreme headache, as a result of working with my brain alone (stimulated by coffee, for it can't begin on its own and as for my nerves, they were probably too weary to receive any impression from outside), I tried not to think with my head any more, and, with a despairing effort, I stiffened all my nerves (as a pectus) to produce a vibration, while holding the thought I was working on at that time, which became the subject of that vibration, or an impression—and, in that way I sketched out a poem long dreamed of. Since then, I've said to myself, in the hours of the essential synthesis, "I'm going to work with the heart" and I feel my heart (doubtless my entire life flows to it), and, with the rest of my body forgotten, save for the hand that writes and that heart which lives, my sketch appears—appears—. Truly I am broken down into my constituent parts, and when I think that that is necessary to have a very unified view of the Universe! Otherwise one feels no other unity than that of one's life. In a museum in London there is "the price of a man": a long box [unreadable], with numerous pigeonholes in which can be found starch, phosphorus, flour, bottles of water, alcohol—and great pieces of artificial gelatine. I'm such a man.

From the depths of its sandy burrow, the cricket,
Watching them pass by, redoubles its song.

Hitherto the cricket used to astonish me, it seemed slight as an intro-
duction to a magnificent line, a line as vast as the ones already quoted:

Cybele, who loves them, makes the country greener yet.[8]

I knew only the English cricket, a sweet-singing caricaturist. It was
not until yesterday that I heard in the young wheat that sacred voice
of the innocent earth, already more unified than that of the bird, that
son of the trees in the solar night, which has something of the stars
and the moon, and a little of death. But above all how much more
unified it is than the voice of a woman, who walked and sang before
me, and through whose voice one could see a thousand words in
which it vibrated—a voice pregnant with the Void! All the happiness
the earth possesses in not being broken down into matter and spirit
was contained in the unique sound of the cricket.

50   AUGUSTE VILLIERS DE L'ISLE-ADAM

24 September [1867]
This is for you, my dear friend, when you have a moment to read
it. Your letter struck me dumb[9] for I *wanted* to be forgotten, remem-
bered by myself alone, in these hours when I refuse to think of the
Past. For the Future, at least as regards the very near future, my soul
has been destroyed. My thought has gone to the point of thinking
itself and no longer has the strength to evoke solely in a Void the
emptiness scattered through its porous being.

Thanks to an extreme sensibility, I was able to understand the in-
timate correlation of Poetry and the Universe, and, to make poetry
pure, I had conceived the plan of removing it from the realms of
Dream and Chance and of juxtaposing it with the conception of the
Universe. Unfortunately, as a soul organized uniquely for poetic plea-
sure, I could not, in the task needed to prepare that conception, emu-
late you and dispose of an Intelligence—and you'll be terrified to
learn that I arrived at the Idea of the Universe through sensation alone
(and that, for instance, to keep an indelible notion of pure Void, I was
forced to impose on my brain the sensation of absolute emptiness).

8. From Baudelaire's poem, "Bohémiens en voyage."
9. On 20 September Villiers had written requesting a copy of the prose poems
and Mallarmé's translations of Poe, for the review of which he was editor, *La Revue
des lettres et des arts*.

The mirror which reflected Being for me was most frequently Horror and you can guess how cruelly I am now expiating that diamond of unnamed Nights.

All that remains for me to do is to delimit perfectly two books, for which I must also create the inner dream, books which will be at once new and eternal, one, utterly absolute, "Beauty," the other personal, the "Sumptuous Allegories of the Void," but (the derision and torture of Tantalus), I am left incapable of writing them—at least for a long time, if my cadaver is to come back to life. This incapability is revealed by a final nervous exhaustion, and an evil and finite pain in the head which only rarely allows me to understand the banal conversation of a visitor and makes this simple letter, however ineptly I try to sketch it out, a dangerous task.

Truly, I'm deeply afraid of *starting* (although it is true that *Eternity* has sparkled within me and devoured any surviving notion of Time) at the point where our poor and holy Baudelaire ended.[10]

So forgive my silence—a silence which has lasted so long since you sent me *Morgane,* that magnificent expansion of *yourself* which I've reread twenty times, and a silence which will continue in the future concerning the riches that your *Journal* will bring me—because of what I am suffering.

P.S. When you see Catulle, who must also have felt insulted and hurt by my silence,—if I'm to go by the friendship I feel for him— shake his hand warmly for me—and do the same to all those whom we love.

51.   VILLIERS DE L'ISLE-ADAM

30 September 1867

Your kind sympathy has been very dear to me. You are a magician and I can refuse you nothing. 1. Strike out "in the behind"[11] because of the great ladies and the little girls; it was a bit of youthful tomfoolery, quite simply, and strictly speaking unnecessary. 2. You'll have for one of the first numbers some poems by Poe, which I plan to continue translating: I accept this task as a legacy from Baudelaire.[12] 3. But not straightaway (they will, moreover, be continued until I have translated

10. Baudelaire died on 31 August 1867 after a stroke had left him incapacitated and all but speechless.
11. Villiers had asked Mallarmé to remove this expression from his prose poem "L'Orphelin," which he was planning to publish in the periodical *La Revue des lettres et des arts.*
12. No translation of Poe by Mallarmé appeared in the review.

them in their entirety) because I want, in a month or two, to send you a Novella.[13] I had a vague plan of it, but was saving it for the future, several years ahead, when my book on "Beauty" is completed. Indeed, it's called "The Aesthetics of the Bourgeois" or, "The Universal Theory of Ugliness." I'll begin, therefore, with what was to have been the end, with Ugliness and not with Beauty, for which it was to have been an appendix.

It is quite simply "the symbolism of the *bourgeois* or where he stands in relation to the Absolute." I want to show him that he has no existence independently of the Universe—from which he thought he could separate himself—but that he is one of its functions, and one of the vilest at that—and I'll show him what he represents in that Development. If he understands it, his joy will be forever poisoned. Don't speak about this work, since I don't want to sell my chickens before they're hatched. And it's very hard for me to work, ill as I am, and moreover worn out with weariness as I'm going to be when the college boys come back from holidays—*the bourgeois's sons!* However I'll try to make up for the poor condition of my faculties by ruses and by the passing of time. *We must* terrify the monster, and I believe I have the perfect plan. I'm eagerly awaiting your sugary mixture, which will make him feel so nauseated he'll vomit himself: you're right, we'll avoid the courts, all the art will lie in making him judge himself unworthy of living. Farewell, then, dear friend, and we'll hope to see soon *le Lac d'Auber.* Oh! if only I had the complete edition of Poe, as Baudelaire did, I'd translate his *marginalia,* the articles on Aesthetics, and what a lot of surprises there would be! That would provide material for each number of the review and would give people the idea of collecting it. But I've never been as poor as in the last year.

Dear friend, take my place, by your good words, with all our friends, especially Banville, whom I adore more and more, but to whom *I cannot write,* and Monsieur de Lisle. Shake Gouzien's hands, but above all your own.

🦋 *In October 1867 Mallarmé was posted to the lycée at Avignon.*

52   FRANÇOIS COPPÉE

Avignon, 20 April 1868

Even disregarding your charming thought of sending me my own copy, your volume went straight to my heart. It revived in me the

13. No trace of this work has been found.

divine poem that a frightful suffering has long held captive, this exquisite collection written to its glory![14] Ah! how wise you are to have wanted nothing except through this work. As for me, it's been two years now since I committed the sin of seeing the Dream in its ideal nakedness, whereas I should have been amassing between it and me a mystery of music and oblivion. And now, since I've reached the terrible vision of a pure work of art, I've almost lost my reason and the sense of the most familiar words.

Your volume, so wise within its restricted frame, has added its voice to those reproaching me for the fault I've committed. And believe me when I say that I only loved it the more for that! I was utterly delighted by it before this coincidence: its melody is in a fixed line, as if it were drawn in India ink, and its apparent fixity has such charm only because it is created by an extreme vibration. But why should I tell you what you set out to do? The only word that could please you, if you don't know it even better than I do myself, is that this series of poems is, quite simply, a *success*. I would give the magnificent vespers of Dream and their virgin gold for a quatrain destined for a tomb or a sweet, provided it was a *success*.

Farewell, dear friend, I don't know whether I'll see you again some day, when I'm in harmony with the tone of things and have returned, but whatever happens, and even if sad insanity should triumph, I'll keep your dear image deep within myself. Assure our masters that I bear them an *eternal* cult, and our friends that at the moments when my brain does not curse itself I chat with them as in better days; give my most intimate greetings to Villiers and Mendès as well as to yourself.

53   Eugène Lefébure

3 May 1868

You are the prince of science and glory, and without any question whatsoever the most astonishing of giraffes, you write to me whenever you have absolutely no time to tell me anything, which is moreover an excellent tactic. Just as silent, I for my part will reply only to your two questions and will omit my principal wish, which is to see you again! I'll just touch on the subject of my health, as I don't want to stir up that disquieting mudpit in the hours when it's kind enough to leave the pure water of my spirit alone. What's more, I wouldn't know what to say to you (for I move from moments which border on a dimly perceived madness, to counterbalancing ecstasies) except that

14. The book in question is *Les Intimités*.

84

I'm in a state of crisis which can't last, hence my consolation! Either I'll get worse or I'll cure myself, I'll disappear or I'll remain, I don't care in the slightest which fate befalls me, provided I don't remain in the state of abnormal anxiety which currently oppresses me. There can be no doubt that I'm descending from the absolute ... but that two-year-long association (do you remember? It dates from our stay in Cannes) will leave me with a mark which I want to transform into a consecration. I'm returning to my Self, which has been abandoned for two years: after all, even poems which are merely tinged with the absolute are already beautiful, and there are few enough of them— added to which is the fact that a reading of them could in the future summon forth the poet of whom I had dreamt. . . . I frequently reread *Melancholia*[15], which is one of the things I most like reading in my state, since it is simultaneously fresh and extremely suggestive. There is a very beautiful line, which constituted my entire life in the period when I was dead:

They pass through the Infinite to create new places.

Turning now to the messages which you want to convey for me: the first task is to be my alter ego for Villiers, should you see him. If I recover, I'll write to him between now and the holidays, for I have a serious request to make of him. In the meantime, ask him for *L'Inter-signe,* which I've not received in its complete state.[16] Is the Review completely dead then? Now laugh, for my rich commissions are com-ing up. You must get from Cazalis the address of the shop where he bought his hammock ... because I'd like to hang a similar one from the laurel trees in my courtyard and and sleep in the flattering shade of their leaves, at least if I can't write some verse! I condemn you therefore to the exact address. . . . Finally, for it's possible that rocked by the hammock and inspired by the laurel trees I may write a sonnet and as I have only three rhymes in -ix, do your best to send me the true meaning of the word ptyx, for I'm told it doesn't exist in any language, something I'd much prefer, for that would give me the joy of creating it through the magic of rhyme. . . .

54   HENRI CAZALIS

18 July 1868

Will I see you? I'm still too much a prey to nervous illness not to mention straightaway what is most precious to me, above all when it

15. Cazalis's collection of poems, first published in 1868.
16. This work had appeared on 8 December 1867 and 12 January 1868 in the *Revue des lettres et des arts.*

overexcites my habitual expectations. But don't come in August, for then it's extraordinarily hot, as it is today, and at such times, even protected by blinds and the shade of the walls, the mind is as indistinct as an aquarium traversed by vague fins, formerly silver. In September, the sun calms down, and becomes beautiful: we ourselves will flee from Avignon from the beginning of the vacation to the first days of September: you'd find us in a village on the Mediterranean, but I'd prefer to have you in our familiar abode; you'll be more present and your memory would remain with me longer.

What's more, you'll see the Félibrige in all its glory, celebrating the Spanish poets, among them the great Zorilla![17] And too, I may be in better health than at present, after swimming in the blue waters of the gulfs. Who knows, you may even be able to bring Des Essarts from Mâcon. Convince him, and I'll be very grateful to you, for I sigh, perverted as I am by the local patois, for the conversation of French poets.

And too, my dear old friend, we'll repeat a certain outing we went on at Fontainebleau! Everything began then, our friendship dates from then, and that's when your heart came alive, to be filled by a delicious child. Poor friend, I suffer greatly from the fact that your marriage has been delayed! But still, don't our souls know how to use the Dream to create happiness from bitterness, and you'll draw ecstasy from thinking of the future, whose entire charm you are perfectly able to evoke, and this time that charm will be supreme! Don't smile, for I can give you no other consolation, and so the consolation I do give is the most natural my heart can offer.

All our friendship and impatience in a single handshake, dear Henri.

P.S. I'm coming to the sonnet![18] Thanks for having thought of me, but you are a torturer to impose on me a limit of eight days, at a time of such enervating heat, when I'm obliged to put up with the hustle and bustle demanded by ridiculous occupations, and when I'm deprived of any intelligent listener, who would make up for my imperfections, given that I'm habitually devoured by my malaise.

I'm extracting this sonnet, which I thought about once this summer, from a projected study on The Word: it is inverted, by which I mean that its meaning, if there is one (but I'd draw consolation for its lack of meaning from the dose of poetry it contains, at least in my view) is evoked by an internal mirage created by the words them-

17. Zorilla is the most famous of the Spanish Romantic poets.
18. A reference to Mallarmé's poem called "La Nuit approbatrice," later entitled "Ses purs ongles."

selves. If you murmur it to yourself a couple of times, you get a fairly cabbalistic sensation.

That amounts to a confession that it is not very "plastic," as you request, but at least it's as "black and white" as possible and it seems to me to lend itself to an etching full of the Dream and the Void.

For instance, there is a window open, at night, the two shutters fastened; a room with no one in it, despite the stable appearance provided by the fastened shutters, and in a night made of absence and questioning, without furniture apart from the vague outline of what appear to be tables, a warlike and dying frame of a mirror hung up at the back of the room, with its reflection, a stellar and incomprehensible reflection, of Ursa Major, which links to heaven alone this dwelling abandoned by the world.

I chose this subject for a sonnet which was empty and reflected itself in all possible ways, because my work is so well prepared and ordered, representing the Universe as best it can, that I couldn't have removed anything from it without damaging some of my layered impressions,—and no sonnet is to be found in it.

I'm giving you these details solely so that you won't accuse me of having deliberately tried to be bizarre—and not even that fear justifies my going into such lengthy detail.

I'll add that I'd be very grateful if you gave me your impression of it, by return, and tell me if Lemerre accepts it for his collection and doesn't find it too abnormal to appear there.[19] Grant this favor to "an absent." But please, I beg you, on my knees, send me a proof in sufficient time, so that I can make any corrections, if necessary. I beg you, undertake this yourself.

In the summer of 1869 Mallarmé began work on Igitur, *which is to some extent a transposition of the spiritual crisis he had been undergoing.*

55 HENRI CAZALIS

[July 1868]

We're placing centuries between us! Truly there is a country in which we must meet very often, but as our two Reveries may cross one another in such a way that the diaphanous natures of both feel no shiver of recognition, so it seems, let's return to our writing desks.

I'll begin, since everything here asks me to: Vève's[20] little nature

19. The sonnet was not published in the original version.
20. Nickname for Geneviève.

87

full of reproach that you're not following her astonishing development, the good laurel tree, in flower just as it was when you were here, and which each day multiplies its tyrannical blossoms, even Marie who threatens me that she'll write and tell you that "we are all well."

I ought to let her do so, for what is the point in letting you know the opposite? And my silence is always caused, ultimately, by the fact that it's painful to cause you further sorrow by referring to what has, for me, dried out the very well of sadness.

At least, dear friend, I'm working, because I see that that is true. Indeed, if I don't, the sorrow increases and all to no point.

If I can extract for you at long last a fine tale, I'll let you have it.

But I'll return to Vève, to Marie, to the garden, which you inhabit, for your presence is entirely a product of summer: the vine, embellished with those clusters of grapes you know, the hammock, the fig tree, all call you back; we cannot see last year's sun burn up the clump of southern shrubs without your being here.

Vève herself, tall and strong in her gray smock, is once again in this consuming heat the Destroyer you used to enjoy summoning. And yet how many new impressions there have been since then: she's already been to school, she sits down in front of music, the alphabet, the German method; often she becomes a little woman, letting a father's foresight glimpse her entire future. You know, every day I noted a thousand things to tell you about, and now I'm not telling you a thing.

Marie has seen you,[21] my poor friend, and how well, from the very night she returned, has she told me the story of every one of your moments together! Her great preoccupation—which is also mine—is with the possibilities of obtaining a tobacco shop, which she discussed with you. If things turn out badly it's a kind of insurance. As yet we have no reason to give up hope. She has a further ambition, which is the restitution of 500 francs of my salary, which I requested as a result of competent advice. The dear girl tells you this because she knows you sympathize with her worries and because both of us are eager that one day you'll set eyes again on a certain well-filled envelope.

And that's forgetting to mention that there is also Vève's piano. We were going to consult you about buying it, as regards price and maker (what do you think of the salesroom?). Advise us a little on this head, for we're very inexpert—don't forget.

21. In May when Mme Desmolins died.

My dear friend, that's the way in which we make you participate in our private lives,—and I was thinking of a good and true letter whose intimate nature would have sprung from the rejuvenation of our two hearts as a result of Vève's presence!

Place the blame on an impotent morning which has undone me— and for your part tell me what you're working on, send me some poetry—and love us as hosts to a part of yourself.

56   HENRI CAZALIS

14 November 1869

Because you didn't come, filling the dark stairway with a well-known footstep, and saying to us as you opened the door: "It's me," and because I'm all alone as I close my book on my Sunday, I'll light the lamp before dinner, I won't listen to Marie and Geneviève telling me about their walk when they return, and I'll place this sheet of paper between us. Breaking the spell of your permanent presence, that sheet will at least initiate you into what the invisible do not see, the minute details of daily life. It's thanks to that pleasant compensation that I've made this decision.

Moreover, since your last letter, whose envelope bears upon it an addition you know nothing about: at Lecques, in the Var (the Bandol of this year, but less shaded with greenery), I've had few tranquil hours apart from a month on holiday which was devoted to the life we dream about, work and study, walks, but all so preciously crammed in because of the brevity of our stay, that there wasn't room for the briefest note. To tell the truth, interminable petitions to the lowest functionaries at the Lycée were already invading my correspondence, and since then there have been countless struggles to ensure that I get a little time of my own! By getting up early, I was able to work for several hours each morning, but in the evening, after thankless days, it didn't take me long to fall asleep over a book of poetry. That, together with a twilight stroll, in my role as autumnal Pan, gives you the picture of my days. The family hour, the one in which we put off writing to you because we spoke of nothing but you, was the time at which we had supper, in our little dining room, to which a grave clock, whose case is familiar to you, lends an air of seriousness. Thanks to its monastic voice, I'll tell you very briefly about my work, which I'll bring to you next summer. It's a tale, through which I want to vanquish the old monster, impotence, which is, moreover, its subject, so that I can cloister myself in my great task, already revised yet again. If I complete it (the tale), I'll be cured: *similia similibus.*

But I'm summoned to supper by the less talkative voice of the clock I mentioned, together with sharper and more impatient voices, I'm leaving you only to find you again in their conversation, at least, since you are not going to Algeria. What a good surprise it would have been if you had come! Farewell, dear friend, I will be more communicative. Let's embrace each other, all four of us. If Marie and Vève, who's already growing up, knew that I hadn't said anything about them! But, too, I've said nothing about you! Talk to us.

At the beginning of 1870 Mallarmé was granted his request for leave from teaching on the grounds of ill-health. He gave private English lessons and considered writing a doctoral thesis.

57   EUGÈNE LEFÉBURE

20 March 1870

You'll receive a letter from me tomorrow morning: you must. The discreet and silent person who is mingled with the muslin of your room and who takes my place beside you and fulfills all your needs, for which reason I detest her, will disappear for a few days. Already the Bour,[22] into whose eyes I gaze during my mornings' work, makes all the minutes that are not transformed into grimaces the confidant of my deepest secrets. Knowing what I myself don't even know, he fades away, and leaves you there, my poor friend to whom I haven't written for three months. But I could ask why aren't you here? There can be only one language between the two of us, a language of half-words exchanged amid silences, allowing each of us to see what point the other has reached. On several occasions I have indeed thought of writing to you, but it was even more essential to redo the pages left incomplete each morning. I saw those ambitious evening projects burst into flames in the fire. Today, it's only because I'm fully convinced that I can't renew them, that I'm going to chat a little with you. Forgive me for always choosing such moments for our reunions; even I hardly recognize myself in any other state.

Nevertheless, what can I extract from myself in this perfectly empty condition, apart from the mechanical repetition of my winter dream, destroyed and scattered around me, a repetition I constantly grant myself in order to prolong the illusion?

22. Geneviève's name for Lefébure.

I had therefore thought, when my weakness forced me to request leave, of benefiting from this rest by reforming my life, both from the point of view of health and from that of my career. To further this latter aim, I was going to prepare for the B.A. exam, and consider the possibility of doing a doctoral thesis. To concentrate my energy, I chose subjects connected with linguistics, hoping, moreover, that that special effort would not be without influence over the whole domain of language, against which my nervous system seems to have conceived a particular grudge. Instead of that, as in days gone by, I *flogged* the subjects I have for poems, which led to an eruption of Dream into study, laying everything waste, heading straight for all the tempting consequences and devouring them. What I'm left with is a little German, with which I plan to begin at Easter a study of a comparative grammar (not translated) of the Indo-Germanic languages, by which I mean Sanskrit, Greek, and Latin. I'll work on that for two years and then take the B.A. Then I'll undertake a more external study of the semitic languages which I will reach by way of Zend. Finally, the thesis, which made all this work necessary, predictably, since I was stupid enough to go directly to my Idea, depriving myself of the successive seduction of its mirages. I think there's five years' worth in that.

In addition to that, there arises, very slowly, the work to which I devote my heart and my solitude, and whose structure I can dimly perceive. To tell the truth, the other task, which will proceed in tandem, is merely the scientific basis of this structure.

I've just recited for you my unconscious and empty soliloquy, as I tell it to myself, so that even if all it gives us is inanity, at least it will give you the exact tone of my current state.

Now many things have been interrupted by a little English course I'm giving from time to time to young ladies, sometimes to young gentlemen, in a room in town or in my house. That gives me more than 150 francs in 100-sou pieces, each month. If it could continue, with the 400 francs a year from the tobacco shop Marie has at Arles, we'd be protected from hardship, but I won't return to the Lycée. If it's a question of being crushed, I'd prefer to be crushed under my thought, I can even escape from that, but not from the other. So don't torment yourself, dear friend, on our behalf: my employers are being very generous for my first year of leave, which allows us to strengthen our future. To return from those sums to the preceding withdrawal, did I tell you that, firstly, the 100 franc note which we weren't touching (you remember it, dear friend), was used to buy my books on linguistics. That would be a reason, even if there were not so many more pressing ones, for you to be constantly in my mind.

And now, what of you? I can only see you, the Bour to whom I'm writing, behind a pile of worries, which are a frequent source of sorrow to us. I know you have a tenacity which I invoked in the very difficult enterprise I undertook, but I learnt at the same time that without strength such tenacity verges on the dangerous. *So, how are you?*

Finally, dear friend, if we can briefly leave so many general questions, a worthy end to this interminable letter in which I've revealed the art of unwinding all the threads of a mind worn utterly threadbare while at the same time lining up the 31 hundred-sou pieces that fill Marie with despair, allow little Vève to ask yet again with her daily voice: "When's he coming, Bour?" Then it would be the real Bour, who would see everything, and not the one who appears to me as an empty shadow of himself and which I've worn out by constantly evoking him. So, farewell, my good friend. The three of us embrace you. Next time I'll tell you about those around me, the garden and our home. For today, I'll merely send you, almost hiding it from Marie, a photo in which the parts of the face that a wolf would hide are a pretty good likeness, whereas those he'd reveal are, on the contrary, deliberately deformed.

To conclude, we all embrace you. Geneviève wants me to add that she can read and knows how to play a scale on the piano.

58   HENRI CAZALIS

3 April 1870

I don't know which of my internal climates I should explore in order to find you and meet you. Why? I don't know why, all I have left of you is this vague last statement of yours: "I want to tie myself to her apron strings." You were speaking of Life.

I imagine you floating in those waters; and now Bour tells me you're writing a very fine book on *The Void*. Sometimes, mingling these impressions with images evoked recently in my mind by an old title I'd long dreamt of: The Sumptuousness of the Void, I think of the luxurious moments of heaviness in a destroyed life, and situate you there: is that right? Sometimes, arguing about the two extreme terms, I try to separate you from me a little and to see you, by comparing your life, visited by the negative Notion, with Belief, where my restored mind currently takes pleasure in being, but, precisely, life refuses to give itself to my mind; and I smile at the contrast. Indeed, it may well be through Belief that I'll succumb; I spent a very strange winter, building up my thought through fine returns to Dream, on the one hand, and on the other through that long and very attractive prelude of the study of a science (Bour must have told you about my plans concerning linguistics), and now an accident, the illness of my poor Marie, tears me unexpectedly away from the abstraction which was necessary to me and from the artificial structure of my faculties which I had arranged with such industry, to plunge me back into disorder and total nullity. I'm going to begin again.

My work is going well. But won't it remain at the half-way point? I told you Marie has been ill: she has only recently got up. The poor dear worried me. She suffered a great deal (I assume it was from her liver, although the doctors say nothing.)

She's sending you a card, a morose card which predicted her illness. From tomorrow Vève is to spend her afternoons in a school. She's a real little weed who pricks her mother's fingers. She'll keep those fingers out of harm's way for a couple of hours a day spent lacemaking calmly.

As for Mademoiselle, who's at a loose end, thanks to her isolation, a little discipline and the chance to spend time with friends will do her good.

That's all of us: what's more, there's the spring and you don't know what spring is like here.

I entrust you to spring and bid you farewell.

59   CATULLE MENDÈS

Avignon, Sunday 22 May 1870

This is indeed a letter from me. It needed the *Révolte*[23] to provoke it. Tell Villiers what joy I felt in hearing his name mentioned, even in an article by S . . . which I find in an English newspaper sent to me from London in error. You will won't you? I'm awaiting his play and your article.

Where your works are concerned, I'm up to *Hespérus*[24] which I believe you wrote for me, up to a certain point, so much does this poem find a perfect echo within me. Moreover, you know what you've always been during my absence far away: one of the landmarks of my mind and an obsession.

It's under that impression moreover that I'm now writing to you

23. A play by Villiers which suffered a spectacular failure (only five performances were given).
24. A poem written in 1869 and published in 1872.

and that's why I began this note in the least intimate manner: to speak to you of everyday things would have been like your writing a letter to Coppée full of confessions, that is if Coppée were in Paris. You are so much a part of all my habits and of my room. So it's only now I'll say in couple of words that I've spent a few very miserable years, oppressed by an illness which all but prevented me from reading and writing, and by a very difficult profession which tended to make that illness incurable: I've been able to free myself somewhat and now I'm truly better. Through some sort of compensation, an old Dream had installed within me a kind of marine grotto, where it created curious sights for itself, if I'm not mistaken. All that won't be lost, and it has left me with the basis of three or four volumes, stubborn and miserly, and they will form my entire life. But between me and their execution and the necessary leisure lies a period of time that I'll fill in the following manner, which leads me back to *Une révolte*. If you really think about it, the future is ours. *Le Parnasse* is a highly amusing invention. You'll have seen that I wanted to send to it some old lines of mine, rather than nothing at all, for the closing date. Villiers has burst upon the stage; I'm preparing something similar for the Sorbonne, a thesis dedicated to the memory of Baudelaire and Poe, which they won't be able to reject if, as I believe, what I glimpse is exact. You, dear friend, should choose some Senate: we ought to seize everything.

My plan will be long: you'll help me during these three years by a few words, copied from a book, but written in your own hand on writing paper, for what I'm lacking is reality. Could I receive reality in a pleasanter way?

This is for Villiers as much as for yourself: you are the two memories I haven't abandoned for a single day; I know, what's more, that you've thought of me.

I shake your hand for your sake and for his and ask you to give my regards to Madame Mendès. Those around me ask to be remembered.

60   HENRI CAZALIS

[April 1870]

I hadn't sent you any reply about the Little Physiology because I was in the process of examining it. You're right, but a book of science can't be too stupid for me, since I'm ignorant enough to place the larynx in the brain. A truly good book wouldn't initiate me into the

ABC of science and would, I think, blend with my own thoughts in such a way as to disappear into them.

What I need for my linguistic studies are a few notions simple enough to remain simple in my memory. So I won't ask you to tell me of a serious Physiology until later on. For the moment, my request is the following: could you recommend to me two works, one of *Physics*, the other of *Chemistry*, books which are elementary and very precise, but which are interesting because of their modernity and their lack of pedantry? They're essential to me, even to allow me to read Huxley.

You must have needed such books for your own studies, at least at the beginning. So I don't think I'm imposing on you any more work than a simple act of memory. If Huxley's Physiology, which you must have examined, doesn't seem to you to offer me a sufficiently complete anatomy, although I don't want anything which isn't succinct, tell me also of a *good little* Anatomy.

I'm asking you this as a service, and I'll even ask you to answer me straightaway if you can.

Farewell, dear friend, Marie is calling me for dinner, which shows you she's on the way back to health. Vève adds her own invitation. We'll take it that they tell me to embrace you for them, since they'd scold me soundly if I hadn't done so.

61   WILLIAM BONAPARTE-WYSE

6 June 1870

What must you be thinking of me! You can add nothing to the horrible light in which I see myself. To put things at their worst, I'll have the cowardice to profit from an accident that really did take place and which led to your precious book[25] reaching me only by chance and then a mere two weeks ago. It came from the Lycée, where I don't set foot anymore, having a year's leave for rest and work. I haven't yet read it, but I've leafed through it and deflowered it by eye. You know the charm and greed the mind feels in wanting to be initiated into a text before reading it. And from several remarkable pages I *kidnapped* what one might call airy couches, of great intimacy, formed of color and music which make me dream of water-colors and pianos at the very moment I write to you. These impressions will gain depth as the result of study, for until now they've only been a distraction from a most tyrannical labor which is giving me a rough

25. Wyse's collection of verse, *Scattered Leaves*. The dedication is dated 28 March 1870.

time at present. So, in the name of the piles of papers cluttering up my desk tonight, I beg leave merely to squeeze your hand.

Moreover, apart from the task which is absorbing me at present, and of which I'll say nothing until such time as I have fully recognized myself, I know absolutely nothing of my Avignon. My only memories are these: Théodore[26] is building himself a villa, in the surrounding countryside, so that he can lock himself away there with the outline of a play, Gras is living at Villeneuve in a house indicated by legal signposts, Mathieu is addressing the Emperor in the name of the Chateauneuf town council, after the referendum,[27] Brunet is one of the best-stocked antiques merchants in the town, and as for Roumanille, I'll wait until I have some indirect insult to make him return from Woolley Hill House and then I'll entrust it to you.[28] Mistral is rarely sighted, but I think he addresses banquets at Agen, and wants the South to crown him king. Of the only two Félibres who ever really existed, you and him, I think that you alone remain.

At Paris there's a pretty thing, Coppée's *Deux Douleurs,* which I'm sending you, for I think I'm right in remembering you were fond of Coppée: moreover, there's a new *Parnasse*[29] and I'll send you my copy.

As far as my household is concerned, I'm sad to report that my wife is ill; Geneviève, who is growing tall and rebellious, sends your fine lad a kiss: the two mothers shake hands.

You are fully restored to health, aren't you, dear friend? As for me, I'll say nothing because I'm able to work. Only, when will see each other again? I almost need some imagination to see you as if it were yesterday.

🕊️ *France declared war on Prussia on 19 July 1870. On 2 September Napoleon III gave himself up to the enemy and France declared itself a republic on 4 September. The capitulation of Paris led to a popular insurrection, forming the commune of Paris from March to May: this was crushed in a week of brutal fighting from 21 to 28 May. Mallarmé remained in Avignon, deeply concerned about the welfare of those of his friends who were in the capital.*

26. Aubanel.
27. That of 8 May 1870: "The people approve the liberal reforms introduced by the Emperor into the Constitution since 1860."
28. Woolley Hill House was Wyse's house in England.
29. The second *Parnasse contemporain.*

Avignon, Thursday, 2 February 1871

I learnt this morning, through the newspapers, the fatal news. Our poor Henri, dead.[30]

You know from your own response at this moment, how lasting is the wound to our affection. And what a sense of revolt there is within us!

There go fifty years of a life of love and glory and all the deep thought of a youth spent in preparing it!

And even if it hadn't been him (that exquisite being), what unforeseen suffering this first gap in our ranks creates, and how much we now know what it is to lose a friend!

You know from the few lines read over and over, that even his corpse has been lost, buried under the remains of soldiers.[31] Would you, my dear friend, like at least to bury him in the folds of our finest thoughts? To dedicate to him, from both of us, certain pages which tell of what he has not been able to do?

I was thinking of that a moment ago. (We'll work out a way, if you're willing, of dividing between us this pious and brotherly duty.)[32] For Henri himself, I'm glad to think that many hearts are grief-stricken at this moment and will never forget. I doubt that there is anyone who did not love him. As for his poor father, it's worse than atrocious.

Farewell, my poor friend. Let's keep our tears and our rage, which can help us bear such a misfortune! Let's embrace one another. My love to Bour. Reassure me about the two of you although I'm certain you're safe. But I feel I'm about to hear from Paris of some foreseen bereavement.

As this is unsealed[33] I can't talk to you about events which appear more important; I confess that the grief which commands me to write this second letter fills me utterly. In reply to my first letter, talk to us about yourselves.

From the three of us.

---

30. The artist Henri Regnault had been killed on 19 January in the Franco-Prussian war.

31. The body was later discovered.

32. Mallarmé published an article in homage to Regnault on 23 January 1872. Cazalis brought out a book on the artist's life and work, also published in 1872.

33. To conform with military censorship.

1 March 1871

I've received your note and although I think your friendly influence can have no bearing on what may happen, I can't resist the desire to write something to you immediately. Over the entire project which currently surrounds me, there floats, reducing my happiness, a shadow so sadly loved (you know whose shadow it is, dear friend!), that I don't know how to say something essential without running the risk of making you smile.

The only English words I know are those used in the volume of Poe's poetry, and I certainly pronounce them well—so as not to spoil the verse.

With the help of the dictionary and guesswork, I can be a good translator, particularly of poets, which is rare. But I don't think that's enough to get me a place in the Hachette publishing house, except through an arrangement according to which I would deliver, at an indulgent price, let's say one volume per year. In a word, do you think that the enterprise I recently discussed with you would be enough for the goodwill Hachette is showing me? I want you to understand me. Having returned resolutely to work, I see the special difficulties I'm experiencing and can decide what regular tricks will overcome the obstacle I've suffered from in these last few years.

At times I'm afraid that a job in a commercial firm, which must employ only those whose presence is effective, and viable, would be less favorable even than the office I glimpsed (perhaps wrongly?) as a result of your last letter, less favorable I mean for definite projects which, after all, form what you expect of me.

That is probably why, omitting any appeal to a grief to which part of your letter alludes, but which is not appropriate in this note, your first letter was more in harmony with my secret sympathies.

Still, as there is not, after all, any excuse, at my age, for finding it hard to work, and as that doesn't concern either Marie or Geneviève or ... I accept gladly something which offers the only opportunity. So, since it's a question of English, I'll have to start by accepting the place at London, which will allow me to recover my English—and I'll be able to return to Paris this winter.

But who knows if a position as correspondent for two or three newspapers might not let me attain the same aim there, and in a way which would perhaps correspond more closely to the future?

I'm expecting the scrutineer.* Thanks for your recommendations. I'm supplying myself with noteworthy and decisive testimonies. Now, dear friend, your hand, so I don't have the impression that I'm talking to myself in all this, so easily do we blend together.

If you meet some of the people who were kind enough to think of someone unknown and far away, thank them for me on both scores now, until I can do so personally later on.

Regards to Mme Judith.

P.S. I posted a jumbled letter to you yesterday from Avignon. Will it still reach you at Trévise? It was announcing the fruit.

*I will moreover find out from him whether, by staying longer in the afternoons, I'll be able to keep my mornings. But on thinking about it I realize that it will only be when I return from London, where I shall have to stay in any case at the beginning, if I want to move in this direction.

64 HENRI CAZALIS

3 March 1871

I, too, have a world of things to say![34] *And I'll say them.* But not write them, no.

Firstly, and always, a sorrowful handshake. No, dear friend, don't abandon hope in yourself. There's only one way of avenging our brother, of making sure the crime is less irremediably committed. And isn't that by letting him live through our different natures? And we can do it! I assure you that for my part I'm already beginning to do it, with this thought, which is a tremendous help and which—it's very simple—does enliven. But the poor child also wants, in addition to our lives, some influence over our existence. It's exquisite of the poor young girl to have perceived the truth of that.[35] You know that I'm in complete ignorance, dear friend. How was he killed? I believe it was by a bullet, and at unexpected moments I have the feeling that I've received it right in my heart, and can't help bursting into tears.

The only consolation I have is that this horrible initial emotion will last and that the moment when I learned of our misfortune will continue unaltered throughout the years.

That's why we can almost talk about us. You'll tell me of your great plans, *which will see the light of day.* As for me, I'm here. A final winter of anxiety spent struggling with the true and good misfortune which finally, by seizing me by the scruff of the neck (you can see that there was still a bit of neurosis mixed up in it), and dragging me through everything alien to my vocation, forced me to exhaust, all at once, the evils and disappointments of the external world.

Once again I've become a writer, pure and simple. My work is no

34. About Regnault's death.
35. Mlle Geneviève Bréton, Regnault's fiancée.

99

longer a myth. (A volume of tales, meditated. A volume of verse, half-seen and hummed. A volume of criticism, or of what in the past was called the Universe, considered from a strictly *literary* point of view.)

In a word, enough to fill my mornings for the next twenty years. I don't know whether it's the springtime that allows me to believe that if I'm careful with my health I'll have another twenty years. This may not bring in a penny, and may only be the equivalent of my deep-rooted internal glory. That's payment enough. As for living by my pen, this is my dream. An article a week (forgive me, dear friend) reducing to a hundred lines or so the pictures and text of the *Illustrated London News* which Villiers is trying to get for me, I imagine for *L'Illustration*. That could come to 1,000 francs a month. But above all, this is the lovely task I plan for the afternoons and which seems destined for me since, through a miracle, it hasn't been attempted before, and it's even a little monument which might tempt an editor (Lemerre, perhaps?), a translation, at the rate of a volume per year, of the great English poets of the nineteenth century. . . .

I'm beginning with the last of them, but one we all miss, Poe alas!, of whom we have only fragments. Indeed I've abandoned that just now to write to you. This may well provide a second 1,000 franc note.

What would be admirable would be if I could do this in a library. (You tell me that Lefébure would perhaps find a place of that kind.) I'll be more precise: would it be impossible for me to find a post in one of the Paris libraries, and wouldn't my knowledge of English make it easier to find such a post, perhaps by allowing me to take on the book section in that language . . . or anything else, in one of those establishments which, because they wouldn't demand a slave-like as-siduity would perhaps leave my mornings free for the intimate work to which I'm devoting myself? You can see that I'd have the added advantage of working on my translations there. In that way, I'd be able to make a living.

If necessary I could add to my salary the fees of ten young English students, who would come to me twice a week for ten months at a sum of 20 francs (to have lessons in French literature) and would thus bring in 2,000 francs. A few recommendations which I could perhaps obtain at the British embassy would be all you'd need to attract them. This has been my system since I left the horrible Lycée, at Avignon, before the war.

I think that all this, when understood, won't appear a pipe-dream. Moreover I'm stressing the figures to make it quite clear.

But you'll forgive me!

In addition there will be (I mustn't count on this) a theatrical dimension. I've gathered together a certain number of scenic themes, to give at the rate of one a year. I'm writing a play at the moment, and think it's good. There are three scenes, in gesticulating prose: but it's very tough. If things don't let me down, I may perhaps bring it to you in a few weeks time! Can it be possible? But if I start on that, I'll begin my letter all over again. I should begin again, for it bears the marks of the great weariness I've felt all day as a result of that dramatic work, which is new and extraordinary. I live so little! And those "chaps"! No, I'm doing it to test my willpower. Farewell, all this is for Lefébure, of course.

I'll say: "Until we meet again" instead of "Farewell."

I wouldn't have dared write to Miss Holmès.[36] But you'll thank her for having thought of me, won't you? As for Mlle Bréton, I want to see her and talk to her. For the moment I'll be silent. Tell her this.

65   HENRI CAZALIS

Friday 24 March 1871

Two words, if I dare believe I can raise again the matter we were thinking about—among so many other things. . . .

My God! how these politics, which (with the exception of the war) we were able to welcome for a moment, have begun to seem encroaching and unbearable!

Moreover, even supposing that, through hatred of the intruder, we return to our own dreams, aren't all our dreams linked to Jules Simon's stay, which has been extended and may be on the point of coming to an end, in the horrors of the moment?[37]

That's why, when I received a note from Sens, in which my mother speaks of the possible protection of a M. Richard (Jules Richard, I suppose who—wasn't he precisely Minister for the Fine Arts?), I was very pleased, should our friendly negotiations be interrupted, to suggest to you this means of perhaps reestablishing them, along different lines.

What are you doing? Do you keep retching, destroying the tranquil decorum of work?

On all my pieces of furniture and according to the various perspectives offered by an old daily constitutional, I'm taking up again those impressions capable of lasting, like a man who is thinking of leaving.

36. Augusta Holmès had supported Mallarmé's attempts to get a post in Paris.
37. Jules Simon was Minister of Public Education. Cazalis was attempting to obtain through him a librarian's post for Lefébure.

Then, I interrupt my drama to see once more in its far-off vistas the ensemble of works I've patiently combined over these four years, in order to go to you and carry all this out, for the rest of my life. This process, new in literature, seduces me on its own; but certain glimpses of the projected task still fill me with happiness, if I chance to see them again and fix them.

This spring seems to wish me well. Nevertheless, I ask it not to cure me entirely, because that would make it more difficult for me to preserve the morbid tang needed to provoke an explosion of empty riches.

Farewell, friend. Marie, do you know, was very vexed with several of the remarks made in your letter about her position which is, moreover, one of utter suffering. Geneviève is a very good little girl. But what's become of Lefébure? Your hand.

66   HENRI CAZALIS

9 May 1871

I'd like to write to you this evening and I'm dropping with weariness. These last days in Avignon (thanks to which I won't have to leave this site and its four years without having distributed the substance of their ill-starred dream according to an unforgettable plan which I can take far away with me) are a little hard, still terrified by the various trials of a move which is fixed for the end of the month. But the result will be that we'll see each other again. That's all that matters.

I feel that things which I've seized and lost many a time, would escape me permanently if I lived a solitary existence. I don't need a crowd, but my friends—you. I'd reached that stage this morning, and was hesitating over installing myself before too much white paper, when your letter came. You can guess how grateful I was. I've reread you and found myself again. Tonight I'm drowsing through my answer to you so that the night won't undo me too greatly.

Poor friend, you're always thinking of me! For my part, I've spent many hours recalling a line in your letter, the next to last letter, trying to discover the tone in which you told me about a marriage floating before your vision in the realm of the possible.

Yes and no, always: therein (reasoning as we do) lies our misfortune. A wife can give everything, loving looks and rest, removed from the necessities of life. But children, who when I last saw you, had become precisely your charming and sole ambition: there is in them a world of suffering which possesses us in the hours we spend with our family: because we are the fathers only of our imaginative creations. We feel our nullity (even if only because of the fatigue of our day-to-day work!) before our terrible duties, a nullity which appears as such, harsh, because, since our organization hoards all that is best in us for its jealous instinct of glorious production, there is the risk that the poor children will inherit only emptiness—and that's distressing for anyone who feels that what they deserved was life, true life.

I'm telling you this in a grave and deep voice. Don't listen too closely, if you don't want to. You know that in the past you were older than I and I scarcely listened to you, following my fate.[38] Now it's my turn to play that role: but be free.

As for the stupid belief that a family prevents one from working, it's quite the opposite. On the contrary, it's only in the family that you find the monastery, with monastic hours, but a worldly freedom. Even taking into account the difficult necessities. For my part, if I weren't still slightly ill (only a little), I'd be in perfect heart.

Moreover, all I ask is a few months. I haven't lost hope of presenting in early October a little play which would adapt itself to the most varied curiosities of the crowd. Who knows that that may not give me the wherewithal to spend my winter by your side? If it doesn't I'll write a second one straight away. For you do understand why all I'm seeking is a corner in a library, don't you? The most lowly literary profession, which would at least let me keep my hand in, would remove me less than an office job from the aim I never lose sight of. There wouldn't be, in any positive terms, any waste of time. Given my task, I really cannot lose a moment. The shrewd thing would be to seize this October: my play is not completely ready and either it or my faculties would suffer from a premature elaboration. This is what I think I'll do: in June I'll be in Sens, and for the beginning of July, too, when the baby is born. Then I'll beg Mendès to get me a post or two as a correspondent, so that I can visit Wyse in England—he's invited me. Then in September I'll return to Sens and complete the play.

You see, my dear friend, that you've *absolutely no reason to torment yourself about me.* I know what I'll be doing for the next five months. Perhaps it will even be advantageous not to rush things. Don't you agree? But I'll see you as soon as you arrive in Paris, if Paris still exists. What a lot of worries, about everyone. You don't know anything. I

38. An allusion to Mallarmé's marriage, which Cazalis had opposed.

have no news. Did you, from Versailles, learn of the death of our dear and revered Emile Deschamps? Lefébure is no longer at Versailles. I haven't heard from him.

I have to thank you, not for writing to me, my old faithful friend, but for being out of reach of the scourge, so that we can breathe after we've mentioned your name.[39]

39. On 25 October Mallarmé was appointed to a post in the lycée Fontanes in Paris. The family moved to 29 rue de Moscou at the end of November.

5 The Return to the Center

🐝 *In May 1871 Mallarmé left Avignon for Sens. After the birth of his son Anatole on 16 July he spent three weeks in England in August, then began teaching at the lycée Fontanes in Paris. The end of the year saw the publication of his "Scène d'Hérodiade" in* Le Parnasse contemporain, *and the breakup of his friendship with Lefébure.*

67   FRÉDÉRIC MISTRAL

1 November 1873

You love things which have a splendid appearance: herewith one such.[1] Open and read the papers accompanying this letter: two copies, one for you, by which I mean Provence since the capitals of the French sections are Paris and Avignon; the other for Zorrilla,[2] whom you know, this page being for Spain. If a subbranch is needed in Catalonia send this sheet to the relevant person, together with a third program that we're keeping ready for you.

Mendès and I, who have thought out the idea described at the beginning of the statutes, are dealing with the general organizational matters, but that's where our involvement ends. Hugo and the masters of all the various countries, those are the people who appear as soon as we withdraw. England fully concurs with our ideas, as does Italy.

My dear friend, what's involved is quite simply a form of free-masonry or guild. A certain number of us love something which is scorned: we ought to know how many we are, that's all, and we should know one another so that we can read each other, and visit each other when we travel. All this, regardless of the thousands of different points of view we may have, and moreover there would not be any differences once we'd studied each other and chatted together.

There it is—you must throw yourself into it wholeheartedly, in the way you know how to undertake a task. Call the Félibriges together and write to those beyond the mountains. Farewell, I won't tell you anything of us, for we're well and I shall ask almost nothing about you since Wyse, who has no doubt described our home to you, will in

1. Included with this letter was a prospectus for a projected international society of poets. Mistral showed little interest in the project.

2. Zorrilla y Moral (1817–1893), the most famous of Spain's romantic poets.

turn tell me about Maillane and Bartelasse.[3] Shake my old friend's hand for me, and tell him I'm looking forward to his return. (There is a copy of the Memorial to Gautier for him, at Lemerre's offices. Do you have yours? This book, which should have been made more international, contains our project in embryonic form.)

It would be a wonderful thing if all the *Parnasse* shook hands with all the *Armana*.[4] All the *Parnasse* and all the *Armana*? No, only those poets gifted with a certain mastery, those who offer something unusual and who will one day be on people's lips. There is, I think, a choice to be made, however small a task it may be, but one shouldn't be excessively severe.

Scrutinize the Statutes so that there is an authentic unity in each section: but yet, act according to local demands. I have moreover annotated them for you.

I'm glad, dear Frédéric, that this task has fallen to my lot so it gives me the opportunity to write to you. Underlying the business letter and between the lines, you can see some very good old memories that nothing can destroy. Do you sometimes think of me? Regards to all my friends and to Mlle Holmès. Those around me, my wife and children, greet you.

68   CATULLE MENDÈS

Monday [18 May 1874]

You really are extraordinary. An important decision changes your life[5] and you let me hear of it from various sources, through strangers: and as a result I am deprived of the right I have, as an old friend, to speak to them to some extent in your name. Fortunately I consider that to be a natural function: and I'm even being the one to break the silence between us.

The whole sum of sorrow that can at first, in the present case, invade someone who loves you but who doesn't see too clearly, that sorrow you for your part have drained to the dregs: it would be absurd to express it to you. I imagine the condolences I include in my handshake must be completely out of date, referring to a time far in the past. I will, on the contrary, say that you're behaving wisely, courageously, with your head held high; given the thousand wrongs that are credited to you, probably, by strangers, as a result of the discretion

3. Maillane was Mistral's home, Bartelasse, Aubanel's.
4. This was the main organ of the Félibrige.
5. Probably a reference to the breakup with his first wife, Judith Gautier. Mendès had for some four years been the lover of Augusta Holmès.

you show in your relations with them, I hardly need to add that you have my complete sympathy. You were counting on it, weren't you? And I'm sure it's not a matter of indifference for you. I see you as one of the most loyal and just of men, someone gifted with immense goodness.

Your only fault is to be at times a little aloof, and strangely enough this produces in me, despite my inner sense of revolt against you, a similar state: therein lies the secret of the hours when we pass each other by without seeing each other. This time there's no cause to speak in such a way, for ever since last Tuesday I've sought you out in my rare free moments, for I long to be alone with you for just a minute so I can listen to you. Yesterday evening, I decided I'd be the first to speak and wanted to see Mlle Holmès. But the annals will relate that you and I will always write to each other and that the best part of our friendship, at least the best part of what I feel for you, will be what I experience when we're apart. I think of how I was closer to you when I lived in another clime, I who came to Paris to be able to be with you. Why should this be? You know that, with Villiers, you're the only man I love in all seriousness, and through an old habit which must not be allowed to pass away, I'll come and see you tomorrow evening, if you still welcome guests at your place: probably after dinner.

🔖 *In August 1874 Mallarmé stayed for the first time in Valvins, near Fontainebleau. This quiet, riverside village greatly appealed to him and he spent many subsequent holidays there. March 1875 saw the family move to 87 rue de Rome, where Mallarmé began to gather around him friends from the world of art and literature. These years are also important for his friendships with Manet and Zola.*

69   Léon Cladel

Friday, 2[4] June [1875]

A serious question: is it you who controls the *Iron Mask*?[6] We'd like to have, in that section of the *Figaro,* a puff, as soon as possible, for *The Raven*. Something presenting it as the height of fashion, very Parisian etc. Such an item, expressed in high society terms, could nevertheless find a few words of praise for the translation and lots for

---

6. *Figaro*'s gossip column.

the drawings[7] (this is important because of the business with Lemerre)[8] and would be of greater value than an art or bibliography article, as far as sales are concerned. That's why we—Lesclide, Manet, and I—thought of it and of you. Write to me as soon as you've tipped off whoever does it, so that we can send a copy which won't go astray.

All yours. Our two hands, Mme Mallarmé's and my own, in yours and Mme Cladel's. Let's hope we can soon spend an evening together in the Monceau park, or a late afternoon. The children can all play in the shade.

70   CATULLE MENDÈS

28 July 1875

I'd have liked to reply to you before the hour when the post is collected, but I had to go to Lemerre's to find out if everything was fixed.[9] This well-meaning chap is so talkative that he kept me for four hours in the Choiseul passage. He brought matters to an honorable and even friendly conclusion. It's true that I haven't yet heard Leconte de Lisle on the subject, but he's not going to deny that he's received the money he was asking and that these lines belong to the *Parnasse*. Lemerre's first outburst of rage, which was violent and simply horrible, fell on me; and truly I was arming absent revolvers in my coat pockets. I thinking I've done all the calming down and reconciling needed for the next few years: that's the result of our efforts and we can only congratulate ourselves warmly on them since the Master's poems are to be published, that's what matters, and that was our only wish! Send off your poem without a moment's delay.

Underlying the misunderstanding were five or six years of daily quarrels and France's[10] subtle clumsiness, to put it no higher than that.

My faithful Dierx will write you better than I can, for I'm crushed by the blackest of tasks and my very pen fills me with abhorrence, even when it's a question of chattering with you.

Another point, my poems have been rejected by the Parnasse committee; but if you speak of it to Lemerre, do so only with a smile and

7. The reference is to Mallarmé's translation of Poe's poem with six illustrations by Manet.

8. Mallarmé had offered the publication to Lemerre, who had refused.

9. Mallarmé had been trying to discover whether the poems of Leconte de Lisle would appear in the *Troisième Parnasse contemporain* despite the difference of opinion which had arisen between the poet and the publisher.

10. The reference is to Anatole France, one of the three judges for *Le Parnasse*.

as a ridiculous possibility, for that's how I myself greeted the announcement of this fact.[11] If I'd taken things on a different tone and it turned out to be true, I'd believe myself obliged to go and slap the three judges in the face, wherever they happened to be; and kick them somewhere. And I'm really tired, oh!, too weary to get the slightest thing underway.

Love to Augusta, and kisses to the children: come back before August 15 so I can shake you by the hand. For if I'm to be in a fit state to start another year in Paris I must disappear for six weeks into a garden somewhere or other, even if I had to get a job as undergardener and water the flowers.

71   ALGERNON SWINBURNE

28 December 1875

On behalf of several friends as well as on my own behalf, I have a very great favor to ask of you. We, contemporary poets and men of letters, belonging to a group which admires you as much as we admire our own masters, are founding a review, *La République des lettres*. The chief editor is M. Catulle Mendès. The bonds of friendship or enthusiasm that exist today between the poets of England and Paris, are such that we immediately wanted to request from over here a benevolent contribution from over there: and before any other we of course dreamed of possessing your name: what am I saying? We seized on it, to begin with, as you may have seen in one of the *Literary Gossips* in the *Athenaeum* before last (in which M. O'Shaughnessy was kind enough to place a little note of mine which he himself had translated.)

The first number of *La République des lettres,* which you'll receive in a few days time, has gone so far as to help itself to one of your most sublime poems, in the translation created by Mlle Augusta Holmès, the poet and musician. As you are now a collaborator in spite of yourself, there's nothing more to do (if we want to be even bolder than we have been) than to beg you to become a collaborator of your own free will and even to do so in French; and send us perhaps late, one day, when the mood takes you, a page or some stanzas.

Forgive us, dear Master, for what was initially a desire to pay you complete homage. The presence of M. O'Shaughnessy, our guest for a few hours, suggested to my friend M. Mendès that he should entrust to him the difficult task of making you welcome us, given our many

11. This information was accurate: Mallarmé's "L'Après-midi d'un faune" had been rejected.

sins and our great ambition. But I remembered your too charming letter[12] and asked to be allowed to present our request myself.

Would you allow me (and this is my conclusion) to send you this time in my own name, two small works, verse and prose,[13] which I'll shortly be publishing: they are very insignificant offerings.

My friend Manet asks me to say in reply to your memories of last summer that his studio would be proud of a second visit, if you return to Paris one day.

72   ALGERNON SWINBURNE

27 January 1876

Forgive me for not having replied sooner; and many thanks for your fine, good letter,[14] for the lines of verse no less than for *Erectheus* and also for something that I'll leave until last. All the claims you list, in so gravely an interesting way, to sympathy and welcome in France as one of those to whom we love giving the title Master, all of those claims have already been recognized; and it gives us fresh satisfaction to be able to link them to two historical facts; but at the time when we were ignorant of those facts, knowing only your genius, which was related in what then seemed a mysterious way to our dearest and most admired poets, nothing would have prevented us from proclaiming aloud that you had in your soul a vast corner which was French, as much as anyone used to dreaming here over our countryside and our books. The surprise we had all already felt at your superb collaboration in our language to the *Monument to Théophile Gautier* arose again in the last few days on reading your cordial contribution—goodness me! to write a poem in a foreign language (no, not foreign but truly your own now), you had chosen the rhythm that poets attempt only in trembling wherever they may be, and by thunder! you produce at once the best Sextine, for that's the form we call by that name, or as near as makes no difference, a form that exists in the language of Hugo and Banville,[15] who themselves, amid so many variations of rhythm, have never attempted that particular form! You can imagine the success it has enjoyed. Sincere, absolute, fervent, such is our

---

12. Swinburne had written on 7 July 1875 to thank Mallarmé for the copy of *Le Corbeau.*

13. *Vathek* and "L'Après-midi d'un faune": see next letter.

14. Published in the *République des lettres* of 20 February 1876. The letter reveals that Swinburne's ancestors had twice found asylum in France.

15. Both poets were renowned for their experimentations in traditional verse forms.

amazement, and it's not because we feel that, despite the charming constraint imposed by the need to obey so many laws, your indomitable musical nature still surges forth; what amazes us is the fact that no expression (and I say this as an uncorruptible and fierce critic) is out of place, either from the point of view of sound or from that of sense. The only slight preference I might have would be to read in the second line:

Pour y cueillir rien qu'un souffle d'amour

instead of

Pour recueillir rien qu'un souffle d'amour,

because of the rather felicitous balance in the line of the two monosyllables *rien* and *y* and because that would reduce the number of times the letter *r* appeared supported by the mute vowel *e* after it's served as the final letter of *pour,* but you'll have noticed this detail yourself on the proofs sent to you as contributor. You may find that there is a blank in the sixth line of the fifth stanza (and on this subject we've kept the numbers between each stanza, in case you're eager for them to appear) replacing the only word that we weren't able to decipher, for *l'orme,* which is what it looks like, doesn't make sense: and before choosing between *arme* and *ombre,* which we thought a striking idea, we wanted to consult you, particularly because it may well not be either of these readings.[16]

The big word of thanks I wanted to say at the end of my letter is not yet for *Erectheus;* for truly, although it was an exquisite thought on your part to send it to me, the enthusiasm I felt after reading a few pages has taken over from the feeling of gratitude and it has ended by reigning exclusively and supremely over all my reminiscences of evocations of ancient art and it is without any doubt the most outstanding of them.

Creatures living in such a state, at once poetical and deliciously human, can exist nowhere else; and neither can that suave and powerful tragic view which disposes, merely on the basis of its beauty, of their presence or their death: with such ecstasy and serenity. When the first general study of your work is written here, that will be the time to recount this book at length and give to it the rank it deserves in modern poetry, but I humbly beg your forgiveness for having deflowered this future interest in the eyes of the French public through

16. Swinburne adopted Mallarmé's suggestion for line 2. The unreadable word was indeed *orme,* which he had written by mistake thinking it meant "trace" (c.f. Italian *orma*) when in fact it means "elm."

a short and banal paragraph that *La République des lettres,* too bulky in its second number, was forced to hold over until the third number. A good opportunity to rewrite it? No, because as your *Nocturne* is to appear in the same third number, it was better to keep the projected long general article for some time in the future. Leaving aside the fact that there are already under my name long fragments of a study I've written on *Vathek*,[17] the original French text of which I'm publishing simultaneously in the form of a volume. These details would serve no purpose if I didn't use them as an excuse to tell you that merely the preface to Beckford's book, as well as a very short little poem,[18] laid out too luxuriously by a printer as a specimen of what he can do, are what I'll be sending you in the near future, I believe, and about which you'll be kind enough to remember: very insignificant publications of my winter.

My supreme, profound, and ineradicable gratitude, dear Master, results from reading in an English newspaper which I've since lost, the noble letter which in my eyes consecrates, as much as a word of satisfaction pronounced by Poe himself, my version of *The Raven.* Moreover it offers to the celebrations held in America our expression of admiration (which but for you would have gone unnoticed) for the genius that they are glorifying. Thanks to your exquisite and benevolent initiative on behalf of foreigners (but that term must be banished from all conversations with you, even when it's used in reference to us), we have from a distance and unbeknown to ourselves taken part in the ceremony where you created two places for us, withdrawing in filial fashion before the great and dear Baudelaire first and foremost. It's a lasting emotion that I feel in this regard and I can assure you, dear Master, that it's one of the most profound I've experienced in my literary career. Manet, who hardly ever writes, given his function as painter, sends you a long and silent handshake!

I had so much to tell you! that this letter is growing long to the point of indiscretion; and it hasn't even told you of Mendès' happiness on reading the friendly passage in your page of French prose which concerns him: yes, he is one of the first to have had the joy of writing your name in France, in a daily paper; what, alas!, has become of the collection of this paper, called *L'Avenir national?* My dear friend will tell you that he doesn't find the article worthy of being sent to you; but I remember on the contrary that it contained not what one says among and for friends (particularly now we are up-to-date with your work) but the impression which it is essential to give in a passage for

17. Beckford's novel, to which Mallarmé had written a preface.
18. The reference is to "L'Après-midi d'un faune."

rapid consumption and for an audience knowing nothing of you: and also something rather better than that. Count on me, therefore, to urge Mendès to do the research that he's promising himself he'll do.

73   EMILE ZOLA

18 March 1876

Forgive me for not having thanked you earlier: I did so when you told me you were sending your fine book. Once I got the book in my hands I read it at a sitting; then, having closed it, I opened it again to study it, over a period of several days. These two ways of appreciating a work, which are firstly the old way dating from the days when novels were written like plays, and secondly the modern way when the very conditions of our existence force us to take up a volume, set it aside etc., *Son Excellence Eugène Rougon* lends itself to either method: for a deep interest is admirably concealed behind the apparent randomness, full of folds and ruptures, that today's novelist must use to fill out his idea.

A book whose special aesthetics are in absolute harmony with whatever mode of reading its readers may adopt is a masterpiece; and that's why, although I prefer, perhaps wrongly and because I'm a poet, certain more tangibly magnificent aspects of *La Curée* and *La Faute de l'abbée Mouret,* I consider your latest creation as the most perfect expression of the point of view that you will always have the honor of having understood and revealed in the art of our times. Everything, from the very profound concept which you both reveal and hide so well of a great force split into two contradictory types, by which I mean at once enemies of each other and avid for each other, Rougon and Clorinde, each of whom completes the other; everything, from that to the style itself which is rapid and transparent, impersonal and light just like the glance of your modern reader, if he sees clearly, yes!, everything maintains an extraordinary harmony which ought to make the most doctrinaire critic swoon with joy, a critic delighted when all the laws of a literary *genre* are well observed, if there were at present a form of criticism which was at all lucid and which believed in anything other than fantasy.

In the splendid evolution that the novel, that product of our century, is experiencing, *His Excellency* ... marks yet another step and a formidable one at that: the point where that genre borders on history, becomes completely superimposed on history and keeps for itself all that is anecdotal, all that is momentary, all that stems from chance; whereas the future historian will have only to sum up a few ideological struggles etc., since the fatal chaps who considered themselves something better than bearers of principles will instantly fall victim to the novelist. What a sudden and unexpected acquisition for literature, which the English call "fiction"!

These, dashed off any old how and away from home, for I've been driven out for the moment by thousands of preoccupations, are some of the thoughts keenly awakened in me by your latest book. Forgive me for this rapid and incoherent scrawl, but I forget nothing and as soon as I have the pleasure of doing somewhere or other an article on "Recent Books," all this will take its place in a general study inspired by your work. One point I still have to clear up, and that we'll discuss when we have the pleasure of seeing each other again, is why you now give certain dialogues for instance (one in the avenue Marbeuf and others when our group meets quite often in various parts of Paris) an air of utter play-acting, as if you were acting out scenes and so forth: isn't that very literary and done deliberately? But I think you're obliged to do this because you so often use the opposite device on every page of your book.

Farewell. Until the first Thursday. I hope that then I'll be able to tell you what is happening at the *Athenaeum:* good gracious! how far the English novel still is, with its handful of habitual devices and its predictable adventures, from understanding what you and the contemporary French generation want!

᪇ *Mallarmé's interest in Poe brought him into contact with several Americans, notably Sara Rice and Helen Whitman, both of whom were eager to rehabilitate Poe's memory.*

74   MISS SARA SIGOURNEY RICE

4 April 1876

I apologize for not replying earlier but I was ill at the very moment your letter arrived. I am really deeply grateful and beg you to accept that gratitude, cordial and complete, in exchange for the photograph of Edgar Poe's monument and for your account of the festivities, for which all those who have been charmed by that man of genius owe you a debt of gratitude. Your work, one of those which most brings honor to a woman in this world, for since time immemorial women have had the fine role of burying the most noble of remains, long ago won you my sympathy and admiration; and that's not all: you want a fine book to glorify your favorite poet.[19] Piously I'll accomplish your wish for my own humble part, by sending you, by a date that you'll be kind enough to fix for me, a few lines written in your honor: by which I mean in commemoration of the great ceremony held last autumn. My friend and collaborator, Manet, who, using his pencil to better effect than by writing a couple of sentences, wishes to reply to your kind invitation, asks what drawing he can do to embellish your book; he'll send whatever you ask of him, in wood or copper, either an engraving or an etching (this latter process being, between the two of us, one of those in which he excells). Finally, but all this is subject to your approval, I'll ask you to leave room for one of those magnificent pages of prose that our great dead poet, my master Charles Baudelaire, wrote as a preface to his immortal translation of the *Tales*. You are certainly aware that he is the one who made Poe known and popular in France.

I'll end this long letter by thanking you again, a thousand times over, for offering Manet and myself such an opportunity to express once again our admiration for one of the most wonderful minds that have ever appeared on this earth.

75   MRS. SARAH HELEN WHITMAN[20]

13 December 1876

A thousand apologies for my silence; I have so little time to myself and I can sense that you must be one of those who always forgive, I can guess it. Your two letters, the admirable story of the poem "Ulalume" and the note where you expressed your fears that you might have put an incomplete address, reached me, both at the same time. It was like a double happiness, which is very rare. Then the new letter, announcing the welcome visit of your young friend, Mr. Brown, and containing the note which I have just handed on to Miss R. Peckham. The welcome I received from this lady and her sister was charming: thank you. But I thank you above all for giving me the opportunity to see a portrait of yourself at their place, based on a beautiful, indeed very beautiful, painting. My first thought was that I would like to be able to translate "To Helen" for the first time today; I feel I'd do it with greater understanding. Let me shake your hand!

19. Sara Rice was preparing a memorial volume for Edgar Allan Poe, and had asked Mallarmé to contribute.
20. Poet, engaged to Poe in 1846. Although she broke off the engagement, she defended him in her book *E. A. Poe and His Critics*.

Perhaps, since the harm has already been done, and since my translation dates from the time when I was translating the others, you'll already have received the review in which I published it. The "Dedication" and the "Preface" will be the last to appear; I'm happily awaiting the portrait of Poe cut out by your own pious hands; and the lines from a newspaper (was it you who wrote them?) struck me as perfect. Your exquisite silence, full of veiled expectation, regarding that ill-starred copy of *The Raven* is something I understood, but with sorrow. The fault is not mine, I beg you to believe me, if that fatal and fantastic bird wanders so long around your abode without rushing in by the casement window (open to doubts and mystery). The editor, a man in the process of performing evil deeds and whom I see little, swore black and blue that he had sent it off for the second time and yet I found the precious packet in a corner of his office, forgotten. I myself informed an agency which fetched it and sent it off and this time I hope that so many accidents and absurdities are at last over. If not I'll send you my own copy and would indeed end by taking it to you if necessary. No, but I'll entrust it to a friend whom you know, for it's largely in talking about you that I first met Louise Chandler Moulton, who lives in Paris and is returning to America at the end of the winter. Nevertheless, I hope that the black wanderer will reach you before that, perhaps even in time for New Year, in which case I'll ask it to convey all my respectful and deep good wishes. As you are such a noble and touching guardian of your memories and represent today, for all those who love him, one of the most magnificent creatures ever to have honored this earth, one of the monarchs of human thought and love, you must indeed live many more years before we see the two of you, yourself and him, in the ideal luster of a double immortality, avenging an unkind destiny.

Forgive me for these emotional lines; but however foreign I may be, Poe is so intimately linked to my mind that if ever I write anything of worth, I'll owe it him. My sole wish is that you should be there to know it. You can guess what a precious relic your precious volume would be for me: and that would make me impatient for the arrival of Mr. Brown, whom I'm still awaiting, both for his own sake and for yours.

Thank Mr. O'Connor for having been kind enough to mention me sympathetically in one of the letters he wrote you; or rather it's you I thank.

P.S. I've just received from Miss Rice a review telling me that the *Memorial* has appeared or is about to do so; and I see with considerable pleasure that the admirable *Memoir* written by our friend Ingram has at last replaced there, as it does in the best editions, the abominable notices which have been current throughout the world for more than twenty years. I cannot fail to think of you, as I take pleasure in this belated act of justice; farewell again and my best wishes for 1877 which is just beginning.

76   MISS SARA SIGOURNEY RICE

12 January 1877

A thousand apologies for replying so late to your letter and the parcel you were kind enough to send. Lately I've done so much work on my own behalf that I threw my pen away during my rare hours of rest, unable to force myself to take it up again to write a letter or even a note. . . .

The *Memorial to Poe* is very good, typographically; and I'd like the cover were it not for the gilded *portrait* and *cottage,* which do not seem to me appropriate to decorative art. Manet, I believe, if he had seen the book, would concur with this advice, which you'd be well advised to take.

Our understanding of such publications is entirely different in France; and in the *Memorial* to Gautier, which was published a few years ago after the death of that great poet, there is nothing but Poems, which I believe to be the perfect offering in such a case. I see by the small number of poems in your book that things are different in America, and I regret the fact from this one point of view, that had I been informed I would have associated myself by a mere letter which would have numbered me among those who participated from afar in the pious ceremony of the monument or at the very least among everyone else. Miss French, who was gracious enough to come and see me recently, told me that the publication is selling well and I congratulate you on that fact—it's a just reward for the many labors you performed. The public likes to keep, in the form of an album, an account of a ceremony related in your newspapers a year ago and which readers have already had a thousand opportunities to mislay and lose. If by any chance there were a second edition I don't know if I'd dare ask you to insert the admirable pages written by Baudelaire, which would perhaps be a little out of keeping with the general tone of the book such as I perceive it today. But I'd be infinitely grateful to you if you would take care to correct a few errors in my sonnet, particularly one of them which makes it completely incomprehensible: it's the substitution of an "n" for a "u" in the word TRESSANT (weaving) instead of TRESSAUT (starting).[21] The bad habit we have in France of relying on the copy editors at the printers for the accents has made me omit a few on the copy I sent and I find them missing in the printed version too.

[...][22] These are mere trifles, infinitely less serious than the error of "Tressant," but in a new edition they could be avoided. If I were entirely free in a new edition I'd also ask you to *remove* the comma in the 9th line before the words: O GRIEF; and to replace in the 13th line the word FOREVER, which is already in the preceding line, with the words HERE BELOW, which are on the manuscript I've kept here. I blame the excessive haste with which I wrote to you, once the business with Manet and the etching was over, for both these errors which must be my own fault. (French is so difficult for foreigners to read that they should be given a perfectly accurate version.) Farewell, and a thousand thanks in advance for being kind enough to remember these details.

77   EMILE ZOLA

3 February 1877

I've just reread at a sitting *L'Assommoir*, which, for some time, I've missed each Sunday when I received my copy of *La République des lettres*.[23] Each section created a really profound impression; how much more profound is that of the complete work! Thanks twice over, since it was in a copy sent by you that I had the joy of rereading you.

It really is a great work and worthy of an epoch in which truth has become the people's version of beauty! Those who accuse you of not having written for the people are wrong in a sense, as are those who lament an old ideal; you've found an ideal which is modern, that's all there is to it. The somber ending of the book and your admirable linguistic experiment, thanks to which so many often inept modes of expression, forged by poor devils, assume the value of the finest literary formulations since they manage to make us cry or almost weep, we who are well-read! I find that utterly moving. Is this a natural tendency in me, I wonder, or an even more difficult triumph entirely due to you? I do not know. But the beginning of the novel remains the part I prefer. The prodigiously sincere simplicity of the descriptions of Coupeau working, or of his wife's laundry, hold me under a

21. The words in parentheses are Mallarmé's own translations: "Start" (in the sense of a leap of surprise) would be more accurate here.
22. There follows a brief list of typographical errors.
23. The serialisation of the novel had finished on 7 January.

spell which the final moments with all their sadness can't make me forget. They're something so completely new you've given literature, these highly tranquil pages which unfold just like the days of a life.

If, at the risk of boring you, I'd spoken to you for an hour or two about everything I admire in this fat volume, I'd let myself say afterwards that the marvellous battle in the laundry struck me as somewhat of a digression, or something out of character with Gervaise, and that Nana changes without visible transition from the depraved and stunted little girl to the beauty she becomes; but you'd find it so easy to answer me that I won't insist. A tiny point; in addition to simple printing errors, I picked up a slip of the eye or pen which will amuse you: it's on page 264, the second line: "Between Gouget who was completely black, the two women looked like speckled hens." Well, it's he who is between the two of them isn't it? Forgive me for this, because of my old mania as a bibliophile. It just proves you've been read with care.

I'm following in many newspapers, with the joy everyone feels when an old denial of justice is at last redressed, (for people will end by discussing anew *La Curée* and *La Faute de l'abbé Mouret* etc. in conjunction with your great success of today), the change of heart the critics are revealing in regard to your works. It had to come, you yourself had no doubts about it.

Farewell. Do you still see visitors (apart from First Nights) on Thursdays? I'd be very happy to come and shake your hand warmly, and all the more so since by chance my fingers are so cold in the place where I'm writing you this rapid note that I'm stopping, unreadable. I've found a copy of *The Raven* which I'll bring to you, from Manet whom you love and from myself, I who love you. Very solitary and working a great deal, I haven't seen you anywhere for a long time; I read you however in the Sunday edition of the *Bien public.* And we have on that other stamping ground, the boards of the theater, if not the same aim, at least the same aversions.

78   MRS SARAH HELEN WHITMAN

18 and 28 May 1877

How I love that wonderful, profound, and poetic image that you sent me the other day, a true portrait whose destiny it is to be placed at the beginning of an edition of your works. However eagerly I await the other which depicts you as you are today, and which is doubtless stamped with a different but very real charm, I have been able these last few days to satisfy myself with the first card, which I constantly look at. My thanks, which I'm expressing to you in one of those hours when, as it happens, I fall back on myself, tired and weary, one of my few hours of leisure, my thanks will remain for a few days at home, so that they can have some hope of bearing with them all my new gratitude on receiving your other photograph. So let's chat a little, even if, as usual, we can do so only briefly. First, for form's sake, I have to apologize to you, although I'm sure you won't accept my apology and will consider it empty. You may have seen, in a number of the *New York Tribune* which has come to my notice, a very unjust sentence regarding your fine imitation of my sonnet on Poe. It pained me to find that blemish in an article which is moreover well disposed toward the French poets and in particular to me. In this regard, let me add in answer to you that I hadn't especially thought of the poem "Annabel Lee" when I spoke of that final song that Death always takes upon itself to break off on the thirsty lips of the poets: what you gave there was an ingenious historical explanation.

You're kind enough to ask me what stage my dramatical work has reached: as far as I'm concerned it at least progresses: but the great attempt to create an entirely new theater to which I'm devoting myself will take me several years before any visible result is achieved. Since I'm too ambitious, it's not just one genre that I want to affect but all those which, in my view, impinge on the stage: magic, popular, and lyrical dramas. And it's only when I've completed this triple task that I'll present all three almost simultaneously, setting fire, like Nero, to three corners of Paris. There's a world of effort in this, both mental and material. And my poor translation of Poe is suffering as a result. It's not that it isn't done; it's here in a box beside me. But I don't have the strength at present to seek out a publisher, which it's always difficult to find, for a translation of foreign poetry, particularly when it's published with the pious sumptuousness I want. My only consolation lies in the unchanging youth of your soul which will let you wait for a favorable moment in the future. To tell the truth my life is at present full of difficulties. I must have absolute solitude to bring my vast theatrical work to a favorable conclusion and I'd go so far as to say that I need to make my name fall into oblivion here for a year or two, in order to reappear, with my three plays to hand, like an unknown or completely new man. As a result I'm losing of my own accord the influence I could exert over editors and reviews, from the day to day point of view.

To reconcile everything I'm looking for some anonymous journalistic work, far away, in America for instance, a Parisian chronicle, even in a publication of scant importance, but which would pay a little. It could be that you could give me some advice, given the experience you must have in such matters, that could put me on the right track.[24]

Forgive me for burdening you with this brief problem; perhaps I should say don't concern yourself with it for a moment if it seems to you indiscreet. But I'm chatting so much I'm no doubt wearying you; moreover my letter is finished, if I'm to judge by the paper, and I've finished it without replying to your question about Ingram, which in fact might be just as well given that this subject causes us both pain. Farewell, dear lady, until the arrival of your second photograph, which my letter will follow, accumulating in the meanwhile silent greetings through its envelope. . . .

Eight days later. Your second portrait has not yet reached me, and I fear you may be kept waiting too long for my thanks for the first photograph. This letter will therefore set off, bearing with it my new good wishes for your health as well as my admiration for the fine poem "Science" which I'd read and which I've now reread several times. You have the eye of an eagle as it soars high and free!

79   LOUISE CHANDLER MOULTON

8 January 1878

What a marvellous collection of lyrics!:[25] melancholy, happy, profoundly humane, by which I mean feminine. I read it, I can tell you, every evening, up to this very evening, so that I could be steeped in them as I write to you. All the delicacy of a soul, vibrating to everything but very isolated in its chaste perfection, this is what I find in these pages, which, though few, are enough to create an ensemble and reveal what could be a special state. Of course there is in this work the most captivating contrast between an unalterable artlessness, perpetually youthful, and (at times) a certain despair, like a gaze directed at a fixed point, a despair which is profound, knowledgeable and intentional. Whoever leafs through it, however inattentively, for the first or twelfth time, has the impression of being in the presence of a soul which is at once intelligible and impenetrable: both; for all your impressions are at first so simple, transparent as springs; but like springs their clarity disquiets and encourages meditation. I, who know you, often find that quality in you, personally, that double charm which is so unusual, so complex and pure. . . . I won't tell which are the poems I prefer; I'd do that in flicking through the book

24. Nothing seems to have come of this project.
25. *Poems,* published in 1876.

in your company, if I had the joy of being with you; a thousand old memories arose in me as I reread the poems I already knew. As for the others, the Sonnets at the end, shall I tell you, my dear friend, that they moved me deeply and there are several I know by heart. I long murmured one or other of the lines to extract from it and retain in my mind all the living essence, its bitterness and smoothness. I adore even the brevity, however fleeting, of those rapid poems. One looks, a fairy appears, smiles with a tear in her eye and disappears, before one has been able to realize how powerful is her brief incantation, of which nevertheless not a single word is lost. But to come back to the sonnets; later, some day somewhere, I'll translate them. What a pretty little book it is from the point of view of publication; everything in it is exquisite (you know that like the barbarians I attach a little value to the box that contains the perfume). I doubt that the English edition can be in better taste, physically speaking.

Farewell, be sure to tell me everything that's said about the Poems of Mrs Louise Chandler Moulton (dear name!) in England and beyond. These are truly seductive pages (even for the general public). I shake your hand wholeheartedly. Forgive me, dear Louise, for not having written to you as soon as I received your jewel of a book, but I felt an imperative need to read it slowly and at length. Even today, my reply to you is very poor. It reached me during a crisis of discouragement and boredom, from which I am recovering, clasping it in my hand as a good luck charm, to chase away the morbid thoughts. Thank you. A year ago, dear friend, just a year ago, you made me wait for a letter which did not come at all.

80   EMILE ZOLA

26 April 1878

A thousand thanks for having listed my name among your first readers: I was very ill when I received your volume[26] which I've just taken off to read in the country, hence the delay in shaking you by the hand.

I'll talk with you at length when I have the pleasure of seeing you on Thursday: but let me tell you today, quite simply and in few words, that I admire your latest book every bit as much as all the others and perhaps a little bit more. It seems to me that for the first time you've succeeded in creating, not something magnificent, for you were used to doing that, but precisely what you consider to be the exemplary

26. *Une Page d'amour* which was first published on 10 April 1878.

modern work of literature. An uninterrupted poem, for it is indeed a poem; and a novel for those who wish to see in it no more than an accurate painting of modern life. The homogeneity of the milieu and the atmosphere, like that of your skill in giving it the impression of exhaustive totality, is extraordinary. As you close the book you have the conviction that it was written at the speed at which you read it or rather that you've had a profound and limpid vision, and that's all. I don't believe an author has ever allowed the paper to talk to that extent or made the pages turn over by themselves, magically, all the way through the book. Then everything is said and the poem is contained, in its entirety, in the book as in the reader's mind, without *any gap whatsoever* through which the *reader* can enter the text and idly daydream[27] in distraction. As for the details, you pursue everything to the smallest corner, with a thousand eyes all having a single gaze: the tone and the attitude of a person or a group, you perceive and convey it all, with a simultaneity which constantly creates the impression of life itself.

I greatly admire your backgrounds, Paris and its sky, which alternate with the story itself: what is very beautiful about them, apart from the incomparable variety and lucidity of the description, is that you don't allow your reader to leave you for an instant, since you provide him with the horizons and the distant views. And at those moments when one normally looks up after an episode in the story, to think on one's own and rest, you appear with superb tyranny and present the backdrop for the reverie. That is a great success. Nevertheless (my one criticism, but made, it's true, from a point of view regarding composition which is quite different from your own, you who play with chance!) I can't find the thread, either moral or arising from any need in the subject itself, which links together these skies, Paris, etc. and the story itself. It may be no more than the fact that Hélène lives in the rue Vineuse which overlooks Paris, but she doesn't have either to sympathize or struggle with Paris later on.... I know very well that the simple presence of an individual near to the vast city, which has nothing in common with her, is in itself great poetry!

I'm chattering away, forgive me; but your book is so stimulating.... Those are really two of the wonderful days of the year, the days one spends in reading one of your books: and how happy one feels at the thought that this happiness will return twelve more times! All my good wishes, however unnecessary, for the success of your

27. A subtle criticism, for Mallarmé shared Flaubert's conviction that the highest function of art was to stimulate reverie.

123

book: when I think of your worries and how you describe as a work full of nuances this novel which is certainly delicate but so vast!

Passy, which I know a bit by heart (having been brought up there), is a marvel of perfection, including the cemetery.

Until Thursday then: please place my respects at Mme Zola's feet, with some of the congratulations I send you, my dear colleague.

In May 1878 Anatole Mallarmé fell seriously ill. The illness recurred in the following summer and Anatole died on 8 October 1879. It was almost a year before Mallarmé regained his physical and mental health after the shock of this bereavement.

81   Léon Cladel

15 May 1878

Now there's a book for you![28]

As a novel this work is placed in the very domain of the novel, beyond the reach of any social power. The man who couldn't exact justice from the law is taking his own revenge, setting the law aside. It's a very high and very pure concept: with which certain facts in your story are perhaps not in complete accord. We'll discuss this next time we have a chat. To have won his suit completely in the eyes of conscience itself, it may well be that Ambrose would merely have needed to let Anzelayr be bitten by a dog already stricken by rabies, and to have done so in a moment of distraction as short-lived as a bolt of lightning. And he could say in his heart of hearts and to the reader that he had probably suffered the tragic and just will of the God he invokes.

That's how a moralist would speak; but what admirable pages the reader would lose: all that new hypocritical friendship, full of hatred, which you paint in such a sinister, extraordinary, and beautiful way! Dear friend, as far as the style is concerned, it makes of those hundred-odd pages a monument which is unique in our tongue. So many new aspects of the language, thrown into miraculous relief, and done so for the first and last time: everywhere one finds that dual charm of something which is unusual or exact or implied by the very nature of the French mind. At every moment a new note is drawn from an instrument which seemed to have given almost all possible notes already. Ah! there is in your book a magnificent instinct, together with a terrible labor: and how few are the things which jar, in relation to

28. *L'Homme de la Croix-aux-bœufs*, published in 1878.

such an ensemble! I even consider necessary to the total effect the few exaggerations, which give the man in the street the key to your art. It's a fine book, a fine book: that's all there is to say, and then one thinks again of each of the pages one has read, for several of them are unforgettable.

Farewell, dear friend; a warm shake of the hand (and my "paw" to Madame Cladel). *Le Bouscassié, La Fête votive,* the peasant tales in *Va-nu-pieds,*[29] your work has such an exceptional and such a powerful savor and is so well concluded, for today, by *L'Homme de la Croix aux boeufs* [*The Man of the Oxen Cross*] (I preferred the title *Celui de la Croix aux boeufs* [*He of the Oxen Cross*]: what a splendid and full youth you have behind you . . .

82 LÉON HENNIQUE

31 October 1878

I'm taking a long time to thank you for sending your fine novel,[30] which I found awaiting me on my return from the country. But I've read you twice. Not that I had any doubts about all the talent which leaps out from your pages! I knew you were a man capable of a great deal. It was only the certainty of your manner which astonished me a little. Leaving aside the conception, it's the sort of novel one expects from a writer who has written twelve; and the mastery of this début overwhelms me. From the walk at Moulineaux, where the true air, the breatheable air, circulates in such a palpable way, right to all the other sections of the book, there is a sense of ease and a studied elegance, both intensity and lightness of touch, in a word everything that makes an artist exceptional. As for certain strokes of inspiration (for instance Octave's start when he recognises himself vaguely in "Amanda's Lover" sung from the window of the room where his fiancée lies), they really are outstanding. The only thing that makes me hesitate concerns Geoffrin, who is composed of admirable details but who doesn't convince me very much: we'll talk of this.

Michelle, in whom I don't see a *modern hero* because she acts unconsciously and entirely passively (and then I think heroism consists rather in slapping evil in the face and sending an evil father to an avenging scaffold!) is nonetheless admirable. All the other characters step out of the book, once you've closed it, and walk about, once more part of the real world, they are (sometimes) so ordinary and true. Apart from the tricolor wooden leg, which is not absolutely charac-

29. Works by Cladel: the first was published in 1869, the second in 1872, and the third in 1876.

30. *Les Héros modernes. La Dévouée* was published on 2 November 1878.

teristic of the modern poet, and your letter from Father Hugo, which fills me with distress, there's not a line to erase. Your work holds together with its perfection of external vision and its undeniable life.

I'm writing to you on the point of setting out for the country, and I've no fire and cold fingers. Laziness slows me down and the clock hurries me up, there were a thousand better things to tell you even in a hasty note. But everything you've sketched there is so clear and remains so indelibly in the memory that I've no fear that I'll have forgotten anything when we meet this winter at Zola's place.

83   LECONTE DE LISLE

17 May 1879

I'll have the pleasure of bringing you, one of these days, a little schoolbook on Mythology,[31] which is in the process of being printed. Before finishing it, I'd very much like to quote a hundred or two hundred lines of the *Poèmes barbares* and the *Poèmes antiques* to show today's youth what a magnificent and lively extension of the fable exists in our own age. My publisher has granted this request on condition that I give him a written note from you authorizing me to quote you. I'm requesting this note from you, with apologies for interrupting you, if nothing restrains you from providing it.

I know you no longer receive visitors on Saturdays: and since I have almost no time for work except Sunday, I've put off from one week to another the pleasure of paying you and Madame de Lisle a visit. Forgive me (you know nothing can make me forget you) if it seems I have forgotten you.

Farewell. My little boy has only just begun to recover from a long illness which has kept his mother by his bedside. She sends her regards to your wife. It's some days now since a friend returning from London told me Payne was very anxious to know what you thought of a poem dedicated to you, "Lautrec."[32] Could you read it between the English lines?

84   CHEVALIER DE CHATELAIN

Saturday evening, 12 July 1879

I have no wish to weary you with a letter, or even to distract the meditation into which you've been plunged by the imminent arrival

31. *Les Dieux antiques.*

32. *Lautrec* is the title of a collection of verse by the English poet and translator, John Payne.

of the hour you believe will be your last.[33] From afar we take your hand in filial fashion, and we will not let it go. Feel us with you, beside you, and with our eyes fixed upon you, and not without some degree of hope still. If you were to be defeated in that terrible struggle against so much suffering, you know full well, my dear old friend, that you would take with you our affection and our gratitude, and that your name will always live in our home, as it does today when you are already the absent but beloved friend. . . .

P.S. Send some postcards to us, even if they're written in English by your old maid, so that we can be kept informed about your condition almost daily. I admire your handwriting, which is so clear and so firm, and in which is truly reflected the great serenity of your spirit, even when you believe your end is nigh.

85   HENRI CAZALIS

9 August 1879

For a long time already I've been wanting to write to you; alas! from the moment when the illness of our poor little Anatole took on an alarming appearance. You looked after him so kindly when all the bad hours that we've just gone through were barely foreseeable that I was eager for you not to learn of our sorrows through some outside source. Here's what has happened. After the note I sent you in reply to your friendly card, recovery was very slow in coming. And, one fine morning, we found the poor little lad strangely swollen, still with his cough and his feelings of nausea. I feel that everything his illness can achieve, without being fatal, everything, including pericarditis, an inflammation of the interior of the heart itself, swelling of the entire body, rendered transparent through dropsy, all this the poor child has suffered. Today, after that severe crisis, which, as it made possible such great dangers, could equally have closed the access to his former illness, we're returning to phases we recognize, and have already passed through on several occasions. You can imagine how despondent we are. The only thing the doctor will tell us is that it's going to last a very long time; and we're forced to accept these words as if they contained some consolation, since one evening we thought we were going to lose the little pet. . . .

Farewell, dear friend, thanks for things you've done several times, as I've guessed, for your little invalid, who kisses you. Geneviève longs

33. Chatelain (1801–1881) was a poet, journalist, and translator. He had written to Mallarmé on 11 July 1879 to announce that he was dying. He was to die on 15 August 1881.

for the countryside, where we're going as soon as her brother can be carried. I'm in great despair and will write to you only when there is a significant improvement. Give our best wishes to Mme Cazalis and tell her we long to see her this winter. I won't tell you anything about Paris, for I'm in total ignorance, in this little sick room.

86.   ROBERT DE MONTESQUIOU

10 August 1879

I believe your delicious little creature,[34] a foretaste of greenery, has distracted the illness of our patient, to whom a trip to the country is going to be permitted. If the first indications of convalescence grow stronger today or tomorrow, or later, we may leave straightaway, if the weather is kind.

Did you hear, wherever you are (I don't know your whereabouts and am speaking to you in Paris), all the cries of joy from our patient, who except to close them on his happiness, couldn't take his eyes off the wonderful captive princess in her marvellous castle, who's called Semiramis[35] because of the gardens of precious stones she reflects? I like to believe that, by granting an old desire which has long seemed unlikely, you have played a part in aiding a state of health which seeks to return; even without evoking the secret influence, which the cage's inhabitant, like a magician with a precious stone, constantly points at the child.

How charming and friendly you've been recently, you who are so busy in so many ways; and it's more than a pleasure to tell you before anyone else that I think all our cares have dispersed into the future.

It's to Valvins, near Fontainebleau, that we'll soon be going; and before the end of the season, for September will be very beautiful, you must come with me, to spend a day deep in the forest. I wish you a wave *from seas far away,* as Poe says, if you're swimming at present.

87   HENRI CAZALIS

[18 August 1879]

We're no longer in Paris. What a stroke of bad luck! I wrote to you on the point of leaving for the countryside, for which our poor little love was longing; and in which we had placed a degree of hope. I wasn't expecting any other reply from you than a handshake; and lo

34. An exotic bird sent to Anatole.

35. The legendary Assyrian and Babylonian queen, to whom is attributed the founding of Babylon and its hanging gardens.

and behold you offer us a chance of hope, which slips from our fingers.[36]—The journey passed off well, for we took a thousand precautions and the weather was good. My invalid is so happy looking at that greenery, which reminds him of the past and of life, that he said of himself in the vehicle that brought us from Fontainebleau: "I don't have a tail of illness left." But that joy was short-lived, like the good weather. A continual nervous cough is shattering him, despite the potions. His color is bad and his stomach is still so swollen! The only advantage we've found is that the poor darling has taken a liking for the farm milk, to which the doctor adds a powder of nitrate. He's an attentive and intelligent doctor but he leaves me very little hope and almost the only thing he suggests may help is a miracle of nature.

Ah! dear friend, I didn't believe I still had so many tears in me! The poor, good little soul.

You were good and exquisite as you've been before in acting so quickly; and truly your letter had the tone of those written in bygone days (in the days of our youth), letters I read through again a few weeks back while I sat up with Anatole. I clasp your hand as an old friend.

Now, I'm worrying away, wondering what to do. Should I go and see Dr. Peter straight away and risk an immediate second journey which may be less fortunate than the other one! Or wait until he causes us a sudden alarm and time forces us to act? Ah! if at the end of a few weeks in the country, when he was a little better or when at least the worst of the illness was over, we could take him to Dr. Peter, to consult him on the long-term care he advises, I daren't say for a cure, but to give the invalid a little life again, even one of eternal convalescence, for we'd be satisfied with that these days!

Would you believe, dear friend, that his little heart beat so violently that it formed a kind of arch, an elevation, on the left-hand side!

Farewell Henri; give me your hands. Our best regards to your wife. Write us a brief letter; your voice is dear to us.

88   JOHN H. INGRAM

24 December 1879

I owe you thanks twice over, for your cordial and good letter, when I'd suffered a terrible blow, and for charmingly sending me the book which I'm still leafing through.

All these hours of festivities which bring the year to a close are

36. Cazalis had sent a letter of introduction to a doctor, in the hope that he might help Anatole. The little boy died on 8 October.

cruel for us, as you can imagine; the absence of the person who was the flame and joy of the house freezes our hearts, as would the cold which is flourishing in the streets outside. Nevertheless, remember that the sympathy you showed us in our mourning gives you forever a place in our home, henceforth solitary, whenever you spend a moment in Paris.

Thanks for your so intriguing *Philosophy of Handwriting*. You've taken from Poe something of his insight; some of your oracles are pronounced with divinatory prescience, which I consider extraordinary. The volume, on every page and under its cover, is exquisite. I tried to acclimatize it as a New Year's gift, in a bookshop or two, but they are willing to take it only as a deposit, which is always a poor arrangement. Another thing! Apart from one (Regnault's letter which I want to own because it has been quoted in part in some specialist works), do keep for your private collection all the autographs I sent you from French writers and artists. I take pleasure in having been able to contribute to the interest of your work, of which you've been generous enough to send me two copies.

Now, if I have a bone to pick with you, it's in regard to all your kind comments about my handwriting; it's too much, especially with a bad pen or in winter, like today. I'll accept only the sympathy which can be read between the lines. But you'd make people lose the courage to write to you.

Farewell, may we meet again soon; all my good wishes for Christmas.

❦ *The Tuesday evening gatherings were attracting more and more artists and writers, among them Gustave Kahn and Paul Verlaine.*

89   GUSTAVE KAHN

13 January 1881

I'm very late in writing to you; and I dare not invoke the excuse of the upheavals caused by these absurd New Year festivities, because then I'd see in their recent return a further motive for blame in that I didn't go and shake your hand in Algeria, where you're all alone.[37]

All you tell me about your very new life both distresses and satisfies me at the same time, because I was afraid when you left that it would be worse and because I consider it hard enough as it is, when one has

37. Kahn had joined the army.

some kind of intelligence, to lead an existence which is idle if not full of peril.

Basically, you know, I don't wish a campaign on you, not at all: you'll see enough of Algeria in the forced marches they'll condemn you to and as for the natives, your evening promenades in the Kasbah let me see them for myself....

Do you have a corner you can call your own? I think I'm right in imagining that you have the necessary pieces of silver, not to make a necklace, but to buy a little solitude and liberty, which are preferable to hashish and drugs, and which are difficult to find wherever you go.

In those conditions, apart from the disgust of living with others, you won't regret this year which will be unusual and, who knows?, perhaps even good for your health. A little nonviolent exercise after your first years spent purely developing your intelligence and living on your nerves will give you equilibrium for the rest of your existence. This is the dream I have, instead of telling you of Paris, where I live more than ever alone curled up in an enormous piece of work destined to last for years. There's nothing to report, except that the publication of *Bouvard et Pécuchet*,[38] Flaubert's posthumous novel, has just started. We'd talk about it well into the night, if you were here.... The style is astonishingly beautiful, but at times it's rendered null, because of the imposing bareness. The subject seems to me to imply an aberration, which is strange in so powerful a mind. Give me your hand.

90   PAUL VERLAINE

17 January 1881

Dare I write to you so late? A slight recurrence of a serious illness I suffered from in the year just ended, the absurd squall of lost hours driving away the first leaves of the entire approaching year, and goodness knows what else. Stupid and unavoidable obstacles have caused a vast delay in the simple handshake I wanted to give you after your book appeared. When we see each other, and we will (where are you? I'm always in existence Tuesday evenings), we'll talk about *Sagesse* at leisure.

Let me tell you, in one of the rare minutes when I take up my pen other than for tasks or for my work, how attentively I read you, how often I'm delighted and how I'm always full of sympathy.

This is a book which it's to your credit to have written, just as one

38. Flaubert's unfinished novel which first appeared in serial form.

loves white curtains in a dormitory in which circulate dreams which are new, simple, and perfect. But, setting aside your preface, which I find monstrously exquisite, none of us, and that includes you as much as anyone else, must forget the Verlaine of days gone by whom we hold dear; my good friend, the *Fêtes galantes* are an eternal jewel. . . . Do you know yourself well by heart? By this I mean, not the old books, but the future poet you continue to carry within you. Well, do you? I doubt it, I think you're whittling down quills pretty much at the whim of your imagination, which, after all, needs only quills to become an angel, under whatever skies it may be.

91   EDOUARD ROUVEYRE

22 March 1881

For several years now, having been put in contact with all those friends of Edgar Poe who are still alive, I've been collecting autographs, portraits, new biographical details, in a word a thousand momentos which may be of interest to the vast posthumous public aroused by the Poet's work. I took things up at the point where Baudelaire abandoned them, when he himself was interrupted by death, that is, at the translation of those extraordinary poems, that everyone has read from time to time in reviews or newspapers. But I've not yet published them as a whole. Add to them eight very fine compositions by my friend, the painter Manet, several of which are famous, as they appeared in my translation of Poe's "The Raven," published in a folio volume, and which I've had reduced for the volume I'm preparing, in the small octavo format. I believe we have here an unusual publication, which will have a real attraction both for those who are already enthusiastic about Poe and for the ordinary reader. Finally, this work will find—this is a question of importance and will need to be dealt with at the right time—*subscribers* in America and England, where it is frequently announced by the literary journals and even indicated in advance in all the specialist catalogues which refer to Poe. The time strikes me as especially propitious because the Charpentier press is preparing, in its usual format, without illustrations, etc. a standard volume by another translator, containing merely the famous Poems. Like mine, it's a translation in prose;[39] finally, one in verse, by Emile Blémont, the critic of *Le Rappel,* is to appear this

39. Albert Allenet's translations appeared in the review *La Jeune France,* but although the book was announced, it never appeared.

40. Blémont published various translations of Poe in periodicals, but these were never published in volume form.

summer.[40] All these translations are by no means bad for my book, which has been ready for several years and successively enriched by facsimile illustrations, which it is the only book to possess.

A few days ago I went to see my dear old comrade Cladel, and spoke to him about my intention of handing over my manuscript in the near future, when he put your name at the head of the list. I am therefore writing to you to ask if this matter would meet with your approval.

So many exquisite publications produced by you have come to my attention recently, all bearing the stamp of a very Parisian and modern taste, that, as a fanatical bibliophile (and I must add, *hard to please* but certain to reach an agreement with you to make something very special), it's a pleasure for me to submit to you at the very least the project outlined in this letter.

P.S. I can add that I own almost all the plates; and that if you were coming to Paris in the near future, as Cladel tells me, we could discuss face to face the organization of this volume which will have about 200 pages.[41]

92   EDOUARD MANET

[11 September 1882]

For days now I've been wanting to have news of you, but laziness and my old confidence in your good health have delayed my letter. The information I gathered from the rue de Saint-Pétersbourg two or three days after your departure, which seemed to me to take place in excellent conditions, immediately reassured me after the ridiculous announcement of a new recurrence of your illness which was made by several papers....[42] I didn't even want to write to you, since I'd no desire to give the impression that I'd believed it for a moment.

How have you been these last two months? A brief letter would give me pleasure. Is the fresh air better for you than last year? Are you working gently? I can see in advance several real garden corners on your easels, which I'll see the next time I visit your studio.

Here there's nothing new to announce: I'm filling a few sheets of paper in the mornings and glide about in my yacht or lie to in the bad weather we have in the afternoon.... In a word, it's a typical Valvins,

41. It was not for another 7 years that Mallarmé's translations were published, and not by Rouveyre but by Deman.

42. Manet had for some time been having problems with his leg. He was to die on 30 April 1883.

from which I'll return with sufficient strength and spiritual refreshment.

I reread, thinking of you who did likewise last year, Jean-Jacques'[43] confessions; yes, it's a superb book. . . .

There, dear friend, you have our usual bit of conversation, with the added charm that I'm not dashing off to college, but with the disadvantage that I can't see you.

93   JORIS-KARL HUYSMANS

[29 October 1882]

Even more than the good recollections you have of me (and believe me, that's not a matter I'm indifferent about) nothing could interest me as much as the magnificent project you discussed with me.[44] It would not have been right for our age to have come to an end without that novel being written: no other age could have understood it. And it's certainly you alone who ought to assume responsibility for writing it. Come and see me, if you have a moment, and I'll give you a copy of the *Faune* which is waiting for you (is it true that you don't have the copy on Japanese vellum?), and we'll have a chat. In my little corner I've taken on the inveterate habits of a hermit, so you'll forgive me for not coming to meet you.—Every Tuesday evening I sit by my fire waiting for any friend who can come along.

And the most remarkable thing is that the young man,[45] having stepped down from an ancestral portrait, and living in the sacrificed world of the dreams we love, really does exist in Paris.[46] I saw him again a moment ago when I read your letter, really I did. Once again, forgive me for making you travel such a distance, but I have so little time of my own, apart from the all-too-short instants I can give to work.

94   AUGUSTE VILLIERS DE L'ISLE-ADAM

20 March [1883]

For many days now I've been reading the *Tales* at every moment of the day: I've drunk the philter drop by drop. I can't refuse myself the joy of sending you, wherever you may be, a handshake,—from the depths of the years—which may perhaps reach you. This book, so

43. The reference is to Jean-Jacques Rousseau's *Confessions.*
44. The ideas forming the basis of Huysmans' best-known work, *A rebours.*
45. The central character of Huysmans' novel.
46. Mallarmé is thinking of Count Robert de Montesquiou.

poignant when one thinks that it represents a life sacrificed to all that is Noble, is truly worth (and this is no mean evaluation) so much sorrow, solitude, trials, and tribulations invented just for you. You have put into this book a quite extraordinary amount of beauty. Truly the language of a god is in every line! Several of the tales are unprecedented in their poetry, which no one else will attain: all of them are astonishing. And that *Annonciateur* which sends me into such dreams, wondering if it's the finest piece of literature I can remember. . . . It's impossible to say anything to you, you laugh.

Oh! dear Villiers, how I admire you! *Mister* Stéphane Mallarmé thanks you especially.[47]

🐿 *On 8 February Debussy set Mallarmé's poem "Apparition" to music. May saw the publication of Huysmans' novel* A rebours, *which contained an enthusiastic response to Mallarmé's poetry.*

95   JORIS-KARL HUYSMANS

18 May 1884

So here it is, this unique book! It had to be written—and you've written it so well!—and it couldn't have been written at any other literary moment than the present.

Truly, as I see it closed on my desk, while under my gaze all the treasure of its knowledge lies stored there, I cannot imagine it other than it is: you know that after one has been reading, one meditates and, almost always, a different book takes the place of the one just finished, even in the case of a book one admires. But that's not so with this book! There's nothing missing, perfumes, music, liquors and the old books as well as those which are almost in the future. And those flowers! It's an absolute vision of everything which can reveal to an individual set before a barbarous or modern pleasure the paradise of pure sensation. What is admirable in all this, and what gives your book its strength, (which will be decried as mad imagination etc.) is that there is not an atom of fantasy in it. In this refined tasting of all essences, you have succeeded in showing yourself to be more strictly documentary than anyone else, and in using only facts or reports which are real and which exist just as much as those which are coarse; they're just subtle, and demand the eye of a prince, that's all. But they are truths which, since enjoyment demands stripping one's pleasure

47. One of the tales is dedicated to "Mr Stéphane Mallarmé."

more and more, will certainly be attained by all who are intense and delicate. That is the very point that will be reached, one cannot go beyond it or reach it in any other way. And the point at which one stops is the point that you've singled out. Thus, your work assumes in our minds a terrifying aspect: for it establishes something which is definitive.

When I have the pleasure of seeing you, and that must happen—how we'll talk about everything, chapter by chapter, in this story where, apart from the trip to London, which bursts it asunder with the brutality of an immediate adventure, all of the past surfaces only when sublimated by the memory of the solitary hero: to conclude with the explosion of the departure from Fontenay, more tragic than a disappearance caused by Death, this return of Des Esseintes into the vast world where he alone has no place. There is nothing for him, nothing, beyond that carefully studied phase of his youth, worse than nothing: one stops and lets the book fall; one doesn't want to know, so greatly does one fear that one won't find sufficient pity for the misfortune of this poignant and artificial man.

Isn't that a sublime finale to a tale?

What I can't wait for, is, not to thank you (because it wasn't to give me pleasure that you spoke) but to say I'm simply and profoundly happy, that my name, as if at home and appositely, wanders through this fine book (the inner room of your mind), a guest adorned with such flattering gowns, spun with the sympathy of the most exquisite art! I believe in only two sensations of glory, each almost equally imaginary, the one formed by the wild joy of a race for whom, through the medium of art, one could fashion a new idol; the other that of reading an exceptionally admired book and seeing oneself appear from the depths of the pages, where one has wandered unawares and at the whim of the author. You have allowed me to know this joy to the point of ecstasy.

Farewell. I laugh as I think of those who believe they now know everything and who have never dreamt of what lies contained in that extraordinary manual, *A rebours*. What a surprise for the simple novelists and what big eyes they're going to open!

6   Love and Friendship

96   Léopold Dauphin

Saturday Morning [10 May 1884]

I'm leaving for the country, still sad at not having seen you the day before yesterday. As for telling you about the organ concert, it's not that I'm unwilling to do so, especially if we could be face to face, for you are always so ready to be charming. But, on my soul, all that I heard and noted cannot be said in any other form than a poem or a book: above all it's the rise of a star of shadow, contemplated at last with joy and terror by a mind that the absolute fills with despair; the shapeless pounding of waves of darkness which, by a miracle analyzed at length, happen to break and beat, here and there, on cliffs pure of all existence, rising up with all the height of their absence. You can see that even Guilmant[1] didn't expect this. I saw nothing that could go in the newspaper; all I did was listen to the organ, with or without the orchestra. I was filled with despair when the audience encored the solos, "Eternity," by Madame de Granval, who accompanied on the piano a gentleman (Quirot), who possesses a bass voice; and "Remember" by Massenét, exquisitely sung by Madame Brunet Lafleur, one of that trio. The real marvel was the largo for organ, harps, and orchestra by Handel, which was like closed mouths and tied tongues accompanying in an obstinate muteness the revealing complaint of a violin, and finally confessing all and saying more than the violin itself. You can laugh, but you see I listen like an incorrigible poet. The same instruments gave a delicious performance of a March based on two Church songs, by Guilmant, and were very successful. But you have the program, in which at a single glance you'll read more than I could tell you and from the proper point of view. There was an enormous crowd, and not just English people and organists as used to be the case: it's becoming absolutely the done thing, thanks, I believe, to the Colonne competition. Once or twice I even felt in this crowd a kind of special intuition of what the great festivals must be like; where the organ, formerly the god, today the voice of the people, will reign, in the future. But you and I won't see that happen.

1. A. Guilmant, composer of a Fantasy March for organ, harps and orchestra that was performed at this concert.

97   MAURICE BARRÈS

Now that's really interesting![2]

I've often thought that the only way to create a review was to do it on one's own; make it above all about doctrine, even more than filling it with your trunkloads of written work, even something as charming as your short story. This year, when we'll be following your progress, can count for you as a decisive campaign. By this I mean that I enjoyed your criticism above all, finding it penetrating and subtle. You're on stage all alone, it's you who must be seen and heard, without the veil of any fiction; but speak and mime about everything.

Moreover, I believe that at present it's impossible for two people to meet and have the same thoughts; and that there is no reason to collaborate on anything.

That doesn't mean one can't often sympathize with you from the auditorium. And that's what I for my part am doing as I shake you by the hand; and firstly for your bravura.

98   LÉO D'ORFER

27 June 1884

It's a real punch, momentarily blinding, that abrupt demand of yours: "Define Poetry." Bruised, I stutter:

Poetry is the expression, in human language restored to its essential rhythm, of the mysterious meaning of the aspects of existence: in this way it confers authenticity on our time on earth and constitutes the only spiritual task there is.

Farewell, but you owe me an apology.

99   PAUL VERLAINE

8 December 1884

Of course.[3] Basically the poet has no other choice; and his destiny becomes too ironic by far if he has to provide free copies to the hundred readers who would otherwise allow him—I won't say to live!—

---

2. Mallarmé had just received the first number of Barrès's review, *Les Taches d'encre.*

3. Verlaine had written to Mallarmé apologizing for not sending a free copy of his poems, *Jadis et naguère,* but explaining that the publisher opposed such a move on the grounds that even for a poet the cost was not too high. Verlaine asked Mallarmé to explain this to their mutual friends.

but to have bread or cigars. In future this will have to become standard practice between colleagues, and something that's tacitly understood.

The only thing I ever bear a grudge against you for is that when you're in Paris you always keep far away from the rue de Rome.

You are the freer of the two of us, even in ordinary times; as for me, my college is at present at Passy and I'm vomited out of the house and into this Gehenna from six in the morning to six at night. That's why you'll forgive me for not writing *immediately the letter I carry within me,* for I'll read you tomorrow or afterwards. (I put off for fortnights at a time the slightest scrap of an urgent letter!)

I no longer see anyone except, on Tuesday evenings, my young friends; and you know that your name is mentioned there with the same enthusiasm by them as it is by me!

Thanks in advance for the pleasant evening which will arise from the pages of *Jadis et naguère.* Farewell.

In 1885 Mallarmé began corresponding with the poetical theorist René Ghil, the symbolist painter Redon and with two symbolist poets, Henri de Régnier and Francis Vielé-Griffon.

100   ODILON REDON

2 February 1885

How you spoil me! and how you grant one of my requests even before I've voiced it, my longing to look at length on one of your works.[4] For two days now I've been leafing through this extraordinary series of six lithographs, without extracting the total impression of any of them, so extensive is your sincerity in the vision as well as your power in evoking that vision in others. A highly mysterious sympathy made you depict in that delicious mad hermit the poor little man who, in the depths of my soul, I'd like to be; and I'll hang this drawing on its own on a wall of my memory so that I can judge the others in a more disinterested way. The head of Dream, that marsh flower, illuminates, with a light known to herself alone and which cannot be pronounced, the whole tragic lantern of ordinary existence; and how you synthesize in plate IV the inner face of many of us, cruelly cut short before there is any withering and just on the point of satisfaction. The female study which you so justly call the goddess of the

4. Redon had just sent Mallarmé a copy of his *Hommage à Goya* (*Homage to Goya*), a series of six lithographs.

139

intelligible, comes to us, regretfully, from nightmare; but my entire admiration goes straight to the great, inconsolable Magician, the obstinate seeker after a mystery he knows does not exist, and which he'll pursue, eternally, for that very reason, with the bereavement of his lucid despair, for that mystery *would have been* Truth! I know of no drawing which communicates so much intellectual fear and terrible sympathy as this grandiose countenance. My other favorite is, in the same order of dreams of Solomon, that "strange magician" whose spirit is shattered by the marvel, in the deep sense of the word, that he has accomplished, and who suffers so much in the triumph of his sage result.

I also adore the caption of a word or two whose aptness shows how far you penetrate into the arcana of your subject.

No matter where I'd seen that work, M. Redon, I would have drawn from it one of the rarest pleasures of art; but since it was you yourself who sent it, you can imagine how much more precious it is to me. There is in this a coincidence so exquisite, that I cannot, however effusively I thank you, fail to see behind all the joy it's caused me, a great deal of the friendship of our dear Huysmans.

101   RENÉ GHIL

7 March 1885

Your book[5] is indeed interesting! The way it reminds me of epochs in myself, is nothing short of miraculous; and I also find in it certain current preoccupations which seem to me breathable only to subtle lungs, in our atmosphere. Few works of youth are created by a mind which has forged ahead as much as yours has. What I praise above all, and what will be done by someone—who? you perhaps—is that attempt to lay, from the outset of life, the first foundation for a work whose architecture is already known to you; and not to produce (however marvellous such productions might be) at random.

Moving from the preface, in which you show toward me a sympathy which is too fervent for the little I've done, but for which I nonetheless thank you, to your series of pieces (I'm talking as I would to a musician) there's reason to feel enormously interested in your effort at written orchestration. I'll criticize you for one thing only: it's that in this act of just restitution, which we must perform, in which everything is taken back from music, its rhythms which are merely those of reason, and its very coloring which is that of our passions evoked

5. The book in question is *La Légende d'âmes et de sangs.*

by reverie, you let the old dogma of poetry fade away somewhat. Oh! The more we extend the sum of our impressions and rarify them, the more may we also, on the other hand, through a vigourous intellectual synthesis, gather all that together in poetry which is clearly marked, strong, tangible, and unforgettable. Your phrases are those of a composer rather than writer: I can fully understand your exquisite desire, for I myself have shared it, but have abandoned it as you yourself may do of your own accord! I'm saying all this as a form of conversation, as I'd like, moreover, to talk face to face with you. I'm at home to several friends, including you, on Tuesday evenings; but I'd like to see you on your own once beforehand. Would you be free on Monday from 11 to noon; if so, with *La Légende d'âmes et de sangs* in our hands, we'll think aloud, I as an older comrade. But with all the sympathy I feel for one of those from whom our Art must expect a great deal. You'll see me full of certain truly remarkable beauties contained in this first collection of your poems.

102   MAURICE BARRÈS

10 September 1885

I feel for you a very special friendship, illuminated by your letter: what conversations I foresee for winter's evenings this year, if you're willing to spend some of them with me!

Ah! the sign *par excellence:*[6] but anyone who thinks he has understood it, must be that Magus called God, whose honor lies in not being himself but the very last last one still to be reabsorbed into pure Simplicity, in order to return to life: from which it follows that it's not even to the entire crowd of a whole day that one must deliver the meaning of that abstruse letter (a meaning which has, after all, been extracted from the fact of death and ignorance) but to Humanity. All is vain save for this ransoming through Art, and the artist remains a rogue. Art implies that, and implies, too, an eternal theater through which the generations pass.

And all this for having got involved with what does not concern us, since there is no one who can do it as of right. The wisest course would therefore be to sail down the river and escape with each stroke of the oar from the obsession of the forest tree bending down toward the water. And that's what I did, instead of replying, straightaway, to your cordial handshake. You'll forgive me. . . .

Every morning I work with a fair degree of fury, and I'm starting

6. This refers to a comment Barrès had made concerning Symbolism.

on my year: perhaps there will come of it, but absolutely at last, a fragment of the only drama I have to create, which is that of Man and the Idea, which is, basically, what veils my article on Wagner which you were kind enough to read attentively.

103   PAUL VERLAINE

16 November 1885

I'm behindhand with you, because I sought out what I'd lent hither and yon, and miles away, among the unpublished works of Villiers. I've attached the very little I possess.

But as for precise information about the dear old wanderer, I have none. Even his address is unknown to me; our two hands find they are together again, as if they'd parted only the day before, at a street corner, every year, because a God exists. Apart from that, he would be punctual at a meeting and the day when, for *Les Hommes d'Aujourd'hui* as well as for *Les Poètes maudits,* you'd like to meet him, when you're in better health, at Vanier's, with whom he'll be dealing for the publication of *Axël,* there's no doubt, knowing him, no doubt at all, that he'll be there at the hour arranged. In literary matters no one is more precise than he is: so it's up to Vanier to obtain his address first, from M. Darzens, who has until now represented him in dealings with this amiable publisher.

If none of this worked out, then one day, especially on Wednesday, I'd go and find you at dusk; and, as we chatted there would come to each of us biographical details which at present I can't recall; not his civil status, for instance, dates etc., which the man in question knows.

Now for me.

Yes, I was born in Paris, on 18 March 1842, in the street known today as the Laferrière passage. Since the Revolution my paternal and maternal families had presented an unbroken succession of civil servants in Administration or the Records Office; and although they had almost always occupied high positions there, I avoided this career to which I'd been destined since I was in swaddling bands. I discover traces of the taste for holding a pen, for other purposes than registering acts, among several of my ancestors; one, no doubt before the creation of the Records Office, was a syndic of the booksellers under Louis XVI and I've seen his name at the bottom of a royal Privilege placed at the head of the original French edition of Beckford's *Vathek,* which I had reprinted. Another wrote light verse in the Almanach of the Muses and the Gifts for Ladies. As a child I knew, in the old interior of middle-class Parisian family life, M. Magnien, a distantly related cousin, who had published a fervently Romantic volume called Angel or Demon which sometimes crops up at the expensive end of the booksellers' catalogs I receive.

I spoke of a Parisian family a moment ago, because we've always lived in Paris; but we're originally from Burgundy, Lorraine, and even Holland.

I lost my mother when I was a small child, at the age of 7, and was adored by a grandmother who brought me up first; then I went through many *pensions* and schools. I had a Lamartinian soul and the secret desire to replace Béranger[7] one day because I'd met him in the house of mutual acquaintances; it seems the plan was too complicated to carry out, but for a long time I attempted poetry in little notebooks which, if I remember correctly, were always being confiscated.

You know that there was no possibility of a poet living on his art even if he lowered it by several notches, at the time when I entered life; and I've never regretted this. Having learnt English solely in order to read Poe the better, I set off at the age of 20 for England, principally wanting to take flight but also to learn to speak the language and to teach it in some corner or other, tranquil and with no other necessary job: I was married and there was some urgency.

Today, more than twenty years later and despite the loss of so many hours, I think, sadly, that I did the right thing. That's because, apart from the prose pieces and the verse of my youth and its continuation, which echoed it, published pretty well everywhere, every time the first numbers of a literary review appeared, I've always dreamed and tried something different, with the patience of an alchemist, ready to sacrifice to poetry all vanity and all satisfaction, as in the past one burned one's furniture and the beams of the roof, to feed the furnace of the Great Work. What was it? That's hard to say: a book, quite simply, in many volumes, a book which really would be a book, architectural and premeditated, and not an anthology of random inspirations, however marvelous. . . . I'll go further and say: the Book, persuaded that when all's said and done there is only one, attempted unwittingly by whoever has written, even those of genius. The orphic explanation of the Earth is the sole duty of the poet and the literary game *par excellence:* for the very rhythm of the book, then impersonal and living, even to its pagination, is juxtaposed with the equations of this dream, or Ode.

There you have the confession of my vice, laid bare, dear friend, which a thousand times I've rejected when my spirit was bruised or

7. A popular songwriter.

143

weary, but it possesses me and I shall perhaps succeed. Not in creating this work in its entirety (you'd have to be I don't know who for that!) but in showing a fragment which had been created, and in making glorious authenticity shine in one place, and in indicating in all its entirety, the rest, which would demand more than one lifetime. To prove by the portions created that this book does exist, and that I've known what I was unable to accomplish.

Hardly surprising then, that I haven't rushed to collect the thousand fragments already known and which have, from time to time, attracted the benevolence of charming and excellent minds, yours first among them! All that had no momentary value for me other than to keep my hand in: and however successful some pieces may be; all of them together barely constitute an album, certainly not a book. It's possible, however, that the publisher Vanier may tear these shreds from me, but I'd only stick them onto pages as one makes a collection of scraps from materials which are centuries old or precious. With this damning word "album" in the title, Album of poems and prose, perhaps; and it would contain several series, could even develop indefinitely (beside my personal work which I believe will be anonymous, since the Text would speak by iself and without the author's voice).

These poems and prose poems can be found (or not) both in literary reviews and in luxury editions which have now been sold out, such as *Vathek, Le Corbeau, L'Après-midi d'un faune.*

In moments of hardship or to buy ruinously expensive dinghys, I've been obliged to write things of which the most that can be said is that they are honest, and of which it is fitting not to speak: *Les Dieux antiques, Les Mots anglais.* But apart from that, I've not often yielded either to necessity or to pleasure. Except that at a certain moment, however, despairing of the despotic book abandoned by Myself, I have, after a few articles hawked about here and there, tried to write completely on my own, including advice on outfits, jewelry, furniture, even theater reviews and dinner menus, a journal entitled *La Dernière Mode,* the eight or ten numbers of which still serve, when I blow the dust off them, to make me dream at length.

Basically, I consider the present period as a form of interregnum for the poet, who has no business to get involved with it: it's too obsolescent, too much in an effervescence of preparation, for the poet to have anything to do other than to work away mysteriously, thinking only of the future or of no time at all, and now and again send a visting card to the living, in the form of stanzas or a sonnet, so that they don't stone him, suspecting him of knowing that they do not exist.

Solitude is the necessary companion of that kind of attitude; and, except for my route from the house (it's now 89, rue de Rome) to the various places where I've had to pay the tithe of my minutes, the lycées Condorcet, Janson de Sailly, and finally the collège Rollin, I roam little, preferring above everything, in an apartment protected by the family, my time spent amidst some old and cherished pieces of furniture, and my sheet of paper, often blank. My great friendships have been with Villiers, Mendès and my dear Manet, whom ten years ago I saw everyday and whose absence today strikes me as impossible! Your *Poètes Maudits*, dear Verlaine, Huysmans' *A rebours* have interested, during my long-empty Tuesday gatherings, the young poets who love us (Mallarmists apart) and there has been a belief that I tried to exert some influence, whereas there was nothing but confluences of minds. Highly refined, I was ten years ahead of the point to which similar young minds must turn at present.

There you have my entire life stripped of anecdotes, quite the opposite of what the big-circulation newspapers have long trotted out, depicting me constantly as very peculiar. After careful scrutiny I can see nothing else, apart from the daily problems, the joys, and the family bereavements. A few appearances wherever ballet is performed or organ music played, for these are my two artistic passions, all but contradictory, but whose meaning will be clear—and that's all. I was forgetting my moments of flight, indulged in immediately my mind grows too weary, to the banks of the Seine and the forest of Fontainebleau, in a place which has been the same for years: there I see myself entirely differently, for river navigation then becomes my sole delight, I honor the river, which can engulf entire days in its waters without giving one the impression of having lost them, nor the shadow of a moment's remorse. A simple wanderer in mahogany yachts, but an impassioned sailer, very proud of his flotilla.

Farewell, dear friend. You'll read all this, written in pencil to give it the air of those good conversations between friends, away from the crowds with no raised voices, you'll run your eyes over it and you'll find, scattered here and there the few biographical details you need, details which one needs to have seen as true, somewhere or other. How sorry I am to know you're ill, and with rheumatism! I know what it's like. Only use salycilate rarely, and then only from a good doctor, for the dosage is very important. In the past I suffered from weariness and a kind of lapse of memory as a result of that drug. And I blame it for my insomnia. But I'll go and see you one day and tell you all this, bringing you a sonnet and a page of prose which I'll create for you, something you can put wherever you want. You can begin without these two trinkets. Farewell dear Verlaine. Your hand. Vil-

145

liers' packet is with the concierge. It goes without saying that I value it as I value my eyes! It's something which couldn't be replaced. As for the *Contes cruels* Vanier will get them for you, *Axël* is being published in *La Jeune France* and *L'Eve future* in *La Vie moderne*.

104   LÉON VANIER

[7 May 1886]

The copies to be decorated with ribbons are ready for you, together with a model: everything, the pasting of the price tag, the tying of the ribbons, and the fraying from the top, must be an exact replica of what was done in the past.[8] You can make up into pages the Poe galleys, which seem to me to have succeeded in the contrast between the two typefaces.

I'm resolutely awaiting the caricaturist, who is unknown to me; but is he an artist? You know I'd hate a portrait which lacked individuality like the last ones, Verlaine's notice in particular being so exquisite and with such control! But I'd prefer to do without any picture rather than have one which was not very good. Now, I'm coming to the proofs of the Faun. On seeing them, I'm dumbfounded, and can't believe my poor eyes. Didn't we say clearly enough and in all manner of tones that if there were none of the 18 elzevir used in *Vathek*, the only suitable one here (I'll explain why), then it would be necessary to search the entire world, even if we had to use the modern type of a newspaper, to make this little volume something quite different from the previous one and having nothing in common with it. Haven't I been sufficiently verbose, prolix, and discursive on this score, and weren't you even going to send me at Fontainebleau two or three samples of different typefaces so I could choose? And what do I get? Exactly the same page setting as the big Faun, with the same characters but less well typeset, that's all! I can't get over it. All we'd be doing in that case is a bastard and bargain-rate counterfeit instead of a new little work unconnected with the other except for the text and illustration.

All this is very annoying both for you and for me. It would be better to stick to the things we've already agreed. So do come in order that we can decide on the conditions of this piece of work, one of these evenings, after your dinner. I find I'm so behind since my return from the country that I can't see a moment when I can escape to see you.

8. This seems to refer to copies of the *Faune,* which Vanier had bought up and which had to be prepared for sale.

Don't have the forms reduced, we'll have to study their dimensions etc. We'll still have to discuss your worries about reducing the run by 500; we'll have to find a solution, but an easy one which satisfies both of us. Farewell, dear Vanier, I'm waiting for you and shake your hands, as a distraught book-lover.

105 Jean Moréas

24 May 1886

Your delicious book[9] debates, in the course of its subtle vibrations, so many important ideas concerning the very form of poetry that I'm satisfied, as I set it down on the table yet again, to thank you for it and to postpone until we next meet a long chat about it. Nevertheless, and this can be said in a few words, you've succeeded in everything you've attempted. It will certainly be impossible to study poetry now, in its so fleeting and almost nymph-like transformations, without having read *Les Cantilènes,* an epoch-making collection of poems.

I believe your obvious originality will consist in having seized, under the official prosody, to which it would now be wrong to limit the education of the ear, an entirely different current, more intimate and no less exact. You, who are by nature an inventor, have chosen this to place in a position of eminence, and you have victoriously revealed it as it is: I see it in more of a subordinate role, but it's your prerogative to act as you have! What I admire is the certainty with which you pursue in all directions and in all kinds of poetry, the new and authentic gold of your discovery: that is already evident, and it promises us truly curious works—and unexpected ones!

106 Auguste Villiers de L'Isle-Adam

6 September 1886

I challenge you
to catch the bus Pigalle-Wine Hall which meets up at the Louvre with the line Saint-Philippe-du-Roule-*Gare de Lyon;*
then get a return ticket valid for two days, cost 6 francs, for Fontaine-bleau, *on the midday train;*
there, when you leave the station, look out for a donkey cart in which I'll be
waiting for you,
and come with me to Valvins.

9. *Les Cantilènes,* published by Vanier in 1886.

What day of the week (except Friday, because the ladies go to a market on that day), quick, let me know; if you remember having promised me this pleasure.

Hug Monsieur Toto[10] for me and let me shake your hand, as a very old friend.

107   JEAN AJALBERT

22 December [1886]

Thank you for so graciously sending me your books, one of which was already familiar to me and belongs to the contemporary library of poetry; the other, the new one, confirms my impression that *Sur le vif* was not an extraordinary piece of beginner's luck with its fluidity of color, its rhythmic poses which seize life through a refined stroke moving as life itself moves, in a word the entire modern mode of seeing and capturing. You had truly opened up, at your first attempt, the perfect path, where you alone could pass. *Paysage de femmes,* which has even more in the voice and is less strictly painted, forms a fine continuation and solves what was perhaps a greater difficulty by setting modernity so to say to music, in essential little prose poems which are pure songs.

Farewell, I'd shake your hand somewhere or other were it not that the lack of time has made me a hermit in my only free moments: but do you never come in the direction of the rue de Rome, on a Tuesday evening, for instance? Believe me, I had to have a doctor's order forbidding me to write, with a blindfold over my eyes and all the associated kerfuffle, to prevent me writing to you sooner.

108   RENÉ GHIL

Sunday 13 March 1887

I close the book.[11]

Here are my thoughts:

Certainly no previous poem has come so close to what needs to be done. With rare intuition, given that our conversations would not in themselves have sufficed to make you conceive it, you've glimpsed the art of the future. I imagine that it's only through long dreams or years of study and not from the moment of the revelatory thunderbolt, that we'll be able to treat it in a definitive manner; but your indications are at least new. Obviously one would wish for a more sharply deline-

10. Villiers' son Victor, born in 1881.
11. *Légendes de rêve et de sang, livre 2: le Geste ingénu.*

ated continuity in the general motif, which is wrongly called a subject and which you feel quite correctly must only be a semblance of the subject. Also, the line itself is not always a sufficiently revealing jewel which the reader can twist and turn under his eye, and whose weight he can feel in his hand—you understand me. We saw that this summer, but how much everything has progressed since then! It's a work of transition, and later you will consider it as such, but not without a sense of pride at the bravura with which you went straight to the most difficult point.

Throughout, a quality of reverie and no music, which, however, sometimes remains hidden and which I consider exceptional. If I were you, I'd push that, in the next attempt, as far as thought and song, since you can always resume, once mastered, your complex and indeed symphonic style. You need, while remaining where you are, to make a move in another direction, toward something which is simply tangible and which you can bring into your art.

You won't object to my chatting away as a chap of some experience, because of the thousands of attempts I've put to one side, in drawers, rather than fail to reach, however late, and as if at my first attempt, the obvious; but I'm also chatting as a very close friend of yours.

109   FRANCIS VIELÉ-GRIFFIN

[7 April 1887]

I've read your volume,[12] as I was saying the other evening and as I repeat to myself, with delight.

You possess the poetic sense superbly, and in particular the instinct for that mysterious thing called a poem, from the moment when there first leaps into existence, felicitously combining several beautiful and exact motifs, right to the time when there falls back again, supple and vast, those thousand of lines which are lines of poetry by virtue of something over and above their external music. Yes, in *Les Cygnes* you have their very pool, under the influence of all climes, torrid or calm or even monotonous, though not without reverie. Your art of sometimes extraneous recollections introduces here something very precious, a song which is not easy to define and which draws on English accentuation; thus more than anyone else and as if by a miracle, you create flights of entire stanzas on the tip of their mute *e,* satisfying the fluttering and silent cadence!

That's why I've studied you: my only criticism would concern an

12. *Les Cygnes,* a collection of poems.

occasional word which has leaped into place rather too easily, if I didn't fear that careful research would interrupt you! and you make up for that by your grace and the ample rhythms.

You must be happy: your book came at the right moment. Thanks for my fine copy; and in exchange for that in particular and now I've said the rest, a warm hand-shake.

110   STUART MERRILL

[8 May 1887]

I'm late in sending my thanks, rushed off my feet recently with work and also because your book is so haunting that one can, without wearing out the charm, wait a little. But at the risk of appearing ungrateful.

It's more than *Scales,* come now![13] You've been in full possession of your fingering technique for a long time now and you find the most diminutive of chords. Perhaps for the first time I've come across a first anthology of which the following can be said: almost no poem, if included in a work of your maturity, would introduce a dissonant note, such a poet you are, intuitive and exact. I'm saying this from the depths of my mind and not without real pleasure. The subtle and fluid song-like quality delights me in your work: with its charge of sudden riches. You are capable of these two lines:

A winged chaos of rose petals

and:

Mirror of golden glories, an excitement of fire

which, each so different, linger in my mind.

I've even noted, during several readings, that you are already, and this is supreme artistry, at the point of hiding the alliterative games, which too much obvious exteriority would betray as method, preventing the miracle of the verse from remaining, momentarily, inexplicable. Continue in that direction.

Now, by what wonder, other than that which friend Ghil brings to the house each week and which makes you familiar to me (this through analysis), by what miracle have you come from your side to be so steeped in everything which is being attempted here by a curious tail-end of a century? I'd find it astonishing were it not easy to understand that the essence of everything is perhaps received, volatile and purified, from a distance.

13. Merrill's collection of poems was entitled *Les Gammes* (*Scales*).

My cordial thanks for placing my name at the beginning and end of the volume.[14] Come one day, at last, but I already know you; and this scrap of a letter I had to write you, after having obsessed me with remorse, has given me pleasure, even though it's belated.

III   GUSTAVE KAHN

8 [7] June 1887

I'd taken your work[15] to the country, so that I could study it very much alone and at leisure: then a fit of the sulks against the poor weather, which was forcing me to write, delayed my letter.

You must be very proud, indeed you must! It's the first time, in our literature and in any literature I believe, that a gentleman, faced with the official rhythm of the language, our old Poetry, has created one all on his own, perfect: that is, simultaneously exact and endowed with enchantment. It's an unparalleled adventure![16] What arises from it is a new point of view according to which whoever is musically organized may, by listening to the special arabesque which governs him and if he manages to note it down, create a personal metrics drawn from himself and removed from the general type (which has become a public monument in our city). What a delicious liberation!, for take good note that I don't consider you as having put your finger on a new form faced with which the old form must withdraw. The old one will remain, impersonal, for all and for whoever wishes to choose a different form of isolation, the choice is our own. You open one of the paths, your own: equally important is the fact that there could be a thousand of them. The very clear laws, which your reader quickly perceives, and which you've recognized as existing in the language, have their place, like many others, no doubt, which a different ear would seize. The charm is great, independently of the very subtle qualities which are specific to you and which are exquisitely connected with poetry. Outside the accepted forms of music there is in your poetry something which seems greatly rejuvenated in the word which presents itself less supported and without preparation, yet by the same token it may also lose some of the intricate fire of its absent facets by not being encrusted in an age-old melodic mold and by not being already part of the reader.

If it were Tuesday, my dear friend, and we were at rue de Rome and not in my corner of greenery, we'd chat about this for much

---

14. The first and last poems of the collection are dedicated to Mallarmé.
15. A collection of poems entitled *Les Palais nomades*.
16. Mallarmé, therefore, saw Kahn as the inventor of free verse.

longer, so greatly does your case interest me, as well as revealing an indisputable success.

🐉 *October 1887 saw the publication of* Les Poésies de Stéphane Mallarmé.

112 RODOLPHE DARZENS

11 October 1887

The value of *Pages in Prose*[17] is that the contents correspond to the title and are in prose; by which I don't mean at all that they are borrowed from everyday discourse. You've understood that given the hieratical music of poetry, from the moment the poet chooses for once not to frame our Thought within it, Thought would find, purely and of itself, a suitable music which is none other than the the sentence led by the internal rhythm of feeling. Therefore it's truly like listening to an exquisite instrument playing solo, an instrument which is yourself, when I let my eyes run from one of your pages to another. Everything, even the vast evocations like those of clouds or cities which partially open in your writing, follows the uninterrupted melody in your mind and in the text, which is the characteristic of Poetry and which is alien to chance, don't you agree?

113 EMILE VERHAEREN

15 January [1888]

There'll be two letters; since Thursday I've been trying to set aside an evening to read you,[18] and have been thwarted. You know what I mean when I say "read you": it means, after great pleasure, a prolonged study amidst the lamplight.

Since you're not unaware, and the echos, which, although they repeat my words so stupidly in the usual run of events, may have brought word to you, each time I speak of you I say this above all: that among the poets of the present generation, here or over there,[19] you're the one from whom can be expected the greatest degree of experimentation. Yes, it's in you that the renewal of poetry best operates and you do it without having anything to do with the farces of the moment.[20] I won't explain what I mean by this, since I'll have a

17. Darzens' collection published in Moscow in 1887.
18. Verhaeren had sent Mallarmé a copy of his volume of poetry, *Les Soirs*.
19. Verhaeren was a Belgian poet.
20. Mallarmé reveals here all the ambiguity of his response to contemporary experimentation in verse forms.

chance to be more explicit in the course of the week, when I'll tell you exactly what I think about *Les Soirs*.

How beautifully they're presented! I don't know a more successful volume than this, modern and traditional, among contemporary publications. Through M. Deman you've made a charming opening for me. But first a word about the major project my card alluded to, for this year. My dear friend, I plan to present myself in public toward October, you know what I mean by that, and to juggle with the contents of my book: it would take far too long to talk about this with pen and ink, so I'll wait for your hay fever.

But between now and then see my meaning through Edgar Poe. I'm eliminating my past and I took to Dentu these last few days (what a shame, but nothing is completely done) a volume of prose poems, 200 pages and 4 illustrations in color and etching by John Lewis-Brown (the cover) and Degas, Renoir, Mme Morisot, perhaps also by Monet. Title: *The Lacquered Drawer.* I asked 500 for it. Failing that, I have *Poems by Poe,* translated, with curious notes: that's also about 200 pages. There's a portrait of Poe by Manet, with a tail-piece and a fleuron, borrowed from my in-folio of *The Raven,* reduced. In all, 200 pages. I'm asking 300 francs for it and am on the point of publishing it because I want this to be the first and definitive edition, the only one to contain the dedication sonnet and the remark: "Made by the author." Indeed, Vanier, who has indulged in all kinds of cheating tricks in dealing with me, has for two years had my permission to print this book, but he's putting it off indefinitely, to cause me problems and because he lacks money. I want to get out of this impasse, as Dujardin helped me to do with the *Faune,* by acting first. This edition, put off indefinitely, has moreover no chance of selling, if it's poorly published and expensive, as it would be through Vanier: what's needed is to make something very attractive in the space of two or three months. Reply to me quickly about this. Then there are my poems, which have indeed sold well through Dujardin, despite the price and lack of care taken by the lithographer, but there are still a few copies and I wouldn't want to interrupt sales.

114   ARNOLD GOFFIN

Sunday 17 June 1888

If Poetry is something situated between music and literature, and if there is, as we can sense nowadays, a rival tabernacle to rhymed verse where Poetry can be housed in a very modern way, or in a way which is completely variegated and mobile, it's certainly not the novel, strictly speaking—that error will pass away—but what you are doing with the book, a subtle series of prose poems, clear and transient. Given your ability to enlarge everything you see, and the acuity of your expression, you seem to me to be one of those created to be among the first to attain that shimmering and deceptive book that we sometimes briefly conceive of. With sympathetic thanks, therefore, for *Impressions and Sensations*.[21]

115   HENRI CAZALIS

18 June 1888

I took your book[22] to the country to read it, while I had a few days' rest and would be free. Today, I needn't add, it's in Dr. Fournier's hands.[23] You know, dear friend, that it's a book and yet it's poetry; I can see that all the better for inhabiting a palace which is different from yours, or a Kiosk. What strikes me as wonderful is that your Orient breathes completely out of your soul, because you are like that and because you've merely juxtaposed an exotic ill with your own thought, as if it were a proof or an illustration; but even your voice, and a certain rich monotony which veils your lyricism, sets free those far-off regions of ourselves, enchanting and sad, vast, losing themselves like a sacred river in the void. I can see you in every page, through that! The intimate you, making chime again so many hours which belonged to us.

Thank you. Embrace the little Lahors for me and shake your dear wife's hand, for I see her emerging behind this name as if from jewels or familiar materials.

116   EDMOND DEMAN

Valvins [30 July 1888]

For the Poe only, I'll be in Paris tomorrow, breaking for the first time in years my habit of forgetting in my time of peace and dreams the very road to Paris. I'll sign copies, according to your numbered indications, they'll then be immediately wrapped by Dujardin's clerk (Dujardin himself is away for a few days); but (and this is where your astonishment will begin) I'll wait, before telegraphing by return the order to take them to the papers, until you've explicitly given your advice on the question of whether it wouldn't be better, since there's

21. This collection appeared in 1888.
22. Cazalis's volume of poems, *L'Illusion*, published under his pseudonym of Jean Lahor.
23. Father of Méry Laurent's doctor, a great book-lover.

154

no longer anything to fear from Vanier who won't publish before the winter, to delay the official date of publication and the press launch until the first of September, when the dead season for books comes to an end. Through unfortunate delays and, recently, through last-minute hesitations, we've been driven back to the worst moment of the year, the moment when a book can sink without trace. This is the thought that has haunted me for the last day or two.

The subscription forms, finally, could, with the agreement of Dujardin, be published in the late August number of the *Revue indépendante* which is read by "my public."

Give me your answer, too, about various details concerning the *Drawer*. Will the illustration be printed at Lermercier's, or will it be supervised by J. Lewis Brown? etc. Let's reach a clear understanding to avoid my having to write a series of letters, for these initial letters already cause me what could almost be called pain, in this corner where I'm used only to writing for myself! In this entirely personal work, I'm of course including valued proofs, like that of the *Drawer*, which I'm expecting almost straightaway, in two or three deliveries, so that I can complete them all at leisure and before the schools go back, in good, intimate hours. With the first packet, I'll send you the revised version of "Le Môme sagace,"[24] in which I'm still letting a sentence doze.

You've always shown yourself to be such a friend to me, that I wasn't indiscreet, dear Deman, in asking you to transmit to me the remainder of my author's rights for *The Drawer*, but I may have been a bit of a nuisance; and as far as that's concerned, now I come to consider it, 150 francs would suffice for the moment, if I'm assured of the remaining 100 for 1 October, a few days before the book comes out, do you want to divide the money up like that? It would give me peace of mind during these months devoted to work and it would give the ladies the possibility of hiring a horse, the promise of which helps them contemplate their solitude more easily.

117 EDMOND DEMAN

7 August 1888

Thank you for the 150 francs, which brought pleasure to those around me. I'm answering your letter, as things occur to me, you'll allow me not to use letter paper, as I want to set aside the very thought of a letter.

---

24. The prose poem eventually entitled "Réminiscence."

The edition seems to me and to the few others who have seen it, notably my neighbor Redon, very fine, sober and traditional, by which I mean everything a book can be in these days, since books are always something from the past. The modernity of the book will come from the large number of white spaces, beautifully set out, and from the exclusive use of black lettering. In a word, it's my belief that the ensemble creates an impression of excellent taste. A few slips, the print is indeed sometimes a bit pale, particularly the first sheet on the Holland paper, but it's superbly rough and primitive, that Holland. On the delicious frosted cover, I would perhaps have liked the raven's head a little more towards the upper left-hand corner. Henceforth we'll put *By the same author* on the verso of a blank page on which the reader can write his name, in a word, on the back of the ex-libris, and we'll place this page first, so that the false title and the title aren't separated, which is an irregular practice. On the title page the line *The Poems* is too isolated, too far from the words *By Edgar Poe,* as a result of a certain lack of proportion between the two typefaces used. And finally, if I'd checked the last sheet I'd have added a List of Contents, or a list of main sections, which the volume lacks, for the one at the beginning is merely an indication of the poems in order. I've not yet reread it with an eye to errors, I doubt there are any more apart from the two pointed out by you, except that the title page itself has "To Someone from Paradise" instead of "in," and in "The Bells" *Tintinnabulisation* instead of *tintinnabulation,* I don't know how that escaped me. Finally on the last page M. L. She*n* instead of She*w*.

I agree with you that we shouldn't consider our first launch in August as definitive, but that we should repeat it to some extent in September, or in October in tandem with the *Drawer.* And for that reason I've left a certain number of press copies with Dujardin, see the attached list. I don't know what result these first packets will produce. Apart from *Figaro,* which has three copies to be absolutely certain they speak of it somewhere or other, I was only able to send one to each of the papers I had in mind and you know it's the rule to send two. So I sent it specifically to the critic at his home, but that involves the risk, particularly in these days of unemployment, that the book will find a home in the bookcase without any article appearing. But that was my only solution. Here, since I receive almost no newspapers, I'll only find out belatedly and by hearsay unless I subscribe to a clippings agency as soon as I'm advised to do so. I think I've telegraphed everything, you'd do better to come under the trees in the forest, my dear Deman, while it rains, oh, to tell the truth, desperately hard!

Farewell, I've received the proofs of the *Drawer,* but I'm waiting for my copy before starting, since I need it; quick! because I'm going from the fifteenth to twenty-somethingth to spend a few days in Auvergne at Royat, since friends have sent me an invitation and a railway pass, both unrefusable, and it will be an interruption.[25]

The illustrations? Everything is ready, except the Degas, I'll write to that sublime but unpunctual painter, and I'll beg J. L. Brown, as he was gracious enough to suggest to me, to supervise Lemercier while he prints them. I know nothing of the prices as yet except that they'll only be slightly higher than the cost of printing a fine etching, but I'll let you know when I've found out.

119   GEORGES RODENBACH

21 May [1889]

It's your qualities, all of them, that this book establishes,[26] in perfect proportions, ranging from the spicy to the poignant: a poem, in which the handful of motifs which make it up never break and in which the soul's song never ceases. How carefully you avoid the veneer and all the bad habits of the novel, properly so-called; and the tale quite simply tells itself, just as the air circulates through your landscape. I'm placing *L'Art en exil* with the books one returns to and whose shimmering, rare text is not exhausted by the initial glance.

It was in 1884 that Mallarmé's love affair with Méry Laurent had begun. Many of his letters to her have not yet been made public, but those included here show the warmth and tenderness of their relationship.

120   MÉRY LAURENT

[12 August 1889]

My great darling, I'm completing yesterday's tasks by writing to Mène esquire, to the Father, to Huysmans, to repeat myself, to be absolutely accurate and to make sure everything is ready.[27] You'll allow me to send you merely a kiss, because I can put everything into a kiss, when I have the chance. Your good presence envelops me, better than ever. You're a rare woman, my peacock,[28] and you renew the exquisite and intimate emanation of yourself to such an extent that I

25. The friends were Méry Laurent and Dr. Evans.
26. The book in question is *L'Art en exil*.
27. For Villiers's marriage *in extremis*.
28. Mallarmé's nickname for Méry, not exempt from a degree of gentle teasing about her vanity.

feel I didn't know you before as I do now, after all these years, do you understand this? Unless you truly add day by day to your charm, which is quite possible. I have for you the loveliest feeling I can feel for anyone. And you're even very beautiful. I kiss you.

121 MÉRY LAURENT

15 August 1889

Your feastday, alas! and we're apart. I'm going to write you some brief sentences, I who would have had so much to tell you, because I have to rest after a few words. I put my arm to too much use during the day I spent in Paris. The worst is that I can't lift my cigarette to my mouth, Geneviève plays my slave for me, would you do as much?

On the morning itself Villiers still hadn't made up his mind;[29] at 4 p.m. we'd only just got all the documents, for Marie is a foreigner, from Luxembourg. So, Elisa, be careful.[30]

When I arrived he said to me: "I'm to be married today, we'll drink a bottle of champagne and this disturbance will bring about my demise." He was very withdrawn, very somber, the entire day; and finally exhausted. What a great change! He's in a new state, which could last for a few days, if he ate; but he no longer eats. He looked 70. Will he last until the first days of next week? This time, I doubt it. A minor employee at the Town Hall, who turned out to be a great admirer of his, took charge of the inscription of the bans and saved everything: what a stroke of luck! It was very silent, the civil marriage, with the four of us: and what a humiliation it was for the poor man, made worse by the fact that Marie couldn't write and said: "I'll sign with a cross as I did on my first marriage." You can imagine the silence. The mayor was perfect, showing respect and deference for the great writer Villiers so obviously is, and that was the only balm for him. So we drank their health, they'd bought champagne glasses, the poor things! and Villiers was complimented on the quality of his wine. Totor was there, sprawling a bit, and he poked a hole in my back on leaving with a stick he'd taken from one of us. Marie was in black with a mantilla. And it was all great and serious. The priest joined their hands, beside the bed; but I understood that there would have to be a mass and perhaps extreme unction; the man of God also

29. Villiers, on the point of death, was persuaded by Mallarmé and other friends to marry his mistress in order to legitimize, and thereby provide for, their son. Villiers hesitated because, believing himself to be of aristocratic blood, he saw this as a morganatic marriage.

30. Elisa Sosset, Méry's maid.

158

took it on himself to let Marie spend the night in the room. Oh! that night! She, stupefied, sobbing; and begging me to write and tell you that you were with us. The beautiful ring "and what a weight it is!" is too tight. Villiers almost dismissed us "to go and dine, all of us" and said: "Now let the death throes begin."

I came home by the evening train and had the time to post my note, in the very box for the Royat express, and I felt I was close to you.

I truly believe you didn't get my scrawl straightaway; you hadn't given me your address, you lady of few words, in your train. And now your two letters reach me together, at noon just a moment ago. You're very kind, and your letters too: I'm glad to know you're well settled in with more intimacy than at the *Splendid:* but, little peacock, you can see that I can't leave here, for so many reasons, one of which you know; and because things will have to be done, immediately, after the death and we'll have to put in train ideas already vaguely worked out!

I'm expecting a wire, at any minute (things are really topsy-turvy, I have still done nothing, there'll be a trip to Paris the day before or the day after, I don't feel on holiday yet and I was hoping to get so much out of these two months): the trouble is that I can't take my mind off things by sailing because of the wound in my elbow which is suppurating. . . . As for the thigh, it's only damaged, which is a very small inconvenience for me, little peacock; yellow and black, the swelling's going down, and so is the pain if I stay still. Do you know all the details? Here, I explained it was due to a door being violently flung open. Keep the truth to yourself, I'm saying nothing about it. I don't know if you realized what happened. The train was moving too quickly away from the stationmaster, with "a minute's halt," I wanted to step down at the very moment when the movement stopped, so that I could discuss everything and fix it all up in time. It was dark, I was thrown headlong with a mad violence, and dragged along under the step, which caught me by the shoulder, for 7 or 8 meters. I felt my last hour was nigh, like Villiers just now; with an impression I'll translate by: "oh! can it be possible! how stupid!" What distresses me is that I cried out loud "Oh! la! la!" but not through fear, I realize it was just in order to speak for one last time. Now the really funny thing is that as soon as the crowd at the doors and the employee came to me, once the train had stopped, I fled like a stag and spoke to the stationmaster. I didn't feel shaken until that night, in bed, and yesterday I couldn't bear to look at a train; but now I'm over that nervous state.

I'm writing you all this so that I can chatter on until the end of the page, the eighth, if you please, and it's close-written; so forgive me for the occasional little card. I hug you, very tight, you know there's someone in you I love very much, and she can never be lost. I miss you.

Some more details. Huysmans tells me he has written to you, I'll thank him and send your regards. Someone (never mention this) opposite, rue Oudinot,[31] let it be understood that he wouldn't be a witness to the marriage, giving as pretext a departure that evening. Villiers understood. I was also obliged, given a state of anguish concerning future seizures of his property, which was ravaging the dying man, to sign with Marie a document transferring his furniture to me. I think I've told you everything, Mme Méry Laurent. You won't mind if I don't reread this. I love you, just a little. And to think I had the revolver in my pocket when I fell, can you believe it.[32]

122   MARIE AND GENEVIÈVE MALLARMÉ

[20 August 1889]

I'm writing you a brief letter before the post goes, and it's the first time I've been able to sit down since this morning.

Villiers suffered no death throes and felt himself dying gently. The funeral is tomorrow, Wednesday, at noon. It will be very decent and dignified, a humble black drape with his coat of arms, all of him; and . . . and we've been able to avoid Pantin, Bagneux, and those horrible overflow tanks of death and for almost nothing we'll have the shady little cemetery of *Les Batignolles,* but what a lot of machinations were necessary. I don't think I'll be able to watch over the coffin. I'll do my utmost to leave by the train departing from here at 6.05 tomorrow.

123   MÉRY LAURENT

Valvins [11 September 1889]

Without saying a word, when last winter you broke an enchantment in which my soul delighted, I guessed, because I know your kindness, that you must have had a serious reason for doing so, and I respected your secret. You can imagine that this is the reason why I didn't have the slightest desire to go to Royat;[33] in this new state I began to reason with myself, and there's no sense in deliberately

31. The allusion is to François Coppée.

32. The Mallarmés felt themselves so isolated at Valvins that they kept a revolver for protection, insisting in particular that if Geneviève were left alone, she sleep with it under her pillow.

33. Mallarmé had spent only a few days in Royat, where Méry was on holiday with her protector.

choosing to suffer. But how could I resist you! ... I went there, to spend two of those days of silence, without any moments free of constraint, each of my feelings of enthusiasm denied by you despite yourself, and those days were atrocious.

I mean, my darling, the absurdity of being like that. ... Existence, a laying bare of my fibers through an excessive literary dream, granting me no alternative emotion but that sharp sensitivity, or an emptiness: sometimes I hardened myself to the point of indifference, you understood what I was doing, but with you it's a complete waste of time. ... You welcome a good friendship, already of long-standing, I do believe that this sentiment, for instance, is one I possess and I'll certainly find, oh you who wanted it to unite us unto death, an occasion of proving it to you, although neither in despair nor illness: wait a moment! perhaps in your present happiness and, at this moment, I swear to you that knowing you are happy makes me. ... No, it's very hard to say—shall we say silent congratulations, believe me, go from me to you. Such a man can do no more, in removing himself: in daily life, it's more difficult, and so, darling, we'll have to space it out.

What else can I do! You are, despite everything, simple and spontaneous (in my eyes, superb) and it's this you, your being, that I adore, completely. The heart, I don't know what that means. The brain, it's with that that I enjoy my art and love some friends. So you see, there is almost no subject on which our two ways of thinking are in harmony, and the attraction you exert over me merely as a woman is wonderful to survive all that, this miracle I've undergone represents fairly generally what is called love: apart from that, what is there? But of course a great and unswerving devotion. You'll have it.

Too many things, and in this you're right, separate our lives for us to be able to draw them together anyway, without falsifying ourselves. Day by day, let's see less of each other; never in that very close intimacy which, unless it remain total between two people each stamped in some way as exceptional, can only be uneasy.

A close and independent friendship can survive this, although it will be put to the test. Rest assured that if you should ever call, I'd come. ...

Finally, you were right to speak, like a good friend, otherwise a feeling of constraint would have lingered, even for you, so that finally whenever you were at my side you would have been constantly on the defensive and ready to repress any act of tenderness, a tenderness which, however, you yourself always inspired. What a torment for me! And that was what lay behind our so attractive meeting.

I've tried (without equalling your lightness of touch) to answer you in the same easy, cordial tone, in which you'll discover some bitterness.

I'm avoiding any expressions of regret, for that would seem a reproach. Nothing but gratitude, Méry. Thank you.

You can't think anything except that my glances at you were not reasonable, and yet you were the cause: let me kiss your brow. Do you know why at this moment I feel a sense of joy, before kissing it, it's from having been able to say the truth, because it was you.

Goodnight, peacock.

7   Verse and Prose

124   OCTAVE MIRBEAU

20 January 1889[1890]

The cordial note you sent me, which was enough to dissipate the storm of cards and letters and destroy the very memory of them, as if they were no more than an imbecile snowstorm, by telling me that someone certainly thought of me, with true thought of a superior kind and not the everyday variety, dear Mirbeau, reached me the day before yesterday, although dated the 3rd, but the number is 89,[1] which, so it seems, makes a difference of a district; but such a mistake only happens when a friendship is involved, and when it concerns such a delightful anticipation as yours, quick, for a shake of a distant hand. The good side of this delay is that I was able to read, in dribs and drabs alas! a few episodes of *Sébastien Roch*[2] which sieze the reader (or create admirably in his mind a mood analogous to that of the novel): how eagerly I'm awaiting the book! You know, Mirbeau, that I love you because you are one of the few who do not pretend: and that's what the public finds unpardonable. Recently we dedicated to you, Huysmans and I, a copy of *Axël*, by Villiers, his beloved work which was interrupted, and we thought that he had paid in the horror of his life for those three hundred pages, not one of them without a flash of brilliance.

Farewell, you independent, isolated, and happy man! The difficulty I have in creating for myself a provincial life and in hoarding up minutes when I can work! When will we meet? Never come to Paris without shaking hands and chatting. Remember me to Mme Mirbeau and pay her my respects.

Mallarmé spent from 10 to 20 February in Belgium, giving a series of lectures on Villiers de L'Isle-Adam, who had died on 19 August 1889.

1. Mirbeau's letter was addressed to 80 rue de Rome, not 89.
2. This novel had been appearing in serial form in *L'Echo de Paris* since 14 January 1890.

Antwerp [12 February 1890]

Laugh! laugh my little children, my lecture, including the papers of my little assistant,[3] lasted two and a half hours. I was still working on it at 8 o'clock, and had been since morning, to get it ready; and I dressed while the carriage waited downstairs, in less than five minutes, and did a very good job of it apart from my shoelace which was dangling as I climbed the step. I didn't read, I bellowed, the rooms are as vast as La Madeleine.[4] The people were angelically patient, but not amused: cold, the subject being sad. The compulsory "bravos!" I'll send the papers, I got a lot of publicity. I made some cuts and I'm counting on a group of sympathetic supporters, when I lecture soon in Antwerp. I was taken to see the docks, which are marvels. As I write to you I'm eating the famous oysters, which have no equal, two francs, ah! I'd like to send you each a dozen. Haven't a moment to write to you, so take that into consideration. Received the letter sent to Antwerp. I haven't slept an hour yet, do you hear Marras? Greetings to the dear guests.

[18 February 1890]

My little ones, the train is rocking about horribly, but I'll try to write to you, although you won't receive my card until after my arrival, probably tomorrow morning. Ah! my poor little dears! Bruges! What a miracle and how I would have liked to have kept you there the whole afternoon: herewith two photographs of it, I'd need a hundred and they don't say anything. I found your note, kitten, when I arrived: but from morning to evening, with lots of people round me and taken around such a lot, I didn't have time to write a word, even to take down notes. A good lecture, a little insignificant, and I was trembling because I'd lost my voice and was competing with the Carnival cornets outside. I've been invited back for next year, as I have been everywhere except at the Brussels circle, with whom I'm at war.[5] This morning went to see the sea at Ostende, and didn't have time to go on a spree because I was hunting for the good stockings of pink wool, knitted and worn by the fisherwomen, but not to be found made up. I'm also bringing back several pretty things.

3. Probably the quotations from Villiers' works, copied by Geneviève.
4. The church in Paris built to resemble a Greek temple.
5. The Literary and Artistic Circle at Brussels complained that Mallarmé's lecture was pitched too high for the normal public.

So at last we're going to see each other again, at last, at last: do you know, Mother and kitten, what I long for just now is a couple of days at Valvins with you. Roll on Easter! The trip, apart from the bad luck of beginning unprepared at Brussels, has been good, for the present and for the future. I hug you already.

127   ROBERT PICARD

25 February 1890

Ah! dear M. Robert, how late I am in writing to you, but I wanted to get some information, as I told you. The exhibition which took place at Durand-Ruel's, on 1 March, was of engravers; you have no etchings etc. and, moreover, the black and white[6] side would dominate here. Well, it's your paintings that must be seen. I conferred with the buyer, Van Gogh,[7] to whom I was introduced by Redon; one day, we'll organize something there, but I have the feeling that before doing so he wants to see some of your work in an exhibition. He assures me that the *Independents,* to whom we must therefore return for the moment, will have a much higher standard this year, with a separate room for the rare ones, including his brother.

That's the current state of affairs, but at the slightest incident I'll be in touch.

Now you, for your part, are also going to play the businessman for me: you must send me the address of the two friends of ours who were kind enough to mediate on my behalf for the food, oysters, herrings, and for the *Three Castles* tobacco, with the bill or the price, so that I can pay. But first convey my warm thanks, because all that caused a great deal of pleasure in Paris.

Another thing, after the exquisite words preceding the fragments of my lectures in *L'Art moderne*[8] and which seem to me to come quite certainly from the ground floor of 47, the avenue etc. convey my thanks! The text, which I no doubt copied out rather hastily in a jolting train, is riddled with errors, words read in mistake for other words and above all capitals and stops breaking sentences in the middle, to such an extent that there's hardly a single one which is recognizable. Well, you can judge that with my reputation for being as incomprehensible as the good Lord, I have to be painstakingly careful. Could you therefore make sure that the proofs, for the final frag-

6. In English in the text.
7. Théodore, the brother of Vincent Van Gogh.
8. A Brussels periodical.

ments, are sent to me on receipt of this letter; I can read them and return them before the Friday morning.

All my compliments and respects to your mother who makes me look forward to the month of May more impatiently this year than ever before.

How lively and sharp-sighted it is, *The Confession of a Poet*,[9] an extract, if I'm not mistaken, from the chat to the XX[10] on Saturdays! [. . .]

128   HENRI DE RÉGNIER

31 March 1890

I've just experienced, in reading you,[11] one of the most intense joys that art can provide. (The previous book, as I said, marked a significant step in the metamorphosis of poetry; already, yes: but it is this book that absolutely demands such a statement.) I've just wandered, throughout an entire week, (oh! how I study you!) marvelling at something new and definitive. The exquisite texture of your poems is surpassed only by the delicacy of your verse, this verse you play with only with the most exemplary modesty; bringing it forth, as if fearfully, by all the subtleties of approximation, to produce it only when it is simultaneously obvious and fleeting, and at the moment when, fixed, it disappears. I don't know how you've been able to do that! but it's one of the most beautiful poetic effects and a phase in art which is completely supreme ... little by little you've reached that point, through a separate sense, that's what it is. Apart from the seduction, one is struck by a feeling of certainty; and a conviction that it had to be like this, that one could no longer proceed brutally, every time, as if one had in one's hand a preexisting instrument. Everything creates itself, discreetly, line by line; even the poem seen as a whole, deliciously borrowed from a rarefaction of a dream. We now march in parallel with music or better, my friend, thanks to such books.

129   EUGÈNE MANET AND BERTHE MORISOT

28 April [1890]

So you've gone, taking with you those Thursdays I'm going to miss; last Thursday, at the moment when I received your letter, I was

9. A series of three unsigned articles published by Edmond Picard in *L'Art moderne*. Robert was Edmond Picard's son.

10. The circle of the XX was a literary club, including Verhaeren and Maeterlinck, publishing in the periodical *L'Art moderne*.

11. The reference is to Régnier's *Poèmes anciens et romanesques*.

getting ready to go and bid you farewell, and not alone but accompanied by my friend Marras, your guest on a famous evening, who wanted, since he's left Versailles for Paris, to pay you a visit as soon as he'd settled in. . . . There it is, and the rain, erasing from the eyes the very memory of the countryside, hasn't frightened you in the least; at bottom, you're right and the leaves reappear, the moment it stops, green and enlarged. The address for the material was received, thank you; my only way of inhabiting the Spring is to drape myself with its hue, plus a spot of gray or boredom. Farewell, and all my regrets that our handshake has to be done on paper, but I hoped to see you the day before, or a few days before, this departure, when Whistler dropped in on me. I didn't hurry and everything punishes me for that error. You know I'll go.—Bibi,[12] how many theological virtues are there? . . . and send my regards to your aunt and cousins.

The ladies of my house send a smile, my dear friends.

130   ALBERT DE NOCÉE

[12 May 1890]

I would have liked to see you in Brussels.[13] I had things to discuss with you concerning the small volume entitled *Album of Verse and Prose*. You took no notice of the observations I made to you when I realized that the new editions were not consistent with the first edition, which, alone, I granted you and which, alone, was submitted to me. I informed you that the economizing of the number of pages agreed on, involving a suppression of white spaces, which I value, together with the numerous errors in the current reprint, displeased me. You took no notice of this. That is merely a lack of politeness, to which I am, however, little accustomed; but there is a certain dishonesty, forgive me!, in putting, or leaving, on the cover of this volume, the name of an editor to whom I've given no rights, above all when, opposite the bibliographical notice which I had carefully drawn up, this individual presents one created by himself and puts forward his own editions (which I disown). I beg you to answer me, and to send me the proofs, if I agree to continue with the publication of these pages, but this I'll only do after a new agreement and on the basis of conditions decided between us. If not, I'll be forced, regretfully, to interrupt the good deeds for which I have given you little credit.

I'll delay sending, until I receive your letter, the notes I hope to have published in two or three Belgian and French reviews concern-

12. Nickname of Julie Manet, who was about to make her first communion.
13. When Mallarmé was there during his lecture tour of Belgium.

ing the modes of operation about which I'm complaining, as well as ordering the seizure in the Vanier printing house of every copy bearing the name of his company—a step I wouldn't hesitate to take, if your reply were too slow in coming.

131   MÉRY LAURENT
[24 May 1890]
Delicious you, I only have time to send you the usual kiss, on leaving;[14] and there are things to say to you, but I'll say them when I'm there. What a Méry you were and ideally perfect, yesterday evening, your shell-ears must have burned all evening with it as we went away. . . . I found five Reviews, I'm sharing them, you'll receive three of them, since you're the bigger. Farewell (what an ugly word!) treasure and [*drawing of a peacock*].

132   MÉRY LAURENT
[29 August 1890]
You humiliate me, I'll never draw your portrait as prettily as you do; I prefer it to the photograph;[15] I'd like to attach it to myself somehow or other, decorated with the order of the peacock. You can imagine what covetous desires the cyclamens aroused.

You know there was no malice in my suggestion about a Tunisian detour. It was only afterwards that I thought of it and I smiled in my very long country beard, that's all, I swear to you. I'm never wicked, as you say in your role of little girl, except when you're there and then I pull your hair a little. Now I send you a kiss. I'm a little hungry to see you; and if you're occasionally absent from the shores of your beautiful lake,[16] it's because you're no longer there but have popped up, unbeknownst to you, on the banks of the river here, amid the reeds, when I'm out wandering. You asked me for a quatrain, I remembered this morning and I'm providing it with the pretext of this little note, which contains kisses instead of a vague text. Raphaël, who's passing through, told me about his mother's enthusiastic return.[17] Until we meet again, my pet.

14. For Valvins.
15. Méry must have drawn herself as peacock, in imitation of Mallarmé.
16. Méry was at Evian, on Lake Geneva.
17. Raphaël was the illegitimate son of Catulle Mendès and Augusta Holmès.

133   JOSÉPHIN PÉLADAN

4 October [1890]

The little card acquiescing to the wonder of a book like yours becomes so removed from the work, during the time we're possessed by it, that we delay writing, indefinitely and quite wrongly, even if it's only to thank you. . . . Whoever writes something other than a novel fills me with excitement, even when they don't emulate you in proceeding to a form which, while unknown, is nevertheless perfectly adequate for your unusual concept: where eloquence mingles with song, to achieve in all truth the Intellectual Music. I'm rereading, in peace, your *Victoire du mari* (which I took with me this winter on my travels) and am thus delighting in it.

But forgive me for writing so late.

134   PAUL BOURGET

5 October [1890]

I'm not sure I didn't read, here, in the countryside I have to leave, your characteristic work, this *Un cœur de femme,* as expansive and as simple as tragedy and so subtle! In this book you hardly tell a tale any longer and all the while the thread of the analysis weaves a continuous moral lace which is absolutely precious. If putting people in a book has any meaning to it, then reducing them to the status of thought is the proper way, in accordance with how we read, and truly superior, of communicating with them: and how, after all, it summons forth their true image! For literature continues to be the performance of an act of intellectuality concerning everything to do with life. You really do control your art, subservient to the old French taste but amplified by everything that has since been acquired, and above all by your own perspicacity and your emotion.

Thank you for thinking of me in sending me this work, and for counting me among your faithful supporters.

Your hand; let me tell you, too, that nothing concerning you is indifferent to me, and allow me to offer you my belated wishes, since I haven't had the opportunity to meet you since your marriage.

135   EMILE ZOLA

5 October [1890]

I promised myself I wouldn't reopen *La Bête humaine,* which I received from you this winter, during a voyage,[18] my dear Zola; well,

18. Mallarmé's trip to Belgium.

now I'm getting ready to read it yet again, this evening, simply before having said thank you for it. The scrap of paper, on which I'm going to write nothing, scarcely floats to the surface in the multiple immediate emotion such a book arouses, and it's easily forgotten. Whatever insignificant addition my belated note adds to the universal amazement, I send it so that you won't think, and this time even less than ever, that I'm not interested.

I admire, with all my mind, and have long done so, this art, which is yours, and which is situated between literature and something different, capable of satisfying the crowd and always surprising the man of letters; and I believe that never has there been such a torrent of life as that which flows in the ravine your drama has dug out between Paris and Le Hâvre.[19]

Thank you or forgive me, I don't know which I should write, receive it like the handshake of a meeting for which we'll set no date but which will be happy.

136   VICTOR-EMILE MICHELET

18 October 1890

Thank you for sending me your study of the esoteric in art, which interests me personally I might almost say, for it would be hard for me to imagine something or to pursue it without covering the paper with a geometry which reflects the obvious mechanics of my thought. The study of the occult is a commentary on pure signs, to which literature, bursting immediately from the mind, is more obedient than to anything else.

On 20 October Mallarmé received a letter from a young poet enclosing two poems and asking for advice. The writer was Paul Valéry.

137   PAUL VALÉRY

25 October 1890

The gift of subtle analogy, with adequate music, you certainly possess that, and that is everything. I said as much to our friend M. Louïs;[20] and I repeat it, before your two brief and rich poems. As for giving advice, solitude alone gives that, and I envy you your solitude

19. The two main locations in Zola's novel.
20. Pierre Louÿs, the novelist.

as I remember the hours of my youth spent in the provinces, down there near where you are; and which I'll never find again.

138   JAMES McNEILL WHISTLER

25 October 1890

Yes, the *Whirlwind*[21] is perfect and interests me, through you and also for itself. As soon as possible I'll send you a mere nothing for it, combining your two suggestions, a letter and a poem. A little sonnet of congratulations, with your name at the rhyme, Ah! Ah! Ah![22]

I'll try to send it before the end of next week, when we're returning to the country, and in such rain! but trusting to some burst of light in the forest, behind us and under the grayness of the weather. Three or four days only.

So the entire Moore family is moved. I went yesterday to shake Degas' hand: "Nothing can break my friendship with Whistler!" he told me, as you can well imagine.[23]

Farewell, dear friend; your hand; and my respects to Mme Whistler, whose laugh I've not heard for almost a year. [...]

139   EDMOND DEMAN

29 November 1890

I'm not going to talk about *Pages,* fear not.[24]

This is the point: it's been suggested that there should be a stage presentation of "L'Après-midi d'un faune," which was, indeed, originally written as a theatrical intermezzo. The very rare and curious way in which I hope to produce it will no doubt give this little work new renown. I'm taking advantage of that circumstance to bring to an end those remains of editions (I'm not talking of the beautiful first edition) which are scattered hither and yon, the edition of *Revue indépendante* which is bereft of interest, and a counterfeit by Vanier, which is costly and abject, drawings by Manet, all of that with no chance of a sale and misleading the public.

I'm preparing a definitive republication, with some reflections of

21. This review, which ran from 28 June 1890 to 27 December 1890, had the aim of focusing public attention on the works of Whistler and Mallarmé.

22. The sonnet entitled "Billet à Whistler" ("Letter to Whistler").

23. George Moore had published an article on Degas in *The Magazine of Art* in October 1890, in which he had insulted Whistler.

24. Mallarmé is referring to the slowness in the publication of *Pages.*

my own on poetry and theater, the recital of this poem and the exact point of view of a stage presentation. If necessary, a color picture representing this; and perhaps some indications on the brief musical overture. In a word, a brochure presenting it all as a monologue in verse with a chance of taking off, through the current rage for live tableaux and spoken recitals, in the salons. Something at once current and tasteful, one of those timely publications which become curiosities. You see what I mean. Price: not more than 2 francs, of which I'm asking a clear 50 centimes. To appear at the same time as the stage presentation, a few days beforehand, that's to say in six weeks time. To be held in Paris.

The press will fire broadside after broadside, from another point of view even than literature; my stage set, which is alive, will, with the help of a few painters, be an event.

As always, putting all my plans before you, I'm turning to you first of all; but I ask you, dear friend, insistently, and you can understand why, to let me know your reply whatever it is, immediately, because I don't have even half a day to lose. All yours. Then, in this case, we'll take advantage of the uproar it arouses to launch *Pages.*[25]

140   PAUL BOURGET

5 January 1891

I've savored in detail, you must be thinking it's obvious from the time I've taken to thank you, *La Physiologie de l'Amour moderne,*[26] to some extent it was my way of going out, this winter. No dinner party's crystal flashes such fire as this book, which opens of its own accord, at pages which are always as one would want them and lives on sharp, subtle glances, so condensed there as to dazzle. I admire you greatly for knowing how to scratch out such a thing, as well as all the rest.

141   PAUL CLAUDEL

5 January 1891

You forgive my delay, don't you? These absurd holidays, when time to oneself no longer exists. . . . But I was able to open the book again,[27] after first burying it in my soul, and I can see it again as it is, human and vast.

Certainly the Theater is within you.

25. Neither the publication nor the performance took place.
26. A cynical commentary on love.
27. *Tête d'or,* Claudel's play, written in its first form when he was seventeen or eighteen and published in 1890.

A development in the gestures of your heroes provides a mysterious accompaniment to that rhythm, so instinctively true, which you've found, a rhythm which is moral as much as it is aural and which controls the imagined world of the spectacle.

It's the authority of your characters which haunts me, particularly; through the stubborn, serious, and simple drama, where everything is absolutely stamped with your mark, my dear Claudel. I know you, but I guessed you.

142 OCTAVE MIRBEAU

5 January [1891]

Nothing to do with the New Year; the only pleasures, intimate and never foreseen, remain beyond any hopes one may be able to formulate. But here's what I'm writing about. One of my young colleagues,[28] greatly talented and of great heart, associated with the painter, sculptor, and ceramist Gauguin, and you know who he is!, has asked me to make a request of you as the only man capable of doing anything here. This rare artist, Gauguin, who, I believe, has been spared few torments in Paris, feels the need to concentrate his mind in isolation, one might say in the wilderness. He is going to leave for Tahiti, build his hut there and live amid what he left of himself over there, begin to work again from scratch, and grow aware of his strength once more. He needs 6,000 francs, for a few years, before returning; and the sale of his current work, in favorable circumstances, can provide him with that sum. Only he'd need an article, not on the sale, nothing commercial; but simply drawing attention to the strange case of this fugitive from civilisation; and how well you could do that! in the *Figaro,* some morning. . . . It's a harrowing adventure. Your opinion soon, and, if necessary, Morice could take you to Gauguin one afternoon, and he'd chat.

You hand: what a pity I didn't see you the other day, with Monet.

143 JEAN MORÉAS

5 January 1891

The page, which distills, in such a rarity of voice and coloration, your written melody, appears to me immaculate, around the words, even the modern ones, which give the impression that you alone have spoken them; and isn't that the greatest charm, to give Poetry the appearance of being foreign, eternally, to the true territory! You excel

28. The Symbolist poet Charles Morice.

in this. And for the first time, so it seems to me, you make one think that there belongs to the corporation of poets, and has done so down the ages, as its heritage irrespective of date and place, a language which is specific to them and perpetual. All that is new, exact, suggestive, it holds me spellbound and you can see it enchants in all its aspects; I'm delighted about it, dear Moréas, and thank you for this *Pèlerin Passionné* and hope to see you soon, to talk about it with you.

144   STEFAN GEORGE

28 February 1891

The fact that at first I didn't have your address explains my silence: for your book was no sooner received than read and translated around me. I was delighted by the artless and proud spontaneity in the brilliance and reverie of those *Hymns* (no title is more beautiful); but also, my dear exile (I'd almost say, yes), I was delighted that your handiwork, so fine and rare, should make you one of us, one of the modern poets.

145   GEORGES DOCQUOIS

8 March [1891]

I fear, Sir, that the poem you need to help your investigation concerning the effects produced on certain individuals by the Spring, may delay it: particularized by the vernal influence on literary production, the case is a curious one—for you or me. Herewith my thoughts: a piece of work begun in late autumn or on returning to Paris sometimes retains an exalted and empty autumn quality which may cause it to be abandoned for months: Spring comes and nourishes and resuscitates the chimaera. So it seems, at least: and winter remains the season of intellectual creativity.

In March 1891 Mallarmé was granted leave for three months on the grounds of ill-health. In May his volume Pages *was published, with a frontispiece by Renoir.*

146   EDMOND DEMAN

7 April 1891

We shall, shan't we, for a few days, since it's a question of establishing this edition of Poems, let each other know our reflections, randomly jotted down as notes. On second thoughts, I don't think we need to publish the manuscript again, that sometimes happens as an exception, but the poems lose out as a result. Poetry is very beautiful only in impersonal garb, by which I mean typographic garb: except of course if one engraves it to give the edition an element of immutability and monumentality. That, I think, was your impression when you spoke of engravings in the past and, in my view, you were right. Find one of the finest Roman types that exists and have it engraved (I say Roman, since poetry seems more definitive to me like that than in italics, which is closer to handwriting).

That will be the definitive edition; of which the manuscript version will have been the first draft or "copytext" and anything afterwards will be the standard, rather humdrum, little edition. Is this your view of the matter? I even believe that, among the book-lovers, several, who have the manuscript version, will, while waiting, take this, since it's stable and completed.

Yes, the Rops frontispiece, if it can be reproduced as it appeared originally and in a way that pleases its creator.

How big will the run be? Perhaps 100: and we'd keep a high price, about what figure, can you tell me, approximately? That's how I see the operation at present: but what's your exact opinion?

There would be, if you were hestitating over the engraving, the possibility of composing it typographically for instance, but brilliantly, and on some watermarked paper chosen expressly for this edition.

My title at the moment is

Vers
de
Stéphane Mallarmé[29]

with a lot of white left between the three lines. I think that's not bad.

As for *Pages* I see in *Jeune Belgique* the date of 20 April: oh! if it could remain so! I'm leaving, at the end of the month, or at the beginning of May, for the country, having taken leave for the summer as a result of nervous tension, and I'd take advantage of the last days to launch the book a little. Over to you.

147 EMILE VERHAEREN

[14] April 1891

I'm not sure it isn't the most extraordinary of the three, this book, *Les Flambeaux noirs.*[30] I've lived with it for several days, so that I could

---

29. Poems by Stéphane Mallarmé.

30. The third volume of Verhaeran's trilogy, of which the other two books were entitled *Les Soirs* and *Les Débâcles.*

really clarify something that has been obsessing me, a truly supreme obsession as far as reading is concerned, and which has now become my conscious and confessed mode of taking pleasure here: Poetry, which is admittedly borrowed from language, has acquired such new strength, corresponding to the fury of your instinct and something else, too, that as a result it becomes, I'm convinced as I recite you in my mind, a new element, unique and individual, naked and devouring its own words. And I'm starting to think that this is what has needed to be done, throughout the ages.—I'm very happy for you, for I am very fond of you—But we'd need to talk. . . .

148 JORIS-KARL HUYSMANS

18 April 1891

I'd cheated, and, for the first time, perhaps, used the newspaper rather than wait for you to send me a copy.[31] An unparalleled book, it seemed to me in fragmented form, and now I grant it that description yet again! for the richness of its insights, for its fury and for its art.

This blatant and dual[32] page of history confounds the reader: and how everything still leaps beyond the recounted facts toward the absolute assertion that God today transforms himself into a Devil and reigns, gold and garbage, thus.

And, how strange it is, how solitary and contemptuous![33] I don't believe, as far as the style is concerned, that I've ever read words as swift and devouring. Let's meet soon, to see each other and chat about it, dear friend.

149 EDMOND DEMAN

Friday 8 April [May] 1891

For two days now I've been turning over and over in my mind the situation[34] you've put me in, without seeing any way out. The box hasn't arrived, I'll need a fortnight (and I'll have to be in Paris) of visits etc. to launch, as I want to launch, my volume in the Press, and

31. The allusion is to *Là-bas,* which had appeared in serial form in the *Echo de Paris,* from February to April 1891, before appearing in book form in April.

32. A reference to the two plots, that of the medieval Gilles de Rais, and the study of contemporary satanism.

33. The word Mallarmé uses here is not in contemporary dictionaries: it may be a slip for "contemplative," but the idea of contempt accords better with the novel in question.

34. Deman's letter is missing. Presumably he warned Mallarmé that the copies would come in two deliveries and that the run would be reduced.

I can't stay that long. I have leave from my college to go to the country, I'm at the end of my strength and must not, both because of my health and because of the undertaking I've made to spend six weeks curing myself outside, remain a moment more here; I've already run into difficulties on this score.

Moreover, it's equally impossible for me not to give this ill-starred book to people who count, to whom I've offered my works hitherto: I can't gratuitously vex them like that.

The only possible solution is to put the book on sale in Paris only when I return at the end of June. Warn Bailly[35] by telegraph that he mustn't release a single copy, or he'll irrevocably harm its announcement in the Press, which must have first access to the book and wouldn't speak of it six weeks after its publication.

On my return at the end of June, I'll spend a month in Paris and will have all the time I need to take this in hand: between now and then, moreover, the second box, my own, will have had time to arrive and I won't be forced to give the volume to the papers while hiding from my friends or keeping silent about it at home, which would have to be my attitude today as a result of this inexplicable decision to send the books in two separate deliveries.

The whole business, momentariy compromised, will take place under better conditions. I needed 75 copies of the Poe[36] to do things properly; and with *sixty, which are essential to me* (I've spent the last two days calculating and I can't make a good job of it with less), I'll try to get it back on its feet, and advantageously so. You are not un-aware, given the literary rank that people have chosen to impose on me here, of how many obligations I have toward colleagues and others (who, rest assured, wouldn't have paid money for it) and you must know that I can't bring out a book here incognito.

The appearance of a work must not,—and this is the least one can say, setting aside other interests I'm pursuing through it,—alienate me from anyone. It's truly strange that this moment, which could be a source of some pleasure for me, should be one which holds nothing for me but vexation. But let's leave that, and I'll talk to you uniquely for the good of the book itself. Nevertheless, I'll devote myself to it, in full health, when I return; and with the satisfaction I'll have gained from knowing that you have taken a more accurate assessment of my position. You understand that I can't be made to suffer, absolutely, through the general reduction in the size of the run, about which I

35. Publisher and bookseller. Bailly played an important role in disseminating the Symbolist message.
36. For the Press reception of the translations of Poe's poems.

think it would have been elementary to speak to me if that were to modify our engagements or my projects; and above all as regards the reduction caused by the last-minute stupidity of that weird printer. I tell you that the book would suffer from it first.

I haven't said a word to anyone here about these slips, and I won't write to you about them any more (it hurts me) after your reply; and we'll continue, if you want, to chat, as one aesthete to another, of the book of poetry, once I myself am a little refreshed.

Your hand; I await your reply which I can have on Sunday, before I take the train, sometime during the day.

150   Geneviève Mallarmé

[22 July 1891]

It seems that it's you who drinks all the wine in the house, so your mother says; *I'm* still filling up the same three or even four bottles, but the level just won't go down. . . . But what makes me most aware of your flight is my lack of enthusiasm for walking: just imagine, I'm obliged to sing *La Marseillaise* to put one foot in front of the other when I go in search of fish or to post a letter. Don't be so inconsolable,[37] the great pantomime maneuvers will take place at dawn on Saturday, between Fontaine-le-Port and Chartrettes and, with the little carriage, at that hour,

You wouldn't even go as far as
Samois where there dwells the Cackas.

(I think that as the troops will be occupying both banks for a long distance, it would, moreover, be very hard to see.) Still, there is talk of a little ceremony here tomorrow morning, just a playful one, at the big farm. I'll escort there only my last glass of water from Montmirail. The house continues to be unbearable; each morning we tie Julia to the acacia tree to sew: and you can judge how hard I work. So, amuse yourself, just by being 100 leagues away. Yesterday, as your mother told you, it was forest and beard: she's not bad, despite the harvest ticks on top of everything else. I have the advantage of being able to ignore them. Lilith[38] has made herself a path through the muslin awning, and she travels through it like a circus rider. My love to your mother and sister of over there.

37. In her latest letter Geneviève had lamented the absence of soldiers in Honfleur, where she was staying on holiday.
38. The cat.

10 September 1891

I had visitors, yesterday and the day before, and was prevented from replying to you.

Obviously, the first typeface is far preferable to the second, which doesn't correspond in the slightest to my recommendations: or something the same as the first one, but one point[39] higher; the truth is, no doubt, that the printer doesn't have this and I regret it, for I find the page in the suggested point for this lettering elegant, I wouldn't want to say not sufficiently monumental, but not sufficiently definitive, do you see what I mean, dear friend?

Concerning the draft contract you've sent me, everything looks very good, apart from two or three details.

In 1. "Everything that has appeared in book form or in reviews," I'd add "except for little verses which have no value and for occasional verse." In a word, it will be the Dujardin edition, plus a few sonnets.[40]

2.—"at the print run, price and format he considers suitable." I want to be consulted about the format, which is that of *Pages,* but squarer, isn't that right? And as I've always been criticized for not producing a reasonably priced edition, let's make this one affordable, so that it doesn't cost more than one of the two prices you've indicated to me, that of 6 francs. That, moreover, corresponds to my author's rights, of 600 francs, and gives me the humble 10%, if my calculations are correct.

This, dear friend, is to allow this edition, which, after all, is a double one, to sell out in the normal time span. Otherwise I'd see myself immobilized forever. All the more so, moreover, in that I'm unable to commit future editions, above all at the same price. Think it over. That doesn't happen anywhere under any circumstances. I owe it to you, and this is the crux, not to "publish a new edition so long as that which is the object of the present agreement," as you put it so well, "has not been sold out." Paragraph 3 is implicit in what precedes.

4.—I'm eager, my dear Deman, to keep to the payment dates first submitted for your agreement; that is, for the 400 francs, I said the 20th of this month, though we could say the 25th, when I return to Paris; and as for the 200 francs, you can spread out the payment until December.

The first sum is really only of value to me if it comes before I leave the countryside. All these are mere quibbles.

39. Typographical term for measuring print size.
40. In fact, Deman's edition of the poems removed one from the Dujardin edition and added fifteen new sonnets.

As for the date by which Whistler will give us an etching, it can't be fixed. God, Himself, wouldn't commit Himself on such a score to anything more precise than a year. You know through his legend this delicious and capricious artist. When I set against your suggestion that we print the Rops[41] my desire to request from Whistler, who had just visited me, something he'd been promising me for ages, I was counting on him returning to France and to Valvins during the end of the summer season, and there were certain chances which have been reduced by his stay in England. Finally, he'll never admit that one of his etchings can be run off a thousand times, he'd want to see them one after the other etc., and I predict so complicated and special a future for the publisher that I think it would be prudent not to have the additional problem of including his name in the contract. We'll be lucky if we get it and if all goes well, that's all that can be said: if not, we'll fall back on the splendid Rops, the effect of which won't have been dulled by the Dujardin edition, since that's unknown to the public, and several people advise me to keep it, as it's a masterpiece in its own right and *my true frontispiece*. This needs a lot of thought: moreover, Rops doesn't oppose, as my dear companion Whistler furiously opposes, acieration and the processes that allow numerous copies to be made.

Finally, there's one last point, my dear Deman, which will be the subject of the sixth paragraph: it's the author's volumes (will they be numbered?). It's fully understood and set down in writing and we'll thus avoid all differences in viewpoint, even amicable ones, as happened with *Pages,* that I'm allowed 40, which isn't many out of 1,100; and you'll establish yourself how many you want for the Press and for yourself.

But all this is less important than the question of typeface: if you haven't anything better, or I mean more imposing than the first one, let's use it: I can only say this, it doesn't convince me.

152 HENRI MAZEL

28 September 1891

Everything that is sumptuous, and not just in terms of external richness but that secret richness which is part of the high Dream and Passion, as well as everything that is subtle and sinister like certain deep recesses of the soul, all this I recognize in your general and stable play *Le Nazaréen* in which the decor and the standpoint appear su-

41. Félicien Rops' etching had been the frontispiece to the photolithographed edition in 1887 and would eventually be chosen for the 1899 Deman edition.

perior to any story, even when they have been suggested by it: and that is truly what one means by pure poetic theater! Add that (miraculously) I don't even regret the absence of verse, which your speech merely dissimulates and holds latent or captive. Thank you, belatedly.

153   ALBERT MOCKEL
28 September 1891

I'm late, Mockel, but *Chantefable un peu naïve* has dwelt in my thoughts all this time; and I wanted to define the work for myself, through my enchantment, and that impression that it towers over everything in the contemporary experiment, as one of the aims achieved. Yes, you have reached that most wondrous point (what a delightful expression, in the note: "imaginary orchestra" and which the eyes have to read. I transpose it from the page of music to your verses, where for me it becomes perfectly obvious!) where the text, because of its original subtlety and its harmonious fusion, prepares for what one might call its own disappearance even while the reader continues to feel the delight it causes; and it fades away, always present, in a sort of silence which is true spirituality. Perhaps there is, yes, certainly, superiority over the use of the real means: brass, wood, etc., since this is the intellectual rarefaction; but free, inborn, general, and without any grotesque premeditation.[42]

I congratulate you absolutely, my dear friend.

154   ALFRED VALLETTE
28 September 1891

Would you be kind enough to convey to Minhar and keep for yourself as well the complete pleasure I had in reading *A l'écart*.[43] How clear and open it is and how you manage, almost incidentally, to touch on multiple and vast matters! and this book indicates exactly the split that is taking place between the Poem and the Novel, marking each with its original characteristics and restoring to the latter, while the other regains its own pure region, all the freedom of the French type of memoir.

On the contrary, one would say, Mme Rachilde[44] illuminates her

42. A frequent theme in Mallarmé's work, this comparison between music and poetry. The reference to "premeditation" is an attack on the "verbal instrumentation" of René Ghil.

43. Minhar and Vallette were co-authors of this novel.

44. Vallette's wife, writer of numerous plays and novels considered daring at the time.

Theater with psychical marvels, and makes up for the error that would exist in treating modernity in simple genre tableaux, in the place which is the domain of wonder. I am most interested in her unique attempt.

155 BERTHE MORISOT

29 September 1891

So I waited until the very eve of your return to give you a thought, no, you really don't believe that! but to write it to you. Simply because I watched the river flow by, that's the only reason, pleated by the occasional wind. And, perhaps because I'm used to vast mental gaps when I put a few sentences together, I feel I'm increasing the distance between myself and those whose thought is close to me: if I write to them. You wouldn't have come up with such a defeat! Yet, do believe that the castle[45] haunts me and I often bet with myself about whether or not you own it. It would suit you so well, there is a certain dark brown cloak I see hanging on the wainscotting of an old drawing room, or brushing along the dahlia avenues in the park. You must reply to me, just briefly, from Paris. This autumnal warmth, which is going to continue, will bring you back only at the end of the month; we ourselves are leaving tomorrow, with the regret that we're not leaving the desolation behind us. Still, there are the Thursdays to draw me back[46] and a few concerts of a Sunday. Otherwise, Paris seems vague to me. You've worked, I'd like to see. My hand in that of Manet; hello, my ward.[47]

156 HENRI DE RÉGNIER

[5 December 1891]

I've never felt, to the same extent as on rereading *Episodes, Sites et Sonnets,*[48]—these!—the enchantment of your art, which creates an independent midpoint, between the object, which you've renounceed, and the word (for it is not the words either, despite their presence and however brilliant they may be, which occupy the foreground): the

45. Berthe Morisot and her husband Eugène Manet were negotiating the purchase of a castle.
46. The day when the Manets gave dinners in Paris.
47. Julie Manet, who was placed under Mallarmé's protection in Berthe Morisot's will.
48. A new edition of this work had just been published.

ideal sense takes delight therein, separates them, too, and without affecting the reality of any decor, evokes a country of the sentiment, pure, which seems to me to be what one understands by Poetry.

Thank you for this pleasure; and I shake your hand, too, Régnier, for the attention given to my volume *Pages:*[49] to be seen and spoken of in such terms brings consolation for more than one secret dream which has met with disappointment, and that, despite the insight you bring, becomes true, for an instant, in the realm of the Mind, where we meet.

157   EMILE VERHAEREN

6 January 1892

A belated thank you, Verhaeren;[50] but I'm incapable of talking about poems like yours at the time when they continue to resonate so vibrantly within me, some with such fury and others through their calm, each one being the necessary integral stroke from which the entire poem seems, in its rapidity, to be suspended. Oh! no prolixity here, but a song almost free of all writing, where the word flashes like lightning. Your reverie is more moving than ever, and, even, unique. My hand for 1892, and our good wishes and hopes to see her, to Madame.

158   EDMOND DEMAN

1 March 1892

Relax, this isn't about *Vers.*[51] Despite my initial haste, I consider that in the long run you're right, perhaps it would be better to leave some time between the publication of this volume and the last one. But once we begin, things will move swiftly, won't they?

On an entirely different subject, I'm tired of writing to this M. de Nocée, who's done some disgusting things to me, such as sell five hundred of me to Vanier, with the name of that bookseller printed on his booklet; he reduced the number of white spaces, there are printing errors; in a word everything I find most disobliging.

He's been able to move 14,000 copies despite all that, simply be-

49. Régnier had published a review of *Pages* in *La Wallonie,* in the number for September-October 1891.
50. For his collection *Les Apparus dans mes chemins,* which had been published in 1891.
51. Discussions about the typeface for this volume were still continuing.

183

cause, as I'm always being told, the need is felt on all sides for something by me which is inexpensive (without necessarily being at 20 centimes a copy). I want to cut the ground from under his feet. Listen to the project I've worked out. Desboutin has kindly proposed to do my portrait in drypoint (which can be done on steel): I'd like to use that for a publication and notably for a spruce little booklet, containing under the same title everything that's in the Belgian Anthology with a few extra trifles. The idea of gathering together a few samples of my work was, or at least proved to be, excellent. I imagine that with the portrait, at ten centimes, and the same again for my royalties, we could make quite a decent profit by selling it at 75 centimes. With the help of the portrait, which would give it an air of completeness and of being a de luxe edition; it would be exclusive to that publication—that, together with the possibility of having a little collection of my writings, would quickly make it become fashionable, there's no doubt about that. I'm mentioning it to you before anyone else, which is only right and proper; we'd need, for instance, an active Parisian agent: think about it and discuss it with me.[52]

People around me aren't in the pink of health, myself included, except for my daughter: have you and your wife come through the winter well? And will you end by coming to Paris conspicuously and together? Your hand.

159   PIERRE LOUŸS

Friday 18 March 1892

Louÿs, I cannot remember anything which has touched me so much; and this sonnet,[53] which is not only beautiful but mysterious and triumphal, possesses even this aspect of the work of art, in which everything must appear miraculous, its unexpectedness: how were you able to think in such a way of such a date. . . . It gives me heart because my golden wedding anniversary with the Muse seems to announce itself through a breakdown of my health; say rather it gives me back my faith. I've staked my life on something, as a hermit; and you show me that it interests people; I can't lose! Touched, I thank you, my dear friend.

52. Deman did not accept this project, so Mallarmé offered it to Perrin, who published the anthology entitled *Vers et Prose* in November 1892.

53. To celebrate Mallarmé's fiftieth birthday, which fell on 18 March 1892, Louÿs had sent him a sonnet.

Tuesday 5 April 1892

What glorious weather, but I'm enjoying it above all with the thought that it may bring you back; you'll become a Parisian again for the month of the Salon[54] and we must see a little of each other, isn't that so, Madame Mirbeau? We'll try to have a few chats together which will make you miss a little less the flowers and the month of May at home. It's nearly a year now since I was your guest, a silent year. What was the point of writing, from the depths of the terrible moroseness of my hours; and then I was ill, almost all winter, to the point of growing worried, since to some extent I've staked my life on my last few days. Not to mention that I haven't even a minute to interrupt myself. But you, dear friend, I heard that you fell victim, you and your wife, to the illness which drags on and fills one with boredom and many a time I've pitied Damps.[55] I don't think many days go by, my dear Mirbeau, without your name coming up in discussions with Geffroy or Monet and others I meet (a sheet of writing paper wasn't to hand when I read your article on Pissaro or I'd have saluted a few astonishing sentences which I sang to myself in my solitude). Just now I discussed you with Whistler and we spoke of seeing you again, and goodness me, since the day had been broken into I said: "I'll write." Writing is an empty gesture, since what matters is less our talking here than something suddenly passing in our glance when your name or mine appears. I've given all letters up: for those we care about we write only through ourselves. I'm back at work, sometimes quite sucessfully: if I'm lucky enough when I finish to make people forget the earlier schoolboy's pieces that appeared under my name, I'll leave the impression of a Gentleman like all the others, astonished to find himself reflected, for example, in a spring.

—You and I, Roujon said to me, and this must remain secret for the moment, will have to think about a monument, which we'll get from the State, in memory of Villiers.[56] I'm longing to see your bust done by Rodin, which must be a marvel. Renoir is to do my portrait. On the subject of works of art, this will make you smile; one of my female neighbors, an old friend of Manet and mine too, Madame Méry Laurent, who knows I know you, asks me to see that in your account of the Salon of the Champ-de-Mars, her portrait, done by

54. The art salon opened that year on 6 May in the Palais des Beaux-Arts.
55. The Mirbeaus lived in Damps.
56. The project remained unrealized.

Gervex (and indeed Whistler has just told me that it's really good) as well as that of Doctor Evans, are not particularly badly treated among the works of this painter, dear friend: it seems that it's a question of great interest to the ladies. As for me, where exhibitions are concerned, I now look only at the Monet placed on the wall there, it delights me and that's enough. How beautiful the poplars were![57] And now he's in front of a cathedral;[58] the man is definitely a genius. Your hand, dear friend, let's say that all I've done here is shake it, and, with yours, that of the most gracious of hostesses.

161 ANDRÉ GIDE

17 May [1892]

Very rare, my friend, this poetic anthology of André Walter.[59] The impression it gives me is very much of a harpsichord, shrill but always in tune; and that double hand, sometimes identical, sometimes like dreaming twins, that relives memories here, is especially charming in its perpetuated duo: so sharp, so familiar.

I must also thank you for giving me such pleasure by sending me this fine first copy, for which I send you a handshake.

162 GEORGES RODENBACH

28 June [1892]

Dear friend, I must nevertheless tell you, better than I could in a meeting or through a handshake, how much I consider *Bruges la Morte* as a work of art. The silences and the deadly transparency of Shadow of that unique city, you, and this is indisputable, are the one who can summon up such charms. I value in this book the poem, which in itself is infinite, but which is literally one of the most wonderfully prolonged of prose poems.

Your human history, at times so erudite, evaporates; and the city, in the form of a vast phantom, continues, or recovers consciousness through the characters, and all that's done with a subtle certainty which instils a very pure effect. All the modern experiments in reading seek to make the poem end as a novel, and the novel as a poem, but there's no doubt the writer is hampered by too many separate items if his juxtaposition is less exact than yours is here: and if he

57. In 1892 Monet had given an exhibition of paintings of poplars.
58. Monet was beginning the famous series of paintings of the cathedral at Rouen.
59. Gide's book, *Les Poésies d'André Walter*, was published in 1892.

lacks your magic. You have a great success and it's growing; and, outside your verses, where I love you for the art you reveal, and the mastery, Bruges will no longer play the slightest role in your success. That's what delights me; your hand, dear friend, affectionately.

163   PIERRE LOUŸS

[15] July [1892]

You can well imagine that I know *Astarté* by heart. There's rarely been so clear-cut a debut, or one which better summed up what had been done and what was still floating, creating a personal fusion. Indeed, you don't omit the art of the past, which is yesterday, and the purity of its sounds; but you also meander deliciously under the changing sail of today. Or, to speak like a cabdriver, in you a very subtle and unexpected Parnassian converges, with (shall I say it?) the decadent; and all that makes a Poet—precise, fleeting, jewel-like and musical, all that I love, and playing directly on a soul composed of the rarefied reflection of everything. Your book enchants me. Thank you.

164   LÉON DESCHAMPS

26 July 1892

How can I tell you how grateful I am, and how proud, to have been chosen by you together with various others, in the name of *La Plume,* to preside over the Committee set up to create a homage to Baudelaire, the gift of an effigy for his tomb.

I know of no cult equal to that of this extraordinary and pure genius. Were you to have conferred this post of honor on one of those already well known or on any other, none among us could have complained, so greatly does the exclusive enthusiasm to support you predominate and, if there are glorious older men such as Goncourt or Zola, they admit that when a poet is concerned the direction should fall to a writer in verse: but, precisely, in the domain of poetry, one name stands above all others for this position as president, that of Leconte de Lisle, admired and revered by all of us and as for me, whatever fervor I devote to recent art, I feel we should remain as we were when we were twenty. It would be peremptory to add that this master of French poetry was the personal friend of Baudelaire and brings living memories of him. It is with all my heart that I offer to assist him in interpreting the wishes of all.

Having indicated this, I applaud every detail of your project, consider everything sensible and perfect, above all the thought of turning to the master sculptor Rodin.[60]

Thank you. I remain deeply touched.

165   EMILE ZOLA

27 July 1892

Thank you. I reopened, after reading it, *La Débâcle:* but in order to study it, since a single reading enables one to seize the overall impression.

So I admire, through the vastness and wildness of this indefatigable and very human book, the beautiful transparency of your art, which never belies itself: I wouldn't change a page, lacerated as they are, and the words, I'd say, placed, finally, with the same sense, in the same degree and in the same vibration. What sureness of touch!

You can imagine that it's not an appreciation I'm sending you here but a firm, admiring handshake; and my eternal thanks.

I'll add that I'd have liked to have seen you again at the cemetery on Saturday to tell you how moved I was by your complete, and cordial, and lofty speech.[61]

166   JAMES MCNEILL WHISTLER

[Sunday 7 August 1892]

Honfleur is a marvellous place, I've never seen so much greenery, combined with water which, although it's not the open sea, is still enchanting: the little old Normandy port, etchings. Whistler isn't here, he's bathing his eyes in the lawn of the rue du Bac at this very hour, on the Sunday when I write to him. We're staying another week. If the terrible architect Madame hasn't leveled the entire little house with her finger, to rebuild it in a style even more strictly Empire, I expect to see some pretty improvements when I return through Paris. Mourey, in writing to give me some information, gave me news of the divine Whistler, a timorous epithet; I'll have to look for a better one.

Your hand, dear friend; I miss you after a week. Madame Whistler, there are such wonderfully perfumed roses at the Honfleur market, that I regret your absence; and everywhere there are blue China plates.

Farewell, here's the card of the neighboring farm where I look for

60. In the end it was not Rodin who made the statue but José de Charmoy.
61. Zola had given this speech at the funeral of the novelist Léon Cladel.

you as I pass by. If my wife were not ill, we'd be truly happy here. Your hands.

167   LÉON DESCHAMPS

[13 December 1892]

There's been a great impediment to my desire, as you can imagine from the fact that I'm writing to you rather than being there:[62] but we've already discussed this in detail and my opinion remains unchanged that the place for the monument to Baudelaire should, like that of Banville, be the Luxembourg gardens [in the margin Mallarmé adds: "a medallion would perhaps be suitable for the cemetery."]. As for the monument itself, a bust mounted on a stele, I think the entire arrangement should be left to the genius of Rodin. You are not unaware, and I've told you unofficially, that at the right moment the steps we've taken with the Fine Arts for the remainder of our work will meet with a benevolent response. As for the volume entitled *The Tomb of Charles Baudelaire* no one will do a better job than you: I imagine that it would be right to increase the invitations to some extent as well as to use a more imposing format than the one you usually choose for the exquisite publications of *La Plume*. A reproduction of the monument, for instance in the form of an etching, would be a fine ornament for the collection; the price of which, however, would not be excessive.

This is what I would have said, and I repeat my regrets, begging you to convey them to those of the Committee who are present.

168   EDMUND GOSSE

Tuesday 10 January 1893

I regret the need to interrupt my reading which I've no more than begun but with what a sense of charm!, of your *Secret of Narcisse,* to thank you for something else: these are exquisite pages where the evocation, free of all excess, is directed entirely by a subtle and fluid sentiment, so delicately expressed! But the article: thanks first of all for its sublime position and for your signature;[63] it's a miracle of divination for, through my own fault, you had so few documents. Poets alone have the right to speak; because they know in advance. There's one sentence in particular where you draw aside all the veils and re-

62. No doubt at the meeting of the committee for Baudelaire's monument.

63. Edmund Gosse had devoted an article to Mallarmé's collection *Vers et Prose* and to his *Villiers de l'Isle-Adam.* This article appeared on the front page of the review *The Academy,* 7 January 1893.

veal the thing with diamond-bright clairvoyance, this is the one I mean: "His aim ... is to use words in such harmonious combination as will suggest to the reader a mood or a condition *which is not mentioned in the text,* but is nevertheless paramount in the poet's mind at the moment of composition." That sums it all up. I create Music and give that name not to the music one can extract by the euphonious juxtaposition of words, this primary condition is self-evident; but the beyond, which is magically produced by certain dispositions of the word; where the word, moreover, is merely a means of material communication with the reader, like the notes of the piano. Truly, between the lines and above the glance, that communication is achieved in all purity, without the intervention of the catgut strings and the pistons of an orchestra, which is already industrial. Yet it's the same thing as an orchestra, but as in literature, meaning silently. Poets throughout the ages have never done anything else, the only thing is that today it's amusing to be aware of it. Use Music in the Greek sense, meaning, basically, Idea or the rhythm between connections; in that case it's more divine than in the public or symphonic expression. This is very poorly expressed, in chatting, but you seize my meaning, or rather you have seized it throughout that fine study which you must keep as it is, intact. The only quibble I have to make is on obscurity; no, my dear poet, except through awkwardness or clumsiness, I'm not obscure, from the moment the reader seeks in my poetry what I enunciate above, or the manifestation of an art which uses—let's say incidentally, I know the profound reason for this—language; and of course I become obscure if the reader makes the mistake of thinking he's opening a newspaper! The other day I found the attached study, by a very solid and astute critic who insists, rightly in my view, but laugh as I shake your hand, on my clarity.[64]

169 JOSÉ-MARIA DE HEREDIA

23 February 1893

The *Trophées* gave me one of my great joys as a poet. Each sonnet was already known to me for its beauty, although there were still some delightful acquaintances to make; but what an effect is created by the ensemble! In addition to the blossoming of your verses, which is total!, this collection is a splendid proof of the unity of the form you've adopted, the sonnet; you've taken it out of the category of knick-knacks to make of it the definitive expression, plenary and supreme,

64. R. Lhombreaud (*Revue de littérature comparée,* 1951, n. 3) suggests that the reference is to an article by Adolphe Rette, published in January 1893, admiring Mallarmé's "wonderful clarity of expression."

of poetry. With its contraction, it binds together under the same glance those very rare magic moments which in the finest poems remain merely disparate. Truly this is the only thing we should be concerned with, and here it is indisputably present. What sureness in the aim, did you even count on success to this degree! This is the modern means of presenting poetry, which has been so much misused. Open the book at any page at all and the two masterpieces thus revealed reverberate together in a multiple and glorious echo giving the monumental impression of a whole, before and after.

Your work, as something eternal, comes therefore at a particularly favorable moment; and as all that delights me, my old friend, I shake your hand, warmly.

170 CHARLES BONNIER

March 1893

I've just been ill for an entire month and I'm someone who never writes letters, feeling either hostile or vague when faced with a sheet of paper. Nevertheless, I want to send a word in reply to your curious and numerous questions. . . . The poetic fact itself consists in grouping, rapidly, in a certain number of equal strokes, in order to bring them into focus, certain thoughts which otherwise would be distant and scattered; but, and this is obvious, they rhyme together, so to speak. Therefore, it is necessary first and foremost to employ the common measure, which must be applied: I mean Verse. The poem remains short and multiplies to form a book; its fixed pattern creates a norm, as does the line. Such at least is how I see it. Now, as for that kind of notation which emotion determines, I savor it absolutely, but as a form of prose, in a delicate, unadorned filigree. The poetic exploitation of the common measure is either lacking or does not come into the picture.—You are one of those who have most succeeded in this type of writing, through your extreme subtlety, and it gives me pleasure to tell you so and to have reread you.

171 EMILE VERHAEREN

14 May [1893]

I find—not belatedly, no, believe in my immediate enchantment, but to reply!—this book admirable:[65] and it's by you, too; and it's Verhaeren who speaks, not merely the verse itself! You have now reached the point, in the life of an artist, that is the perfect life, where

---

65. The book in question is Verhaeren's *Les Campagnes hallucinées*.

what he does and what he is are as one; no more magnificent efforts in one direction or the other, everything is established and comfortable. After so many studies which bordered on the prodigious, your work now becomes your way of being, quite ingenuously: other than being literature. This is what I see as an intimate handshake, this reading of your collection of *Campagnes hallucinées;* but if only we could discuss it in detail, closely!

P.s. My thanks, with equally warm congratulations, to the editor and friend:[66] it's presented exquisitely.

172 ANDRÉ GIDE

June [1893]

With *Le Voyage d'Urien* you have made something which stands alone and which will remain, with Poe and a few others, one of the books I read. I don't know anyone who has begun with such, shall we say, naturalness following a taut and pure thread of fiction; and yours leads to the totality of the Dream! And so plausibly! to use a big word; or rather thanks to the transparent flow of thought which never abdicates and which seeks the collapse of too many marvellous things grouped together for the credulous touch, merely for the pleasure of rebuilding. Well, the supreme satisfaction lies in one's being aware of the magic. A certain group of words which have appeared with no pomp and ceremony haunt one and count among the most beautiful ever to have been written. It was your duty to do this, Gide the pensive and musical one; nothing surprises me, except, perhaps, the nimbleness and exactness of the analogies, which I hadn't guessed anyone was capable of.

Believe me happy; and how I'm touched by a certain number one,[67] authentic as a gauge of admiration! Thank M. Denis; his decoration, with its strange suaveness, is masterly and ingenuous!

Your hand, may we meet again soon; what a pity about the abortive Sunday visit.

173 JULES BOISSIÈRE

Tuesday 25 July 1893

A kind, sea-blue arrow which today passed through our home to set out again (I'm talking about the letter to my daughter who is

66. The reference is to Deman.
67. Gide had sent Mallarmé the first of the specially numbered volumes of this edition.

192

spending a few days at Honfleur and which bears the writing of Mme Boissière) awakened a sense of remorse in me. You can guess the cause: that of not having given you any sign of life. This reminder, together with my impending departure for Valvins which will, I fear, bring with it a few days of airy laziness, is what I need to make me take, for the thousandth time, a sheet of paper destined for you. I'm reduced to the writer who mechanically replies to those who have sent books; when they pile up to scandalous proportions. Never a letter letter. It's not that I'm working, or at least publishing. The miserable college which devours my time more than ever, has held sway this year for the last time. I'm counting on not returning, on retiring and making my real debut in literature. In the meantime here is a little volume, *Vathek*, to which I believe you possess the preface. The tale is worth reading so you'll allow me to offer it to your wife. I'm late with Jean Robert,[68] having greatly enjoyed his two *Souvenirs d'un fumeur d'Opium*. What beautiful sentences it contains, in a superior rhythm, as ceremonial as dream and greenery; and with immediate leaps of life, with no dissonance! And always in this book there watches and persists a sense of humanity, as if faced with danger. You must therefore continue to rarefy yourself, but in a virile way, my dear Boissière.—Farewell, this note is very brief and even derisory, when it ought to be saying everything. Take from it only our handshake from my wife and me (my wife is in gentle health), with all that we include of affection and longing for the two of you.

On 6 January 1894 Mallarmé officially retired from teaching. In February he went to England, where he gave his famous lectures on music and literature in Oxford and Cambridge.

174   EDMUND GOSSE

Saturday [24 February 1894]

I'm lecturing next week, Wednesday at Oxford and Friday at Cambridge and in the meantime will rest at a friend's[69] place in a spot I know as yet only under the name of *Sussex Bell*. I've been suffering from an affliction of the eyes caused by my cruel insomnia and am overburdened with work at the last minute; were it not for which I

68. The pseudonym Boissière adopted in writing his reminiscences of an opium smoker.
69. Charles Whibley.

would have written to thank you for the excellent information and to say I understand that the case of Verlaine was very different etc.[70] I'll skip London, more or less, on my return from my lectures because of a very pressing engagement which recalls me to Paris; but I'll take the time to shake your hand, to see you again, if only in haste and in the impossibility of accepting your kind invitation, as I don't have a Sunday free.

Please convey my regrets to Madame Gosse.

175   MARIE AND GENEVIÈVE MALLARMÉ

Wednesday [28 February 1894]

Your letter gave me a double pleasure, little cat, in half-opening to me each door of the apartment, and because you write so prettily, o singer, with a little song running under the words. You'll permit this sense of pride in your old literary daddy.

My letter, if I work it out, will arrive tomorrow evening just as you're imagining an echo of my lecture and will interrupt you, poor little ones. It doesn't take place until Thursday, during the day at one o'clock, and I won't be wearing evening dress. Today, for the English one, I'll have to: I'll participate as a mere listener, for the perfect, charming, and splendid M. Powell spent the night translating it. I remain astonished at this for I took more time to write it and am distressed for him at the work needed, but he does it happily and in a masterful way. He'll read it, first, in his language; which is almost mine, truly, for I interrupt him in our conversations in French, to continue in a different way, which has become, yes, easier for me, having improved in this since my time with Whibley.

Oxford is a marvel; twenty cloisters, or more, exquisitely medieval in the midst of parks and water; there's even a town and people, but one forgets them. Under my window there are meadows with cows, deer, and age-old trees, with lacey towers revealed by the lack of leaves. I visited a lot of that yesterday, in sunshine; dined in the refectory which is as beautiful as a cathedral, with a high gas pipe on wood panelling on which hang portraits of famous men who were formerly pupils here—I'm sending you the menu, stolen from the table of honor, to amuse you. Then, an hour spent in the drawing room, where the dons take various wines, having taken off the gowns in which they

70. Mallarmé had asked Gosse to arrange a lecture room in London, as had happened for Verlaine, but Gosse replied that since Verlaine had already lectured in London, and was known there, an audience could be assured, which was not the case for Mallarmé.

dine, and that bizarre headgear, midway between a schapska and a blotter. Finished the evening at the home of the excellent Bonnier. He came to meet me yesterday, together with M. Powell, at the station.

Everything would be perfect if I could sleep: nothing, not a wink. In addition, and it's the one inconvenience, the only things to appear regularly are those I can't drink, such as tea or white wine and I must dip my lips in them, little mother, through politeness. As for the liqueurs, I say firmly: No. I lap up water, in secret, but it doesn't put things right. Beer is nowhere to be seen, I'll drink some on the boat when I leave.

The trunk is intact and I'm using it as a cupboard admirably packed by your dear hands. Farewell, lots of kisses, my dears; oh! you do miss me a little, don't you? And Lilith misses me too.

176 MARIE AND GENEVIÈVE MALLARMÉ

London [1 March 1894]

At last I'm able to write to you, my children! I left Oxford. The excellent Mr. Powell treated me maternally throughout. Yesterday evening there was a great dinner in my honor. Apart from the champagne, sherry, and all the other things that are so terrible for me, or water, it was perfect. I've just dined at Payne's and drank my first beer, with a sense of joy. He wasn't able to put me up in his little lodgings which are a long way off. I'm not displeased to be, at long last, on my own, for a moment; and feel almost at home in a hotel.

Then tomorrow morning it all begins again.

The lecture, good God, if I'd only known! Two teachers, or perhaps three, a few pupils; all the rest were ladies: I'm not complaining, they behaved perfectly well, with the correct, lengthy applause offered a little mechanically at the end. But it's my fault I gave them a pretty stiff piece of aesthetics when I could have chattered almost without preparation; I hadn't eaten, it was in the middle of the day and I was merely in a frock coat. I'd already suspected that, the afternoon of the preceding day, when Mr. Powell read my lecture in English. It strikes me as odd to have come so far and taken such trouble merely to entertain sixty people, who were either of the teaching profession or looking for a chance to hear French spoken!

We'll see if things are any different at Cambridge; perhaps they will be, since an audience which has had to pay wants something for its money.

Little mother, you'll receive at the beginning of next week, in your name, the money Mr. Powell is sending you; I wonder if that's wise! The hour of the cake is approaching, or rather, I can't see myself buying it before Monday, the day I'll spend in London on my own behalf. If you're writing for Sunday (there's no point) or Monday morning, address your letters to the Charing Cross Hotel.

Kitten, your information about *Axel*[71] was so good that I hardly needed the papers: did you, however, get the *Figaro?* If so, send it. Still, it's not a work that should have been performed. Madame Laurent has written to me and I think it was Eva that she was staring at so much through her lorgnon. The weather here is awful. Farewell, my dears, I won't reread this, will I, for I'm falling asleep. Am I going to have my first sleep?

177   MARIE AND GENEVIÈVE MALLARMÉ
Cambridge [3 March 1894]
While the water comes to the boil, for my wash. Good morning, ladies; this morning kiss.

I came to Cambridge in a rather glum mood because I felt all too well despite Whibley's kindness that there'd be very little in it as regards money. Twenty places, at 5 shillings, 125 francs for the English banknote. Honor has been upheld, but that's all. I neither lose nor win anything: and as it's fine, for a few days, it seems to me it will be better to see Cambridge too, which is another marvel.

The tickets were simply put on sale through the town's bookseller, who didn't want to take anything, as was also the case for the printer of the announcement which I'll send you: isn't it a fine piece of work! I was competing with a touring group at the theater.

But, let's come to the lecture. If ever I missed you, my poor absent ones, it was yesterday evening. No lecture has ever given me and never will give me such an emotion of uniqueness and beauty: such things do not come twice. Those twenty people, of whom two were ladies, were an absolute élite, and I can't say they were friendly without adding that they were discreet. To be listened to religiously, to feel between each word I uttered a sense of sympathy and intelligence. It has to be said that the setting was exquisite: a superb wood-panelled room, with beautiful furniture, in Pembroke College, nine in the evening, with the audience in shadow, one or two tables, at the back with a few candles. And in front of this, enthroned and framed, Father himself, alone in the light cast by two high silver candelabras. The

71. Geneviève had described the performance of 27 February 1894.

applause on my entry and when I left had nothing banal about it and revealed perfect tact. The lover of rarities in me was seduced. There you are, my little ones. This evening I return to London, spend the Sunday with the Paynes, do a few errands or at last! stroll around on the Monday. Afterwards I'll tell you when I arrive. How are you? I don't hear too much of you here; there must be a letter missing. Many kisses. And you Lilith, how are you?

178   MARIE AND GENEVIÈVE MALLARMÉ

[3 March 1894]

The cake is approaching.[72] With me. The address was considered so surprising, sagacious, and elaborate that at Pembroke College they asked if they could keep the envelope.[73] Write to me for Monday or Tuesday morning, not at Charing Cross Hotel, where I'll drop in just to see, but at 93 Jermyn St. London W.

Kisses.

179   W. M. ADEY AND R. B. ROSS

9 April 1894

My dear colleagues, I accept your magnificent present[74] and, given my long-standing cult for Maturin, consider it precious not least for your spontaneous and charming attention. I'm placing this *Melmoth* in my library beside *Bertram* and will not be long in taking them up again and renewing acquaintance with this extraordinary man who is nowadays too often forgotten.

180   RAYMOND BOUYER

April 1894

I've just finished reading *Le Paysage dans l'art*:[75] thank you for this reading or rather for this delicious, inner conversation, of the sort one would love to have and which envisages so many mysteries and explores them page by page, always charmingly, and rationally when

72. Mallarmé is replying to a letter from Geneviève where she conveys her mother's plea for Mallarmé not to send the cake but to bring it.

73. This envelope has not been found.

74. A copy of Maturin's gothic novel, *Melmoth the Wanderer*, of which Adey and Ross were the co-editors.

75. An exploration of art and poetry, comparing descriptions of the countryside in literary works and the depiction of landscape in art.

reason is called for; that's all one needs to do and nothing goes further. What exquisite words you use, both as art-critic and as passionate enthusiast, combining the two attitudes in a perfect whole, for whoever is able to feel, throughout your writing, your veracity!

181   Méry Laurent

Monday [13 August 1894]

Quick, a kiss for your feast day, free of all chatter so that you can receive it better and on its own. Do you know that August 15[76] is one of my fundamental dates; and that were I even further away I'd still think of it, you good, dear, and great person, joined to some extent to my existence, you know what I mean. So you feel completely well, let's hope you continue to do so! I don't even hold it against the sun for not shining here in order to shine resplendently where you are; indeed, it's only doing its duty.

My poor friend Fénéon[77] (no he has a very interesting physiognomy) has been acquitted and this gives me happiness. The fruit has not yet arrived or been eaten. The ham reigns supreme and Geneviève considers we put it in its trousers (the bag) too soon after the meal.

How many [drawing of seagulls] are there here?

Your S. M.

181   Charles Morice

Wednesday [5 September 1894]

I was going, through this little card, to shake your hand, for a cutting from *Le Soir,*[78] to be exact, where your old faithfulness shines out. I'll do so first of all.

As for the subject of your letter,[79] here's how things stand. Huret, who went almost directly from Morocco to the Tyrol, wrote to me from Innsbruck saying he'd ask Magnard to do the Interviews in the *Figaro* as soon as he got back or at the beginning of September; this was agreed between us before the article. Too much time has gone

76. The day on which the assumption of the Virgin Mary is celebrated.

77. Fénéon had been arrested on 27 April 1894, charged with being a member of an association of criminals, and with planting a bomb at the Foyot restaurant on 4 April 1894.

78. An article in the number for 31 August 1894 contains a highly complimentary review of Mallarmé's work by Morice.

79. Morice was planning a response to Mallarmé's proposal in the *Figaro* of 17 August 1894 concerning art. He had written to ask Mallarmé's advice.

past. I doubt that Magnard would be willing to take things in hand again. It's a matter of some importance since it's this that alone will bring in the aid for Literature (not to mention that literature has every right to it) so we must push this project and I count on taking it in hand, presenting it to the minister etc. after everyone returns from holiday. You can guess, Morice, how valuable your collaboration is to me. Perhaps you could sound out Magnard on his intentions concerning a repeat in the *Figaro,* I have my doubts, and if he does reply in the negative, I'll be my own master and won't appear to finish in another journal, thereby undervaluing a hospitality which was perfect and it would be possible for me to sum up, through a letter, in *Le Soir,* all your interviews—for it must be interviews, Morice, you wouldn't get enough replies through letters: above all from the editors.

I don't really have anything to add to the *Figaro* column, apart from one point, that I was wrong to omit although I knew I was doing it, but I wanted to take it up again later on. It concerns the estimate of the tax. There must be a certain percent of tax on the highest and lowest sales prices, but it must be tiny so that it's an insignificant sum to pay, for the editor, in the case of a publication which is really inexpensive. The great reason against it which has until now been adduced has been that the authors would sell less if the public had to pay more. Similarly, when a deluxe edition goes over the usual bookshop price because of engravings or for any other reason unconnected with the text, it would be possible to charge tax only on a standard maximum price, which would have to be fixed. No other case, and I didn't even want to single out these ones, but they lead to equivocal replies. I have here an entire dossier which is very interesting, opinions in Paris and abroad, which I'd put at your disposal with a chat, if you were to lunch with me as soon as possible. There is a direct train from Paris at 9.35. I'd be pleased, Morice, from all points of view.

182   FÉLICIEN ROPS

7 September 1894

Wherever you are, an affectionate handshake and this note on Deman's instigation. I'm taking it on myself to ask you to be kind enough to authorize him to reproduce, at the head of a printed edition he's going to make of the first book of my poems, your masterpiece which opens Dujardin's photoengraved edition. This frontispiece, one of your pure works and a constant source of admiration for me is, in my opinion, inseparable from the humble text it decorates or, at least, confers on it such honor! Your silence can be taken as agreement; this will avoid forcing you to write a letter which is always a minor form of torture. Except in this case which gives me the pleasure of describing myself as your Stéphane Mallarmé.

183   EDOUARD GRAVOLLET

Sunday 7 October 1894

Thank you for your kind regards, dear Gravollet; but I was hoping for better things at the beginning of this autumn, in other words, that you would be coming. Madame Mallarmé's health is returning, certainly, but slowly.

We'll be returning, but when? The time is coming when I'd love to remain, or better still would choose to arrive, for that's the only time when the countryside is intimate and nature corresponds to a few dreams I cannot abandon.[80]

The ladies think otherwise and I detect from the cunning revealed in various indications, such as the scented waters being allowed to run dry in their flasks without being renewed, the discreet suggestion of a departure. In consolation I have affectionate friendships, such as yours, which prepare their welcome and are certainly worth the most glowing and crimson leaves here.

I've been working, mainly on myself, having reached an age where surface repairs are necessary at each season; and I can see my year ahead. Your hand, then that of B. . . .[81] A smiling homage to your wife.

184   MÉRY LAURENT

Saturday [13 October 1894]

Good day, little peacock. M. Mallarmé has reestablished himself in his little study overlooking the river, as if nothing had happened, and yet everything happened, since he saw you and even had a very good view of you. He carries with him your delicious presence, which will long remain with him; but, fear not, he won't make this an excuse to spend an eternity at Valvins. Paris, you see, means you and music; and what's more, since the concerts haven't yet begun again, it means you alone. Méry, you are the dearest and most beautiful of friends.

I didn't miss the fatal 5 o'clock train and I gave pleasure with the little gifts of food I took back, including the oysters, the excellent indication of which I owe to you. Our invalid[82] is somewhat better

80. Autumn had a deep significance for Mallarmé.
81. Edmond Bonniot.
82. Marie Mallarmé had just recovered from a worrying illness.

but will recover slowly, since the alert was intense and yesterday, having received visits from neighbors, she lost some of her strength. What lovely weather! It extends as well to the little Talus,[83] which I cherish, as I do, moreover, the rue de Rome. I kiss you as an old friend (the old means me!!) and tenderly.

185 FRANCIS VIELÉ-GRIFFIN

4 November [1894]

Thank you for [*in Greek letters:* Págai],[84] dear friend, it gave me joy; not only to see you reimmersed in the days of ancient Greece, but also because the source, above all, of so much serene condescension toward those high harmonies which are fate can be seen in you yourself.

And yet, with a perfect sense of decor, you bear fate's tribute to the ancient altar. What a delicate and firm extension to the possible keyboard, in suspense and far off, is offered by each of those delicate and very proud dramas, in which the opulent silence between the words nourishes the spirit in all purity. I like that very much, Griffin, and you.

186 LUCIEN DESCAVES

December [1894]

How did you manage to write that book,[85] one of the strangest that exist and one which almost abolishes the reader's sight in order to give him supernatural senses: unless, perhaps, your despotic and prodigious instinct for every analogy, which, if it is to explode, demands that the eyes be closed or burns them first, indicated this poem to you as the cave in which it could blaze forth in all its wonder, feeling its way to illuminating the most secret and forbidden recesses. Always, both through the subject and the details, you place your finger on something which is literally fatal and mysterious. What is admirable, too, is that even for someone not looking at the book from this very rare starting point, this is still a perfect novel, special and comprehensive, written with mastery. The exactness of your language on every line proclaims a miracle! Many thanks, therefore, for real pleasures.

---

83. The house where Méry was staying.
84. This work consists of three poems in the form of dialogues with the Greek poet Pindar.
85. *Les Emmurés,* published in 1894, described the inner life of the blind.

187   CHARLES GUÉRIN

[24] December [1894]

Forgive me for replying so late,[86] but the crush at the end of the year! Everything, I'd like to grant you everything, if only because we're at the time of year when people exchange gifts, and especially the unimportant gift you suggest to me. . . . But your letter touches on a special point, and one which is a sore spot for me. I detest *Prefaces* even when they're written by the author, and I find them all the more out of place when they're added by someone else. My dear, a real book has no need of an introduction, it works by arousing love at first sight, as a woman does in her lover, without the assistance of a third party, the husband. Less figuratively, I think it shows a lack of bravery not to act like that, or a lack of gallantry, and it strikes me as old-fashioned, let's say provincial; and I'm seized with distrust. All this to explain my thoughts to you clearly: something that could be done, that is in the case of your not wanting to appear alone, but you are surely in a position to do so, is that I could read the proofs of your book and send you a friendly and almost irrelevant note which you could publish in deference or homage,[87] it's discreet but I wonder whether it's even worth the trouble! I'm answering you as I always have and to very dear friends, they took good advantage of it, when they sounded me out on this subject.

188   CHARLES BONNIER

February [1895]

How is it that I haven't written to you, my dear Bonnier, you ask me and I reply: it's because I was so discouraged I gave up writing letters, my real work being put in jeopardy by sinister insomnia. Still, I'm pulling myself out of all that because I feel ungrateful; having read and reread, you, in particular, in *Chères Faces,*[88] all this time with a certain degree of lucidity. Your preface is one of the most admirable pages ever written on Poetry—the stairway of magnificence, the only step, etc.[89]—what richly intelligent evocations, creating what I hold most dear, the critical poem! Then the book itself contains such en-

86. Guérin, in a letter of 15 December 1894, had asked Mallarmé to write a preface to his volume of poems, *Le Sang des crépuscules.*
87. This is the solution Guérin adopted.
88. Published in Brussels in 1894 at the author's own expense.
89. In his introduction Bonnier speaks of a lost stairway of luminous sounds which poetry sets out to rediscover: he claims that if one neglects to apply a single rhythm to a single emotion, poetry's steps all disappear.

chantment, the successive spontaneity of your emotions which drop within its limits of congeneric art, spread out as if in an immediate pond which fixes and preserves the images which burst forth only from a pure instinct and according to the needs of rhythm alone, all of that bears wonderful witness to the holy operation, intense and guided by you from the moment it wells forth. If we were chatting, I'd add that some of your incidental strokes stand out, for the mind, with such sureness that their typographical isolation doesn't seem to me a necessary artifice. As soon as one speaks the lines aloud one sees them, such as they should be. I myself have determined only to separate out whole sentences, very short ones, or ones which are deliberately broken for the sole purpose of counterbalancing other long complex sentences, removing the length in order to begin again. These are mere bagatelles, compared with your precious quality, in this collection which is rich in emotion and dream. Farewell, my dear friend; consider me negligent, or, when I'm obsessed, letting everything drift somewhat; but never inattentive to any production of your far-off evenings, for they are imbued with a thought which is deep, rare, and dear to me. Your hand, which I beg you to stretch out, in my name, to our excellent friend M. Powell.

189   HENRI DE RÉGNIER

Sunday [24 February 1895]

Thank you, Régnier, I won't say for inscribing my name on an exceptional page,[90] where that's concerned I'll just squeeze your hand; but thank you for the most wonderful hours of reading that I've had for a long time, this fortnight, why did various things have to interrupt me and the enchantment aroused by *Aréthuse,* after your *Trèfle noir!*[91] I knew the *Flûtes*[92] and admired them: you have succeeded in the most enviable of achievements, that of creating a definite poem, one which is, precisely, a musical air with a greater or lesser degree of fingering, and more or fewer lines, although the number is similar; and all that without having recourse to fixed forms. It needs inspiration, miraculously precise, and even, my dear Régnier, when one isn't constructing a poem, like "The Man and the Mermaid,"[93] but limits oneself to sections, none, humanly, goes beyond that measure of a

90. The third part of the collection *Aréthuse* is dedicated to Mallarmé.
91. A collection of three tales published in 1895.
92. The first volume of *Aréthuse,* like the third part, was entitled "Flutes of April and September."
93. The title of the central part of *Aréthuse.*

page, more or less, which is your great discovery. Your great wave of impassioned sea-chanty, which would on its own be a book, and what a book!, sometimes fluid and sharp, headlong or slow—the watcher on the prow at the beginning and end, the pure echo, in different silences, which is his voice!—there I was truly enchanted with the word, equal in the three fine moments, or supreme moments, of pure Music. As each day passes and without hallooing about it, you are accomplishing all that needs to be done now. The slender and very precious thread of dream which extends your sentence, here in the work of prose, reveals a new virtue, one which is just as rare, in the pleasures of a feigned simplicity which ends by being a real simplicity; for you can reach that point!

All this verbiage means that I'm full of admiration and would like to say so.

190   OCTAVE MIRBEAU

Sunday [3 March 1895]

I am the messenger of a truly terrible piece of news, our poor friend, Madame Eugène Manet, Berthe Morisot, is dead. Her tact was such that she didn't want any letter announcing her death to be sent, but that only those who were not unknown to her should be informed personally. Under no circumstances could I have considered not in- cluding you. Let me add, in case you are coming to Paris, that the funeral, to which only her intimates are invited, will take place on Tuesday at 10; we'll meet, a little before, rue Weber, 10.

191   JULIA DAUDET

Monday [?6 May 1895]

If a woman, being a woman, turns her hand to any art, she pene- trates it, instantly, simply, miraculously. Your book of poems[94] contains something rare, which could result from its own grace; but one real- izes immediately that it's the exquisite relationship with the very in- stinct of poetry—or, the rightness of each of your poems, the way in which the emotion and music are given exactly the right time to create a harmony, enchants: it represents a perpetual success, poem after poem, with a tact which is beauty. I shan't mention, fearing that I may return it clumsily, after reading, the very precise and filmy detail which allows one to follow the delicate flowering of the intimate thread of what is, almost, an entire life; we were entitled to expect

94. *Poésies*, published in 1895.

a marvel, and here we have something even higher, with a loftier meaning.

I send you my affectionate compliments which I shall bring personally as soon as possible, and I beg you to remember me to M. Daudet's good friendship.

192   PAUL VERLAINE

23 July [1895]

Ah! Verlaine what a delicious book when it growls, once or twice, furious in its tranquillity and, above all, supremely elegant as regards the heart: your natural and witty *Confessions, Autobiographical Notes.* I speak here not just as someone who is very fond of you, but who is also very fond of sentences when they go on infinitely long, from all points of view, in the mind and in the text, there are some, here, which I followed with anguish and charm right to their imperturbable conclusion. Dear Grammarian, I'll say this; you truly control your syntax.

Now, let's talk of things: I was forced, because of the greatest of problems (I recount them in *La Revue blanche* for 1 August and won't swell this letter with them), to live between the country and Paris, without seeing you again; what a pain! I met Dierx, chatted of course, as the good chap is in the Ministry, of the subject you mentioned to me;[95] he is entirely at your disposal when the time comes to try, directly and without new fraternal signatures, to obtain a sum equal to that given last time. Unfortunately, he seems to believe—knowing what usually happens—that it's not given more often than once a year; without, however, there being any desire to turn it into a pension, for these are granted only to former civil servants. All things considered, I believe, in my incompetence, that if you make a request, let's say eight or nine months after the last allowance, you won't be refused. In that case, let it go through Dierx's hand in the Ministry. How's your foot, dear friend? Do you go out a little, when they're not making music in your courtyard? Or do you stay behind the pots of flowers?

193   PAUL VALÉRY

Friday 6 September 1895

The article[96] has, then, appeared and I was enchanted, not surprised, on reading it, for I had guessed what it would be, with all its

95. Verlaine was trying to get a grant from the Minister of Education.
96. Valéry's famous article, "Introduction to the Method of Leonardo da Vinci" was published on 15 August 1895.

subtle contours; many a time, in the course of conversations you revealed your thought aloud, dear Valéry. I'm struck by the way you've arranged and grouped with an almost invisible fingering the present symphony of your new mind, such a comprehensive and sharp symphony; and truly, it's not inappropriate that the figure of da Vinci should accept such a tribute. We'll go over more than one page in chatting, Valéry, when I've stopped dragging my heels in this spot which knows you. Yes, this philosophical debut brings you honor, dear friend.

194   JOSÉ-MARIA DE HEREDIA

[Friday 25] October [1895]

Your double parcel arrived here late, through my fault. Let me say how happy I am to see a little book, timeless, which will dwell in libraries for as long as language exists, and while there is simply Poetry, I mean your TROPHEES: I also see them, in this regard, reduced, more closely imitating the precious way in which I possess them all, *by heart*. The DISCOURS DE RECEPTION[97] is at once familiar and superb in its expression and makes me regret having applauded it only in private; but these pages, the glorification of Lamartine, gave me, when I read them, a vast, contemplative joy, and I understand you. The countryside is closing its doors this Autumn, we're returning and I'll come and shake your hand, the first Saturday, having been with you from afar in all the festivities of these recent weeks.[98]

97. Heredia's speech on his election to the Academy in May 1895.
98. Mallarmé is alluding here to the marriage between Marie-Louise Heredia and Henri de Régnier.

8   Prince of Poets

Verlaine, who had been elected "Prince of Poets," died on 9 January 1896. On the 27th Mallarmé was elected by the review "La Plume" as the new prince of poets.

195   LÉON DESCHAMPS

Tuesday [28 January 1896]

Beyond all I'm touched, by a mark of sympathy, and I accept in that light, under the auspices of your friendship.[1]

Perhaps there is, indeed, a common concern between the young who are good enough to be fond of it and my name—in that up to now I've never combined poetry with anything else.

So much for the pleasure; which I admit, since you wish, dear herald, to make explicit and public a consultation which normally takes place mentally, all on its own. But, oh no! no banquet, to celebrate this, for that would destroy the meaning of the gesture, through excess: I'd suffer, and all the more so since I have a profound memory of presiding in my turn and in normal circumstances, over one of the twelve banquets held by *La Plume*. Two, even, for I stood in for Leconte de Lisle. And since that time there has been a real celebration, you remember, for the election of Verlaine,[2] an election he truly deserved, genius and misfortune! In his case, perhaps, since anything done had to be exceptional, given the man himself, there might have been a reason to call together, as a surprise, this one time, the group you have in mind; since, faced with a great injustice to redress, it's not a bad thing to make a personal sacrifice. But that's not the case now; and let's say it, dear Deschamps, under no circumstances, even through a friendly presence, can we allow Verlaine's death to give rise to a banquet.

So, I'm utterly opposed to a banquet, very moved by the election as if it remained tacit with, moreover, a sense of gratitude to *La Plume*— and I shake your hand with all my heart.

1. Deschamps had announced to Mallarmé the latter's election as Prince of Poets.
2 Verlaine was elected Prince of Poets in August 1894 after the death of Leconte de Lisle.

18 February 1896

I'm going to utter a blasphemy, by saying that I don't know whether I value more the sense of space brought by your letter,[3] or your friendship. That will indicate to you just how tired of this place I must be; since you know that first and foremost, I have a liking for you. It's just that you are to be congratulated and I believe you're taking charge of yourself by not being in Paris or in my shoes. My dear friend, there is no way of escaping the crowd and if one tries to evade, let's call it the Press, for that's how the crowd reveals itself to us, then it drags us out of our retreat to make us more absurd than its immediate servants; and to make the hermit a buffoon. You'll see I've been promoted, after a vote! Prince of poets; so the papers have stuck on me a kite's tail with which I try to escape in the streets, having no other means of hiding myself than by joining the Mardi Gras parade. Imagine being a mask despite oneself, Claudel, and when one wants only to be forgotten, except by you. I miss you too because you'd shrug your shoulders furiously, there, on the little Tuesday sofa and that would give me intimate comfort. There are the jokes drawn from Verlaine's tomb, in the cause of topicality, profaning the beautiful disappearance, which indeed is less easy to understand. All that in order to paint Paris, even setting myself apart; and, dear friend, to make sure you won't miss it. You are one of the strong who need to breathe a solitary air. Nevertheless, one evening I heard Léon Daudet speak superbly of you and that remains one of my evenings this winter. I spoke of *Pagode, Jardins, Ville, La Nuit* to the *Revue blanche;*[4] when they're ready you should send them there. I'm not publishing my articles straightaway, they need revising; but since you are willing to read them as a friend I'll send you the collection as they are, one of these days. The package will mean that I've gone to the Ministry and extracted, for now it's more or less time, the seal I dream of.[5]

Farewell, dear friend, I shake your hand wholeheartedly. I'm sad we're separated by such an uncrossable distance and, through some strange confusion, moreover, I imagine that when I take flight, in spring, towards Nature, I'll find you there.... The ladies ask to be warmly remembered.

3. Claudel had written from Shanghai.

4. These are titles of prose poems which later appeared in Claudel's book *Connaissance de l'Est.* Some were published in *La Revue blanche* in 1897 and 1898.

5. This allusion remains obscure.

197 JULES BOISSIÈRE

Sunday 8 March 1896

Ah! my dear Boissière, by dint of spending ten days, leaving the house as soon as I got up, and returning late, I've just established and set in motion the commemorative Exhibition for our great Friend, and I'm sending you the catalogue....[6] Not an hour has gone by without my wishing to write to you, but I'm so tired; I felt the time slipping away. You at least, are you still staying at Avignon, or will this letter pursue you absurdly and will you have left without my last handshake, the one into which I wanted to put all my love for the *Fumeurs d'opium*?[7] The book is absolutely fine, written equally by a man of letters in the strict meaning of the word and by a gentleman of the world. There is nothing as interesting as having avoided the monograph of Opium, even written as a poem, and having made of it the terrible enchanted cloud hanging over a region and over beings successively or fragmentedly evoked. It's a thousand times better, for it demands, without the facilities of the song and of a continuous progression, that the writer discover incidentally a subtlety of impression. In a word, it's the work of an artist, and of a fine writer; the reality of your style, never immediate, always appears or can be perceived in an ambiance of thought, mentally, and where it is direct or abrupt in order to strike the reader, it always obeys the ensemble, and proceeds with a sentence of luxury or one steeped in dream; under that can be discerned the depths of a thoughtful resonance. But we'd chat about it at length if you were to come this evening, after the concert. I miss both of you very much, because you are sincere and charming, each of you bringing to this blend your own qualities and even a little of the qualities of the other, as a reflection.

Farewell, I hope it won't be for a long time and forgive me, if, by bad luck, this letter should reach you only when you've arrived.[8] In that case, my letter doesn't seek to welcome you, there, where it doesn't suggest you should remain; but acts as a faint reminder of your pied-à-terre.

198 EMILE VERHAEREN

March [1896]

I don't know why, Verhaeren, I feel, after the celebrations, after the unanimous and beautiful acclamation of a great Somebody, an old

6. The Berthe Morisot exhibition.
7. Boissière's book had just been printed.
8. At Tonkin where Boissière was vice-regent.

desire to shake your hand on my own behalf;[9] and to tell you how *I* too love, in my own little corner, *Les Villes tentaculaires*.[10] Your voice, dear friend, has often been powerful in its loftiness and solitude; here I find it vast, because of its generality, an eternal echo repeated, as it were, from very massive walls, colliding with the crowd. Soon I'll take the *Poems* off with me to Valvins, in the coming Spring and leisure, to reread them.

You did come with me one day, didn't you, to Madame Manet's place, and I'd like to take your arm here and spend the afternoon together at her commemorative exhibition, but I can only send you the catalogue.

199   MARIE ET GENEVIÈVE MALLARMÉ
Valvins Sunday evening [17 May 1896]
My last letter. I'm arriving Tuesday, for lunch.
I learn from an all too brief note from Madame Laurent, who must have found the sad news in a newspaper, of the death of Madame Whistler. Should I write, with so little information; but if I wait for information, it will be very late.

The mason has finished cleaning the downstairs rooms, washing the tiles, which was really necessary. Everything's done, except for a thousand important trifles. I'll go over everything with a brush in my hand, for the joins and other minutiae. Guérin is at last going to move house. Tomorrow we're going to be really busy. In all, setting aside the inexperience of the workers, it will be pretty: and the errors of execution will disappear in the overall effect.

Half the bakery is repaved; the rest will be finished in a fortnight's time, because of Pentecost which falls next Sunday.

Madame Pubelier, seized with emulation, is arranging for the whitewashing, at her own expense.

I was eating the first fried potatoes around my cutlet when I heard myself called by female voices. The two Natanson families, inviting me to lunch at Les Plâtreries. Madame Perrier[11] even more clinging than usual. Visit to Madame Biard's garden, who cooed such Ohs when she saw me that Mischia shouted out: "It's love!" She and Thadée are, I think, going to take the Prunaire house. So, Vève, get ready to ride the steel. What is it, little vixen,—the sole owner, let's

9. Refers to the banquet given to Verhaeren in Brussels on 22 February 1896 at which Mallarmé's toast to Verhaeren was read out.
10. Verhaeren's collection of poems was published in 1895.
11. The innkeeper at Les Plâtreries.

210

say contractor.[12] What strange weeks, almost two, that I've just passed; it's no longer suitable at my age, when everything ought to have been in existence for a long time. I may think back on it, however, with curiosity. I'd never order something to be built; reinstalling oneself is quite enough!

200   HENRY COUTANT

[Wednesday 20 May 1896]

I've never tried riding a bicycle,[13] through a sense of loyalty, perhaps, to older sports, which are quite sufficient, such as fencing or river-sailing and horseback riding, which I'd like to try. But one recognizes what a practical marvel it is. Its action on the species will have been important, for it has liberated the female sex, which in many cases was confined to the dubious gender of the school friend. As a distant spectator I criticize the clumsy and ungraceful movement inflicted on the legs, in this exercise: the human being does not approach anything mechanical with impunity and cannot become involved in it without suffering some loss. And moreover, it is said that this habit harms dancing, another source of vertigo; which I shall always prefer to the bicycle.

201   CHARLES MORICE

Sunday [7 June 1896]

Here, dear Morice, with good wishes for the success of the project and for a pleasant journey in Belgium.[14] I would have liked to find an hour at my desk earlier; but I was renovating the house here, with my own hands, red, lilac or green, and that's one way of really thinking about the subject. I offer you one of them, nevertheless, and affectionately.

Beauty and Usefulness, with this connecting term, Truth. Beauty, when gratuitous, tends to ornamentation and is repudiated: Usefulness, on its own or at least in this case, when it's involved in mediocre needs, expresses a degree of inelegance. To fashion something exactly,

12. Mallarmé is responding to a comment in Geneviève's letter of 16 May criticizing some of his projects for the house and asking him not to behave as the sole owner.
13. Coutant had sent Mallarmé a questionnaire with the aim of finding out what writers thought about bicycles.
14. Morice published an inquiry on the relationship between beauty and utility in Le Gaulois of 21 August 1896. Mallarmé had promised to provide his opinions.

the artisan has to forget both the use to which the object is put and the knick-knack itself—and think merely of the way in which an idea is being directly expressed in the object, the way it appears, to give pleasure or to be useful, creating an entirely modern impression of truth. This transformation of the creative sense is not accomplished nowadays without a degree of unconsciousness and errors; but, what a marvel, when it's successful, is an umbrella, a black suit, a carriage. A bicycle is not vulgar when wheeled out of the garage, and soon becomes sparkling in its rapidity. Yet whoever mounts it, man or woman, reveals something disgraceful, that of human being reduced to mechanical object, with a caricatural movement of the legs. Too bad! That cannot but be the case: often there is a passing error. For instance, the automobiles where the engineer exults brutally, believing himself to be their master, through a chain of reasoning as elementary as this:—the dynamic horse, steam, electricity, is just as good as the other kind and doesn't eat (no more than you *think*, engineer): so, we'll suppress the *trotter* and cut off the shafts. I answer:—Your conclusion, my friend, is false; it's a question not of distorting but of inventing. The vehicle, with harness, complete, requires the inconvenience of a cabdriver, hiding the view; he's allowed to enjoy it, transformed into a chef at his oven. Something utterly different ought to appear. A gallery, glassed-in, in the form of an arc (a bow window) opening onto the view, over which the eyes can rove, without anything in front of it, magically: the mechanic sits behind, his upper body higher than the roof, and he holds the wheel, acting as pilot. Thus, the monster moves forward, with novelty. This is the vision of the passerby, the man of taste, a vision which perfects things. Yes, as a result, a jury of artists, and a few writers, would perform a valuable function, at competitions: and in addition the intervention of such a jury would never destroy the ugly completely (for it is important to conserve it as an exception, to create a decor for souls who themselves are street peddlars).

202 FRANÇOIS COPPÉE

Friday 26 June [1896]
You can't have failed to notice in the newspapers that there is talk of erecting, in the Luxemburg gardens, a monument to Verlaine, crowned with the bust done by the sculptor de Niederhausen. To this end, a few friends of the poor Lélian[15] have formed an Action or preparatory Committee, and have entrusted me with the presidency;

15. A sobriquet for Verlaine.

Rodin is vice-president. In the name of the members, whose names you can read on the attached card, I would like to ask you to accept the presidency of the definitive Committee of Patronage, or Honor:[16] you would be at the head of all the contemporary poets.

Personally, I'm delighted to have been asked to perform this task. Everything seems to me well defined and clearly established, the preliminaries have already been dealt with. The Academy of Fine Arts have given an indication of their interest. Permission to place the monument in the Luxemburg Gardens will, beyond any doubt, soon be accorded by the Senate. It's less your cordial activity, in the midst of all your current occupations, than the prestige of your name and the vast current of sympathy which it would attract to the work we've undertaken, that's what everyone expects. Nevertheless, I'd add that the desire has been expressed that one of the Thursday articles[17] should throw a warm light on this subject. Your voice can achieve so much.

Above all, don't take any note of an infamous commercial attempt to enhance the Vanier bookshop in this matter.

Farewell, I've been very slow, Coppée, during my installation here, in thanking you for sending me *Mon Franc Parler,* fourth series; you know how much I enjoy that chat with you, wide-ranging and exquisite as it is. I heard, too, that you were ill; and would like to know that you're better, or completely well. My letter brings you wishes for a beautiful summer, one of work and health.

203   PIERRE LOUŸS

Sunday [19 July 1896]

What a marvel! I've been counting, these last few days, on meeting you in various places and of talking about *Aphrodite* better than through this handshake. It's delicate and ample, without those heavy foundations which normally, in novels, testify to the power of the work; every time you turn the page the wing-beat is present, dazzling and light. You reveal a city of the past, limpidly, or in other words by leaving it the charm it holds for us, that of a luminous dream. This hymn to pleasure stems from a high literary intelligence, for, as the philosophy of the work announces exquisitely, it is that silent, human music which words can translate, and it falls within our scope. Your language, so splendid and pure, which I'll always admire, gives a rare joy. Thank you, affectionately.

16. Coppée accepted this task.
17. The chronicles Coppée published each Thursday in the *Journal.*

Friday [25 September 1896]

I'm very late, aren't I! the hours not spent on my work were taken up by a lunatic correction of proofs, for a book I have in mind. . . .[18]— Yes, we'll chat, in Paris, about your book, this autumn, I think I can see a way out; there's no point in thinking of placing a book of verse with a publisher, I mean a first book: but you could get a loan and repay it, little by little, through sales. At a pinch and although the least possible amount of prose is suitable for a book of verse, I could write you a letter of a few lines, after you've shown me the proofs, and that could be put as a preface.[19] Even beforehand, we'll make a bouquet of the poems for a review. All this means that we'll need to discuss it better than in a letter. All your corrections to the envoi are excellent and in the right tone—for they embody you, Dauphin, a name that should be written throughout the book, given that there is no longer any Pimpinelli.[20] After *Fumées,* which was exquisite, *Et c'est l'Automne* has a fine, sure rhythm, in control of its movement. The *Sonnet* which reveals a grave fervor, seizes me like a single and ample cry. You said good things to me, after I sent you *Variations,* and you understand so well: musicians, decidedly, are readers, for I've received on this same subject a perfect letter from Vincent d'Indy who was kind enough to rediscover, in some of my sentences, the laws, so he says, of musical composition. How's that for revenge! Farewell, all around me kisses are raining down; and my hand in all yours. I look forward to winter and having you all with us.

Sunday [27 September 1896]

But you must have caused even more damage to your orchard than the storm, and all for us; I have the impression that a great wind has blown these fruit down from the garden at Arpajon to the garden at Valvins, which has only flowers. We thank you and scold you. My wife is slowly getting better, she was very ill. Geneviève, however, has been able to leave her for four days: she's roaming about, with a lady friend and three companions, somewhere or other, either Le Havre, or Rouen or Honfleur or Caen. I'm just coming out of one of my most painful attacks, two months without closing an eye, when everything seemed so promising in spring; autumn has given me back a little

18. The volume entitled *Divagations* which was to appear in January 1897.
19. Dauphin did adopt this suggestion for his book *Raisins bleus et gris.*
20. Dauphin had used this as a pseudonym.

sleep. Nevertheless, I haven't stopped my morning work, two hours at least, and I'm not unhappy. My only interruption, the correction of the volume *Divagations* which is to come out at the beginning of winter. It contains *Pages,* selections and, alas!, those variations which are not for M. Ch., the sculptor. You'll look on them with an indulgent eye. I've straightened them up a little: so the most recent one pleased you, did it? I wanted, just once and without seeming to, to reply to the stupidity which torments me and I was doubly successful, since I interested you as well.

Vincent d'Indy, who spontaneously wrote me an exquisite letter, was kind enough to find in my article the rules of musical composition, I daren't say the laws. Now there are a few expressions of fellow-feeling which avenge me! I still don't know when we'll return, in October I'll charge you with the usual commission; convey all our triple affection to your wife and our wishes that your son may be free of all illness.

206   ALFRED JARRY

Tuesday 27 October [1896]

Quite simply to admire *Ubu Roi*[21] and shake your hand, on the basis that it's better late than never. . . . I truly believe, apart from the cares of summer and the few letters, that everyone apart from me is too steeped here, at the Natansons', in this exceptional work, declaimed aloud, read in all the real spirit of the work, to be able to write a word about it. You've set on his feet, using a rare clay, one that lingers on the hands, a prodigious character and his family, and you've done so, my dear friend, as a sober and sound dramatic sculptor.

He'll take his place in the repertory of high taste, and he haunts me; thank you.

207   JULIE MANET

Friday evening [13 November 1896]

I don't want to stay far away on the day you turn 18; I'm moved, just thinking about it: what a real grown-up you are! I believe that dear eyes, watching your destiny from another place, are still happy, at the sight of you, serious and good and even a little happy as youth demands, surrounded by people who are affectionate and ideally suited to allow your mind and your emotions to develop freely.

21. Jarry's famous play, which points forward to the absurdist theater of the twentieth century, was first performed, with marionettes, in 1888 and published in 1896.

I embrace you and take advantage of the custom to do the same to your cousins.

I would have been charmed to tell you about Valvins, but I haven't seen it all afternoon, I had to reply to thirteen books[22] which had been sent to me and I've still 47 to do for tomorrow or afterwards. The countryside is turning wintry, our chateau existence, as we're driven through the final magnificence of the forest, is coming to an end, for my friends the Natansons are rushing to other spectacles in Paris until Sunday. I'm locked away to perform tasks which resemble packing up and announcing our return, I'm told your linen has arrived, without either you or the others, which I find insufficient: oh! you've all missed some beautiful things, I'd have you know, with your habit of going away, especially a tide of golden leaves, which stayed slack for a long time, under the Denecourt tower.

Farewell, affectionately, all three, whose portraits by Mme Rosalba, and this will be their function, keep in order while I work the papers scattered on my little desk. Some morning there will appear before the Parisians Paule, Jeannie, and yourself, your very rustic neighbor.

208   EDMOND DEMAN

[Friday] 20 November [18]96

No! decidedly, we haven't reached the end, I'm very sorry. Neither the format nor the characters are a good choice—not at all worthy of your art nor suitable for our enterprise.[23] I took fright at relying on my own taste, and thought this was an isolated impression, but there's only one opinion, people came to see me and each of them made the same grimace when faced with these experiments.

Everyone, moreover, expects the same format as *Pages* and I share the general feeling: what's more we need a somewhat monumental book, a role long fulfilled by *Pages,* and it should appear before the publication of the standard edition, which is going to be produced by the Charpentier press under the title of *Divagations,* from a group of pieces into which this one has been poured back. So, at a certain point in time, after the period that we can plausibly devote to this fine standard edition of my poems, there will appear an ordinary publication, at a price to be fixed: for the moment, it must be the stable, high, and noble publication that we're at present attempting.

I know that you'll make the objection that your preparations, the frontispiece and the ornamentation, were not made with regard to the

22. Ten letters by Mallarmé dated 13 November have been found.
23. Mallarmé is responding to the specimen copy of *Poésies* sent by Deman.

format in question, that of *Pages* or of the Poe; I regret this and that it wasn't submitted to me beforehand. Despite the distance and my reluctance to write letters we would have decided on something already. As for today and given what's done—it'll still be better to fit the ornamentation to a different format, rather than continuing with what we've got now; no, it is not beautiful. So you'll find some beautiful and large modern characters. I'll add that the people who pay more than three francs fifty will go to the price of *Pages* and even a little higher; and those who wouldn't pay the price of *Pages* moreover wouldn't go beyond their habitual maximum of three francs fifty. We know that all too well, you and I.

Hérodiade, nothing, not ready: the proofs of *Divagations* on which I'm still working have prevented me from working on it; but I'm counting on doing it, after a task I have to carry out soon, in January. But it'll be done for a separate publication, immediately or as soon as it has appeared in the *Revue blanche* and it will be essential to let a moment elapse before republishing it in the Poetry, to the collection of which it will form, when complete, a Finale.

Your hand; that's our current position, I wanted to chat with you at leisure, before returning to Paris and all these last weeks I couldn't see the necessary quarter of an hour under the lamp, over a sheet of paper, to do so.

209   EDVARD MUNCH

Wednesday [30 December 1896]

All my regrets to learn of your indisposition and my hopes that you will soon be free of this illness. We'll put off until later our meeting which, moreover, was for last Monday. Today I'll only send you my good wishes for restored health, in a handshake.

210   ANATOLE LA VIEILLESSE

[January 1897]

You terrify me by referring to such a subject.[24] So you've noticed— it hasn't escaped your attention—that our contemporaries wear on their heads something somber and supernatural. Perhaps you're going

24. La Vieillesse may be a pseudonym: nothing seems to be known about him, but Mallarmé is replying to a letter in which he asks what Mallarmé thinks of the top hat in particular and modern dress in general, and whether he feels the exhibition of 1900 ought to create a revolution where dress is concerned. An article appeared in *Figaro* of 19 January 1897 entitled "The Top Hat: is it ugly?" with comments by a range of writers, ending with Mallarmé.

to be marvellously daring and exhaust this mystery in the column of a daily paper: as for me, it has for some time provided almost the sole source of my meditations and I cannot believe that science can resolve it and go beyond it, except by several volumes of a compact, copious, and abstruse work. It would be possible, you believe, to leave aside here all that disquieting philosophy concerning the device or the embellishment or whatever it may be that this shadowy Meteor presents, and restrict yourself to a hat-trade discussion, as your questionnaire indicates quite clearly. For example, you suggest the question of whether this modern complement, called a top hat, will haunt the dawn of the twentieth century. What—it's only beginning in its furious diffusion to sweep aside the diadems, the feathers, and even hair itself: it will continue!

Sir (I add quietly), given that it is, at a certain date in man's history, on heads, then it will always be there. Anyone who has put on such a thing can't take it off. The world would come to an end, but not the hat: probably it even existed from the beginning of time but in invisible form. Doesn't everybody pass by it today without noticing it?

Nevertheless I have to say that I consider it, on others, with whom it seems to make a whole—and if they doff their hats to me, I don't separate the hat, mentally, from the individual; I still see it, during this polite gesture, in place. Immutably.

Once it appeared, the object suited man, it was as evident as it was unexplained, and it is neither ugly nor beautiful; it is beyond judgment. A sign, who knows?, a solemn sign of superiority and, for that reason, a stable institution.

211   PIERRE LOUŸS

[Monday] 11 January 1897

We've received some bananas, which, even pronounced by Ubu, wouldn't be a banal form of fruit; they come from afar and from your hand, my dear Louÿs. The ladies thank you and most warmly; we need, on a day when invisible coal smokes away, to remind ourselves that there do exist countries which are full of light and I'm happy that you live in them,[25] even tomorrow, Tuesday, when I'll be expecting friends among whose number you could be.

25. Louÿs was in Algeria.

218

Saturday [February-March 1897]

A few days ago I read the third part, which is as good as the other two; I opened the *Carillonneur*[26] again, at every point where there is a marvel, in a word at every page. You prepared it by the novels you had written before, it was predicted by them, but one couldn't have suspected it would be as it is, with that definitive grandeur of a major work, your own, absolutely—and, moreover, it's prodigious, the way your own art, unique to you alone, proceeds from the Carillon. The vast flights of the whole, the powerful blows, which reverberate throughout the work and are diluted in it, my dear chap, are of the soul's richest metal, the most profound, sonorous, and imaginative that literature can provide, all this whirls through it and fades away like a tempest of beauty; and so for the detail in every line, ah! I delight in a minor miracle of thought, fallen from heaven and infinite, your very own bells. It's a work of maturity which has lost nothing of the primitive flower: you must be very sure and very happy, Rodenbach. As for me, I admire it greatly and shake your hand, just as greatly.

213   ELÉMIR BOURGES

1 March 1897

On carnival Monday, while the Mallarmé ladies gaze upon the fatted ox, from a window in the rue de la Paix, I've sensibly remained at home, with other aims in mind, and I'm writing to Bourges. His very good letter cut my winter in two and an entire half of the time I miss him will plunge into the past, while the other half invites me to step into it without as much despair as at first; the reunion coming at the end. I'm even tracing dates in my mind's eye and imagine that in mid-April, I'll put on the mottled smock of the house painter for an initial preparatory stay and then return to look down my nose at the Salons, before returning definitively, supplied with a few summer utensils. May, the rose bushes, intoxication! and the two of us will go and breathe each other's gardens. The Ladies, more serious, will agree to come in June, to note that all is green. These are the projects you set before me, dear friend, and have done since your letter came: before it, I certainly thought of you, but not at all of nature. I was, so it seems, like a ferocious beast, a wild animal in a cage, the first

---

26. Rodenbach's novel, published that year.

months; I didn't stop fuming; then my fury was spent and finally one is always tamed. People harass me here, nothing interests me, so I shut myself away and work, deprived of fresh air, no way of going out, in the worst of conditions. The insomnia I suffer from every night digs itself in through a day of weariness, a useless day; and every day is like going down a step into emptiness and disgust. Above all the unbearable awareness that I'm doing something absurd. Paris and your servant have got nothing to do with one another. Ah! how I envy a winter of regular work or inspiration like yours! have you at least profited from it, are you happy? I want to know when I arrive there. I like you very much, Bourges, and wherever I may be, your name is spoken and you can guess whether I then become its harpist.

Our friendship, from the three of us, one says in English our love, to Madame Bourges and yourself. Why aren't you, as sometimes at Valvins, here for the five o'clock tea, including Sita. Madame Normant inquires after Samois, meaning you, the "little" ones as well. They held an evening entertainment, if you please, with music, Mauclair, Natanson, Degas, orangeade and their dresses! Julie, who has been ill all winter with bronchial problems, is better. I find Geneviève a little below par, she takes her mother's place a great deal, while her mother, as brave as she is weak, defends her own domain. The attacks of last summer have not recurred and we are predicting better things of next season. Farewell, I want to say everything at the end and I'm being summoned: we're dining with the Natansons, your name will often be mentioned but that's not enough. So, nevertheless, I'm not abandoning you altogether and even missing you is dear to me.

Your hand: thank you, for this affection, Bourges, which finds a tender echo in me.

214   LORD ALFRED DOUGLAS

[Wednesday 24] March 1897

Your *Poems*[27] which can bear that title proudly and simply, reached me in Paris, this winter, late, through complicated circumstances. I have the pleasure of reading them in the original without nevertheless neglecting the translation which renders them miraculously well; but even more than in the parallelism of the two languages, I delighted in the first, your own, the original version, which fuses a double instinct which is both French and English. For your verse, depending on your emotion, however much it takes flight and trembles, infinitely, as in your greatest contemporary masters, retains a sureness of touch, un-

27. A bilingual edition of Lord Douglas's poems, published the previous year.

broken and lucid, which is characteristic of us here. I'm sorry to have to offer as many apologies as thanks.

215   FERNAND CLERGET

[Wednesday] 7 April 1897

You requested, dear M. Clerget, for teachers—several of them poets—my assertion that Verlaine, that Master, did indeed teach: certainly, English language. I used to call him—since some of my hours, too, remain on the frosted windows of high-school classrooms—smilingly, my colleague and comrade in arms, for he told me of the outstanding successes of his teaching, I think it was at Rethel, and when we met he would wink at me, as a connoisseur inquiring if my own teaching was flourishing: he had escaped long since and I used to attribute to that interval of oblivion the serenity he revealed in willingly discussing a subject which for me, whose trials lingered on, had no attraction. By chance I sorted out his son, in a course, at Rollin, and told him about it, and this may have contributed to this interest on his part in the technical details of my obligatory pastime. Thus, he enjoyed making many quotations from English, bombastically, like a man who knows some exceptional language or one which few can master, or to be more accurate, which only a small number of poets can master. Pedagogical reminiscences, bits of advice; he used to show me in particular something he'd invented himself and into which he initiated me, a source of pride! He had (so I understand it) seen, correctly, the persistence of the guttural intonation or the stridency against the teeth, which is inveterate among English people trying to pronounce our language, as an unquestionable proof of the ability to pronounce excellently and without any effort their own language rather than ours. The perfect performance, which a conscientious French teacher demands of his pupils, he felt could be attained immediately, by inculcating into them, even when reading Boileau, the habitually defective pronunciation common to Dr Johnson's compatriots,—not in the form of a coarse varnish which would deceive no one, nor in order to proceed, straightaway, through a facile reversal and argue that if the pupils altered French in imitation of barmen and jockeys, they'd be all the more capable of emitting a pure English: but, according to a mystery appropriate to linguistics, because the organs, falsified into an authentic grimace, must lend themselves better, perhaps, to the miracle of foreign elocution, which, who knows, will therefore be automatically produced in the speaker. Verlaine, then, had taken measures never to enter his class without the children standing up and greeting him in chorus (how can this be transcribed, except by borrowing from the spelling of the theater or comic opera): *"Baonn-jaur, Maossiur Vœu-laine!"* during the time it took for the educator to reach the rostrum.

🏵 *Mallarmé spent the spring of 1897 at Valvins, working on "Les Noces d'Hérodiade" ("Hérodiade's Wedding"). In May he published* Un Coup de dés *(A Throw of the Dice).*

216   MÉRY LAURENT

Sunday morning [9 May 1897]

I'm counting the days,[28] reducing them when I consult myself and increasing them when the rain begins. I think it's going to be a bad week which will end well.

My companion abandoned me, almost as soon as she'd left her carrier, for the Lover himself, a splendid chap of a cat, named as such by the neighborhood, and all evening she flirted at him, while I shouted from the window Li-Li-Li-Lilith, in rivalry with the nightingale.

When I arrived, I found an agreable surprise, the letter in which you invited me for last Monday, it's still something of you waiting there. Only the enclosed letter from Madame J. B. struck me as out-of-date, since so many things have not happened since then on the way to the publisher Colin.

The countryside is powerfully green, entirely different from what it was like on my first voyage and very lovely, doubtless through your approaching presence; and to think I'm going to see so little of you, with my worries about the workmen and my need to lend a hand. I want you to see everything perfect. Farewell, dear lady, my good and great darling whom I embrace.

217   ANDRÉ GIDE

[Friday 14 May 1897]

Ah! dear Gide, what literary generosity you have and how typical of you your letter was.[29] So this attempt, this beginning, this trial essay,

28. Until Méry's arrival at Valvins: eventually she arrived on 15 May and stayed until 17 May.
29. Gide had written to Mallarmé to express his excitement at reading *Un coup de dés* in the periodical *Cosmopolis*. Gide compared his emotion on reading the last page of this difficult poem to what he felt on hearing a Beethoven symphony.

didn't shock you even though it is ill-presented. *Cosmopolis* behaved gallantly and deliciously; but I could give them only half the work, and even that represented for them such a risk! The poem is being printed at this moment as I conceived it; as regards pagination, in which lies the whole effect. A certain word, in large characters, dominates on its own an entire white page and I believe I can be certain about the effect created. I'll send the first acceptable proof to you in Florence, and from there it can follow you elsewhere. In this poem the constellation will, fatally, assume, according to precise laws and in so far as it's possible in a printed text, the form of a constellation. The ship will list from the top of one page to the bottom of the next, etc.: for, and this is the whole point at issue (which I was obliged to omit in a "periodical"), the rhythm of a sentence about an act or even an object has meaning only if it imitates them and, enacted on paper, when the Letters have taken over from the original etching, must convey in spite of everything some element of that act or that object.—I'm chattering on, instead of shaking your hand for your very noble and lovable enthusiasm; farewell, place my homage at Madame Gide's feet.

218 EDVARD MUNCH

[Tuesday] 15 June [1897]

The fact that it has been slow and needed several occasions to settle in here, from where I'm shaking your hand, hardly excuses my failure to thank you for the arresting portrait;[30] in which I feel myself intimately portrayed.

All my affectionate gratitude and a thousand thanks.

219 THÉODORE DURET

[Saturday] 11 September [1897]

How are you: are you in Paris despite the rain? I read, this summer, your fine page, logical and perceptive, in the *Revue blanche:* it makes one impatient to read your *Napoléon.* You know I never leave Valvins, without interrupting and compromising my work, so I'll charge you, if it's not a nuisance to you, dear Friend, with a little commission I've been asked to do myself. You'll do it so well, in one of your daily

---

30. Munch's portrait of Mallarmé was described by Geneviève, in a letter to her father, in these terms: "It's fairly pretty, but it resembles those heads of Christ imprinted on a saint's handkerchief and underneath which is written: 'If you look long enough you'll see the eyes close.'"

walks, particularly given your sagacious and delicate eye for Japanese curios.

My friend, Prince André Poniatowski, on his return to San Francisco where he's been directing the railways, after a recent short trip to Paris, is haunted with regret for certain "Japanese engravings, about fifty of them, backed with cardboard," which he glimpsed at Bing's, "in an upper room." He would like to buy four of them, chosen from the most beautiful. So I'd ask you to track them down and let me know the price. Once I've sent the information to San Francisco, Poniatowski will send, by telegraph, the sum requested, on the very same day, to M. Bing, who will send them or if necessary get Durand Ruel to send them in one of his American parcels· but don't worry about this, I'll look after the details. All I ask of you is to be gracious enough to make the choice for me, my friend will gain thereby; and to let me know the price. And, too, give my regards to M. Bing.

You're wondering what one can do in the country in such weather, or, at least, the Ladies assure me you ask this question. The same as at Paris, more calmly, I work and think and, as we're now going to be without the Lamoureux concerts,[31] which played a great part in calling me back, I for my part wonder if it's ever worth going back: were it not for several old hands to shake and dear voices to hear, and you, Duret, are one of those I'd miss if I prolonged my solitude. The Ladies, although they will precede me back to town send their warm greetings, already.

220   CHRISTOPHER JOHN BRENNAN
[Thursday] 16 September 1897
My dear Brennan,

Let me call you that, instead of Poet and marvellous poet—yes, this cordial and enchanted handshake implies everything, or that you and I are certainly linked by some kinship of dream; thank you for your special, delicious copy, which you had bound for me, applying on it an advance, like the seal on a book placed in my library within reach of my hand, my monogram.[32] *Towards the Source* is no empty title: you retrace, wildly, powerfully and limpidly, the ordinary current of

31. These famous concerts were under threat as Lamoureux had sacked his musicians in order to found a theater. The concerts, however, continued under another director, until Lamoureux took charge of them again in 1898. Mallarmé greatly enjoyed these concerts.
32. The book in question is Brennan's collection of poems entitled *Towards the Source*, published in Sydney in 1897. Brennan had it specially bound for Mallarmé.

poetry, returning to its rarest source. The words chosen by you, you use correctly, because that's essential, and you've steeped and purified them in some original flow of life, amidst an essential breath of air. Certainly, although the language is absolutely English, I truly feel your song has passed through ours: but it also gives the impression that alone and on its own it would have been like that.

Thank you, as a reader, as a friend or, since this name is dear to you from afar, as Stéphane Mallarmé.

221   MÉRY LAURENT

Monday [24 January 1898]

You're quite right to stay where the weather is fine; especially if you feel new-born, Peacock. Here, it's merely sad, it's already that: not too bad however: but the season is glum, or at least as far as things are concerned. I assert that I'm fed up already with going out in the evening or with anything other than remaining calmly at work without disturbances. Paris, in these conditions, becomes useless. . . . Saw Whistler, however, yesterday evening, dined in a very attractive and old-fashioned French room in the Café Cardinal.

Apart from that, nothing but the unending Dreyfus affair and the "Shout them down"s in the street. Degas seemed so terrible on this topic to the Manet girls, who were going to invite him for last Thursday, that they withdrew without mentioning the object of their visit. I wrote to "little Monvel" for the Ladies' bath. They haven't seen *Paris qui marche*[33] which is coming to an end.

Breathe deep, look around and fill yourself with views of the horizon, which is a preferable spectacle, in which one can live. I hug you warmly.

P.S. If Madame Noële is still there, Princess[34] is to smile at her and offer her paw, on my behalf.

222   GUSTAVE KAHN

[Saturday 30 April 1898]

I dote on *Petites Ames pressées;*[35] and I believe that you'll often take up that tune again in the future; there is a you who is delicious, all but unknown, that you're trying out and establishing to the point of

33. A three-act revue which had its fiftieth performance on 12 December 1897: it was to reach its hundredth performance on 28 February 1898.

34. Méry Laurent's dog.

35. A collection of six tales published in 1898.

unquestioned originality, a humorist of a very new kind, and a poet of immeasurable prestige, with a mastery of words while always giving the appearance of improvisation. Charmed throughout the book, I nevertheless single out the last story and rank it as unique, I'd say a classic, in my memory of short novels.

I'm sorry not to be beside you this evening; but I trotted out, since I find them authentic, all my old reasons when we last chatted: it's as much a question of the impossibility for the past and the future, of breaking the habit I imposed on myself of not coming to Paris, as it is of my dislike, which you know, of presidents, particularly when I'm the president. I'm with you all in spirit at the banquet, the founders, the interpreters, the winners of those poetic matinees at the Odéon (about which I, in particular, have too much cause to praise myself): shake Mendès' hand, and those of the friends who are kind enough not to forget me; and keep for yourself, Kahn, the unwearyingly affectionate and loyal, in your attractive functions, toward all who take part in poetry, my affirmation here of my already long-standing friendship.

Good day; say, why do you no longer cross the bridge at Valvins, in your military costume. . . .

Be good enough to convey my respects to Madame Kahn.

223   MÉRY LAURENT

Valvins, Saturday [14 May 1898]

Yes, I'd be pleased if I were transported, tomorrow evening, to the Talus; but, apart from the pleasure of gazing upon you there, I don't want to budge. The endless rain, on the window panes, places a gauze over a countryside which is admirably green; the stove snores, I'm working fairly well and am enjoying having elbow room and being able to walk up and down in one room and in several, all spacious. In Paris, I would mold, shut away, in the rue de Rome. The problem is that the sun, which ought to have dried "your" Plâtreries and the whole of the house before the Ladies arrived, has left the interiors in their winter condition. So you're better off getting a cold at the Talus, which is a hothouse. Or losing your voice, which is a shame for your musical scores.

The oafish way the Men-of-Letters have behaved toward Rodin[36] is perfect; I haven't cooled off yet, and it makes me feel ashamed even though I'm hardly one of their number. Ah! these lords, paid so much

36. The Society of Men of Letters had complained about Rodin's first version of his Balzac statue, which they refused to accept.

the line, faced with the evidence of genius which for them can never be anything but a mystification.

Farewell, the clouds are bursting again, and will they deprive me— last time I was able to escape them—of carrying this kiss to the far-off letter box at Mother Perrier's: I'm afraid of that; and that my good-evening won't reach you in time. Lilith, whom I've asked to carry out this errand, is dozing and lets me know that she fears water more than I do. At least welcome our good intentions.

224   MARIE AND GENEVIÈVE MALLARMÉ
Thursday [19 May 1898]

A little greeting, before getting down to the afternoon's work, be-cause I won't write to you this evening since I'll be dining with the Dujardins. The terrible icy wind has dropped, there'll be more rain; it's warm and, at the moment, I'm lighting the stove for the blaze of the day. I'd also like to light the Poet, who is fairly inert. Don't tell anyone, from Moréno on, that I'm working especially on *Hérodiade;* that could reach Vollard's ears and as far as he's concerned the poem is finished. Imagine how I mutter at him here! There's nothing wrong with you, is there?—Not the slightest incident here, apart from the daily passage of Madame Dony in her short skirt, her apron, with her milk jar and, too, a cap like my own on her head. Yesterday, predinner walk toward the Russian prince's dogs, which are my own exhibition, sleepy and hidden; but you can't imagine how marvellous the Made-leine wood is, in all its fresh greenery. Don't hurt your hair, today, when you visit the little ones.... Ah! Julie! I still deplore Paule's dress. You'll probably meet Madame Normant. What are you doing with your "Sunday"? My kisses this evening when I come home, like you, probably a little late.

225   VICTOR MARGUERITTE
Valvins [Wednesday 22] June 1898

You treat me like a king; and I'll allow my name, on the dedication page, printed, to blend more impersonally with the book because the lively astonishment it arouses in me borrows nothing even from our old friendship. I've read *Au Fil de l'Heure,*[37] letting memories of pieces already known sing within me, admiring the very numerous other pieces, like a book one suddenly meets and has never, in fact, consid-ered as an ensemble; it's a completely fine book, of which the author

37. Margueritte's collection of poems, published in 1898.

ought to be proud. This, my dear fellow, is how I judge, do you see, the thoroughbred poet: it depends on all the archetypal forms of Poetry being reproduced, as if unbeknownst to him, in the work, perpetually causing the delights of novelty. You use—certainly, having clearly foreseen in the early pages, the extraneous games—the eternal verse as if it presented itself to you quite obviously and you were the first to use it; in all its freshness, inborn: this will be done on yet other occasions but rarely with such a spontaneous aptitude. The more I consider our art the more it implies a competition, to see who, on a perfect instrument, will play with originality. Your imaginative and emotional repertory moves from a superb frankness to very fine subtleties; you put your finger on what is needed, directly, and you add an infinite delicacy of fingering.

Thank you for *Le Parc enchanté*[38] whose luxurious and serious opulence you guessed was bound to seduce me.

You are either moving house or are newly installed today: find in your new house our triple smile, even though we're absent.

Ah! your aunt buys you castles, she's still the same magnificent person: yes, yes, we'll go to Vétheil, not from here but in some escapade, once, in the future. I'm very happy with this little spot, which will be a place of work and familiar to all. The country is said to be very fine; Monet lived there, for years. The news, announced in the papers, that Poincaré is refusing all offers of a ministery, is precious to us; his help remains assured for our dear Paul. Ah! this must be brought to an end.[39]—Shake his hand, embrace the two ladies and, Victor, believe me also yours tenderly.

226   LÉOPOLD DAUPHIN

Valvins June 1898

Good day, *old* Dauphin, meaning *very dear.* The one who's aging is me, by the hour. One proof, for instance, is that I've not once opened the sail of my boat to the pleasant winds: I work, trot out the same things, botch things up, add a head and a tail to my poem about Hérodiade. I'm saying all this to be done with it; better. . . . The fine project you paraded before my eyes, of being present at that open-air performance, I enjoyed in so far as it has any semblance of reality for me, that is, in your friendly lines; really I don't travel any more: I just grow dozy, here, among my thoughts. Accuse too the *Hérault* which comes to me; my dear friend, truly your way of putting everything

38. The section entitled "The Enchanted Park" is dedicated to Mallarmé.
39. The reference is to the divorce case of Victor's brother Paul.

228

into your poems is perfect and each times creates a rare music. Have you read *La Chair et l'esprit,* by M. de la Hire d'Espie, one of those on the *Aube méridionale?* It's very good. What do you think of Mauclair's novel, *Le Soleil des Morts;* do you recognize the central character, my humble self, magnified? Your hand, my dear fellow; are you well? and we send our kisses.

227   LÉOPOLD DAUPHIN
Valvins Saturday [20 August 1898]
Oh! my poor Dauphin, what, you're suffering in such a way:[40] I'll only take your hand from afar, without saying anything. Everything irritates you and particularly, perhaps, this page which I send only because you demand it. Take heart, and above all read my friendship. Around me, they're whispering pleasant things to your Ladies, I join with them.

228   GENEVIÈVE MALLARMÉ
[Valvins] Saturday morning [20 August 1898]
I'll risk this note (it's morning and the window is open) before the postman comes, since you're not here to open my shutters. The night was really hot . . . yesterday evening, however, there was a little breeze on the bench in front of the door where we chattered late into the evening like two old people. A storm, which we would have clasped in both arms, passed over the region, deceiving it, heading north and perhaps to Pontoise, Mother says. A visit yesterday from M. Currey, Schwob's Englishman. Moreover, the afternoon's work melted away. We send our love and beg you to divide our regards equitably among your dear hosts. Mother finds the continual heat wearing, she can't sleep and has no appetite: she and I kiss you again. The cats are weary.[41]

40. Dauphin had complained to Mallarmé that he was finding it very difficult to write.
41. This is Mallarmé's last letter to Geneviève, who had gone to spend a long weekend with friends. He died on 9 September.

Index

Desmolins, André, 1789–1865
S. M.'s maternal grandfather, 3, 5, 6, 7, 18, 28, 56, 57, 58
Desmolins, Louise, 1799–1869
S. M.'s maternal grandmother, 3, 4, 6, 7, 88, 142
Dierx, Léon, 1838–1912
poet, associated with the Parnassian movement, 76, 108, 205
Docquois, Georges, 1863–1927
journalist. Interviewed Mallarmé about his cat Lilith and published this interview in a study of writers and animals, 174
Douglas, Lord Alfred, 1870–1945
minor English poet, best known for his notorious liaison with Oscar Wilde, 220
Dujardin, Edouard, 1861–1949
founded several important symbolist reviews, 153, 154, 155, 156, 179, 199, 227
Duret, Théodore, 1833–1927
art historian, author of the first book on Impressionist painting, 223, 224

Félibrige
movement whose aim was to restore to the Provençal language its former status as a literary language, 25, 42, 86, 96, 105
Fénéon, Félix, 1861–1944
critic greatly admired by Mallarmé, editor of several reviews, 198
Flandrin, Jean-Hippolyte, 1809–1864
painter, best known for his religious works, 32
Flaubert, Gustave, 1821–1880
French novelist best known for *Madame Bovary* and *The Sentimental Education,* 36, 123, 131
Fournier, Alfred, 1832–1914
doctor and great bibliophile, 154
Fournier, Edmond, 1864–1926
Méry Laurent's doctor, 154
France, Anatole, 1844–1924
essayist and novelist, 108

Gaillard, Anne-Marie, 1843–1884
eccentric society hostess, known as

Nina, who gathered round her many young writers and artist, 7, 9, 10, 41
Gaugin, Paul, 1849–1903
artist, 173
Gautier, Judith, 1845–1917
novelist, author of several volumes of memoirs, 99, 106
Gautier, Théophile, 1811–1872
novelist, poet, short-story writer and art critic. Very influential as a literary critic and guide to Baudelaire and Mallarmé, 30, 32, 34, 106, 110, 117
Geffroy, Gustave, 1855–1926
writer and art critic, 185
George, Stefan, 1868–1933
German poet, whose early work shows the inspiration of the French symbolists, 174
Gerhard, Marie. *See* Mallarmé, Marie (born Christian Maria Gerhard)
Gervex, Henri
artist, 186
Ghil, René [pseudonym of René Guilbert], 1862–1925
Creator of "scientific poetry," which attempted to systematize Baudelaire's ideas on correspondences and Mallarmé's notions of music and letters, 139, 140–41, 148–49, 150, 181
Gide, André, 1869–1951
novelist and prose writer. Highly influential in the period between the two world wars, 186, 192, 222–23
Glatigny, Albert, 1839–1873
Bohemian and wandering player whose chance encounter with a volume of Banville's poetry transformed him into a poet, 31, 34, 36, 38
Glazer, Emmanual, Hungarian poet, 69
Goffin, Arnold, 1863–1934
poet and novelist, but best known for his studies of Belgian art, 153–54
Gogh, Théodore van
brother of Vincent. Ran a small art gallery, 165
Goncourt, Edmond de, 1822–1896
novelist and art critic. With his brother wrote a highly informative *Journal* of literary life of the time, 187
Gosse, Edmund, 1894–1928

236

Stahl, P. S. [pseudonym of Hetzel], 1814–1886
published works of Hugo, Verne, and many others, 75
Swinburne, Algernon, 1837–1909
poet, 109–13

Taine, Hippolyte, 1828–1893
French historian and critic, influential for his positivist views, 48, 49, 54
Titian, c. 1490–1576
Italian painter, 73

Vacquerie, Auguste, 1819–1895
close friend of Victor Hugo, acting as his spokesman during Hugo's exile, 31
Valéry, Paul, 1871–1945
French poet, philosopher, and mathematician. Mallarmé recognized and respected his considerable potential from the early letters Valéry sent him, and the two became close friends, 170–71
Vallette, Alfred, 1859–1935
journalist, cofounder of the prestigious review Mercure de France, 181–82
Vanier, Léon, 1847–1896
published many of the works of the Decadents, 142, 144, 146–47, 153, 155, 168, 171, 183, 213
Verhaeren, Emile, 1855–1916
Belgian symbolist. Mallarmé considered him the most important and original poet of his generation, 152–53, 175–76, 183, 191–92, 209, 210
Verlaine, Paul, 1844–1896
Mallarmé's friendship with this poet dates from his days in the provinces, 70–71, 77, 130, 131–32, 138–39, 142–46, 194, 205, 207, 208, 212, 221, 222
Vieillesse, A.
journalist, 217 n.24, 217–18
Viélé-Griffin, Francis, 1864–1937
poet, best known for his experimentation in vers libre, 139, 149–50, 201
Villiers de l'Isle-Adam, Auguste, 1838–1890

poet, dramatist, and short-story writer. Mallarmé admired and respected him, particularly for his play Elën, 47, 48, 51, 57–58, 67, 69, 79, 81–83, 84, 85, 93, 94, 100, 107, 134–35, 142, 145, 146, 147–48, 158, 159, 160, 163, 164, 185, 196
Villiers de l'Isle-Adam, Victor, 1881–1901
son of Auguste, 148, 158
Vollard, Gabriel
printer, 227

Whibley, Charles, 1862–1930
journalist, invited Mallarmé to lecture at Cambridge, 193, 194, 196
Whistler, James McNeill, 1834–1903
Impressionist painter, close friend of Mallarmé, 167, 171, 180, 185, 186, 188–89, 210, 225
Whitman, Sarah Helen, 1803–1878
fiancée of Edgar Allan Poe in 1848. Inspired "To Helen." Broke off the engagement but defended him in her book E. A. Poe and His Critics. She was also a poet herself, 114, 115–17, 119–21
Wyse, William Charles Bonaparte-, 1826–1892
A rich Irishman who became a great friend of the Félibrige, 95–96, 103, 105

Yapp, Harriet [Ettie], 1845–1873
English girl loved by Cazalis. Close friend of Nina Gaillard, 7, 8, 9, 10, 13–14, 17, 20, 28, 37, 65, 76, 86
Yapp, Kate
sister of Ettie, 14

Zola, Emile, 1840–1902
naturalistic novelist, author of the famous Rougon-Maquart series of novels. Also wrote important studies of artists, 107, 113–14, 118–19, 122–24, 126, 169–70, 187, 88
Zorilla y Moral, José, 1817–1893
Spanish poet, 86, 105